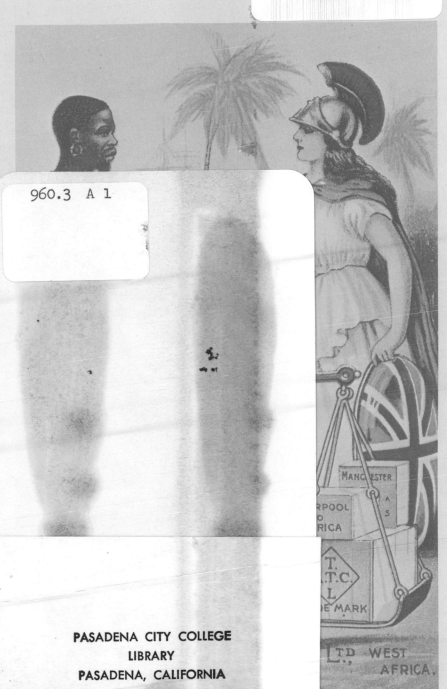

# TALES FROM THE DARK CONTINENT

ALSO EDITED BY CHARLES ALLEN

Plain Tales from the Raj

Raj: A Scrapbook of British India 1877–1947

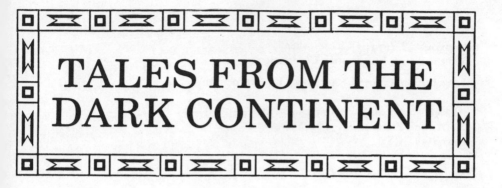

# TALES FROM THE DARK CONTINENT

EDITED BY

**Charles Allen**

*In association with Helen Fry*

INTRODUCTION BY ANTHONY KIRK-GREENE

ST. MARTIN'S PRESS

NEW YORK

Library of Congress Cataloging in Publication Data

Allen, Charles.
Tales From the Dark Continent
I. Title.
79-54148
ISBN 0-312-78389-2

Filmset in 11/13 point Imprint
Printed and bound in Great Britain

# CONTENTS

List of illustrations                                                        *page* vii
Preface                                                                              ix
Introduction by Anthony Kirk-Greene                                                   xiii
 1   Running Up the Flags                                                             1
 2   White Man's Burden; White Man's Grave                                           17
 3   To Africa                                                                       33
 4   Taking Up the Ropes                                                             49
 5   Keepers of the King's Peace                                                     65
 6   Going to Bush                                                                   79
 7   Men with Sand in their Hair                                                     95
 8   The DO's Wife and the Governor's Lady                                          109
 9   Winds of Change                                                                125
10   The Flags Come Down                                                            139
Notes on Contributors                                                              151
Glossary                                                                           158

# ILLUSTRATIONS

*Between pages 30 and 31*

British society in Sierra Leone, Freetown 1910 (*Royal Commonwealth Society*)

Kitting-up for Africa; Walters of Oxford in the 1920s (*Walters & Co*)

The gateway to Uganda, c. 1910 (*RCS*)

Trading company 'canteen', Liberia c. 1920 (*United Africa Company International*)

White ducks and 'Bombay bowlers', Lagos 1919 (*Clifford Ruston*)

The opening-up of the African interior, Uganda c. 1907 (*RCS*)

'Blues ruling blacks'; the Sudan Political Service, 1910 (*Sir Angus Gillan*)


*Between pages 62 and 63*

Native Authority headquarters, Ashanti, Gold Coast 1940 (*David Allen*)

Zaria Races, N. Nigeria 1926 (*Clifford Ruston*)

The Rex Cinema, Ibadan 1939 (*Mrs Betty Moresby-White*)

The District Officer's house at Mandera, Kenya 1936 (*Sir Richard Turnbull*)

The District Officer's office, Mandera 1936 (*Sir Richard Turnbull*)

The District Officer and the tribal *baraza*, Tanganyika c. 1954 (*Charles Meek*)


*Between pages 94 and 95*

Touring or 'going to bush' in West Africa, Nigeria 1959 (*Michael Crowther*)

On safari in classical style, N. Rhodesia 1935 (*Royal Geographical Society*)

The District Officer setting out on safari, Uganda 1925 (*Mrs Mavis Stone*)

Camping in the bush, N. Rhodesia 1935 (*RGS*)

Ablutions on safari, Mbulu District, N. Tanganyika c. 1955 (*Charles Meek*)

The local Emir or district head and the touring Resident, N. Nigeria 1959 (*Michael Crowther*)

The 'Officer-in-Charge' confronting a deputation of Turkana near Lake Rudolf, 1947 (*Sir Gerald and Lady Reece*)

*Between pages 122 and 123*

Margaret Gillan, Jebel Marra mountains, Western Sudan 1935 (*Sir Angus Gillan*)

Betty Moresby-White at breakfast, Ibadan 1939 (*Betty Moresby-White*)

The Governor in full ceremonial regalia, Gold Coast *c.* 1945 (*Sir Alan Burns*)

The Governor in mufti, N. Tanganyika 1958 (*Sir Richard and Lady Turnbull*)

The Governor's Lady boating down the Rufiji river, Tanganyika 1959 (*Sir Richard and Lady Turnbull*)

The reality of Mau Mau, Kenya 1953 (*Popperfoto*)

Julius Nyerere shortly before Tanzanian Independence, Dar es Salaam *c.* 1960–1 (*Charles Meek*)

# PREFACE

This reconstruction of part of Britain's recent Imperial past was assembled from the recorded experiences of some fifty Britons who lived and worked in Africa in the days of British colonial rule. Drawn chiefly, but by no means exclusively, from the former ranks of the Colonial Administrative Service, these men and women were kind enough to let me interview them at length for the BBC's Sound Archives. Without their co-operation, candour and generosity neither this book nor the radio series of the same title (first broadcast on BBC Radio 4 in 1979) could have been compiled. Many extended their help to include most useful advice and suggestions, as well as offering private material in the form of photographs and illustrations – of which only a small proportion could be included in this book. From among these contributors I must single out especially Anthony Kirk-Greene, now Senior Research Fellow at St Antony's College, Oxford, whose advice both in the original recording project and in the compilation of this book proved invaluable. Adding the historian's breadth of vision to the practical experience of the man in the field, his Introduction provides a salutary counterbalance to what is essentially a social panorama rather than any sort of historical record. Both to him and to these many friends of Africa past and present I must express my sincere thanks, with the hope that this distillation of their experiences will to some extent justify their kindness.

The chequer-board of colonies, protectorates, trust territories, mandated territories and one condominium that until the mid-1950s and early 1960s made up the sum of Britain's African Empire had very little in common beyond the imposed system of government that briefly linked them together. Rather than attempt to particularize British rule in each of these territories I have concentrated on the general form of Crown rule itself – on the shared experiences rather than the differences or the distinctiveness of each country. I have, however, concentrated rather more heavily on certain territories than on others, so as to reflect the relative importance – in colonial terms – of those territories. More is said about British West Africa

(Nigeria, the Gold Coast, Sierra Leone and the Gambia) than British East Africa (Kenya, Tanganyika, Uganda, Zanzibar and British Somaliland), which is, in turn, better represented than British Central Africa (Northern Rhodesia and Nyasaland). A lot more is quoted (both about themselves and the country) from those who were in a 'top division' territory such as Nigeria (with a population of thirty million and enough land to bury France, Belgium and Italy combined) than from those who served, for instance, in the Gambia (which is little more than a three-hundred-mile strip of territory on either side of the only navigable river in West Africa). I also make no apology for including the Sudan, which falls naturally within the scope of this book (even though it came under the direction of the Foreign Office rather than of the Colonial Office), and for all but excluding Southern Rhodesia, which does not.

In this panorama I have made no attempt to confront the political issues of colonialism. I have confined myself simply to putting on record and in their own terms something of the manner and style of those who were there, placing them and their beliefs in the context of the times in which they lived and worked. Within this framework I have retained a colonial sense of geography, in which, for instance, modern-day Ghana, Zambia, Tanzania, Malawi and the Somali Republic appear as they were then – as the Gold Coast, Northern Rhodesia, Tanganyika, Nyasaland and British Somaliland. Similarly, I have referred to my witnesses in the text as they were known then. Brief details of their careers and their distinctions will be found in the appended notes on contributors.

Britain's colonial involvement in Africa was so remarkably short-lived and has been so recently brought to an end that in 1977–8, when these interviews were conducted, it was still possible to find witnesses to what was almost the complete colonial cycle of occupation, consolidation, emancipation and withdrawal. This wide range of experience spans the first sixty years of this century, as remembered by three different generations: those who went out to Africa before the Great War (Chapters 1 and 2); those who went out between the wars (Chapters 3–8); those who followed during and after the Second World War (Chapters 9 and 10). At one end of the time-scale are men like Chris Farmer (Nigeria), Patrick Mullins (Gold Coast and Nyasaland), and Noel Harvey (Nyasaland), all of whom went out as administrators in the 1940s and 1950s and now occupy senior positions within the BBC. At the other there are the last survivors of that momentous age known – from a somewhat partisan point of view – as the era of pacification; the years before the Great War when men like Sir Angus Gillan (born in 1885) and Sir Alan Burns (born in 1887) went out to the Sudan and to Southern Nigeria, and when Mrs Sylvia Leith-Ross (born in 1883) was one of the first white women in Northern Nigeria. Chapter 2 is devoted entirely to the early experiences of these three veteran witnesses.

Although this cycle of events is mainly recalled by those who came out as administrators, as well as the wives who followed them, I have also included a limited number of contributions from other ex-colonials. If this concentration on the life of the District Officer seems to have been made at the expense of the Education Officer, the Superintendent of Police or the Agricultural Officer, or if the contributions of the missionaries and the pioneering work of surveyors, bridge-builders, Public Works Department men and B class officials appear to have been neglected, then let me emphasize that it was the administrator in his role as government servant who first and last provided the common thread that bound so many different territories together under one flag. Off-duty and in many ways he shared a common life-style with other expatriates, but his work and all that went with it was unique and has no modern-day parallel.

Whatever their background and working experience these witnesses shared the exercise of power in one form or another in British Colonial Africa – and as such they may be regarded as representative of their time. Accordingly, I have not always identified quotations when commonly expressed attitudes or experiences are given. Nor have I presented the spoken words of my contributors as a series of individual experiences, but have edited and assembled them as interrelated parts of a whole. For ease of reading I have made minor amendments and conjunctions but as far as possible excerpts have been quoted as they were spoken. I have also sought to exclude, as far as this is ever possible, all views and opinions other than those expressed in the original material. For this and for the way in which the spoken words have been selected and related, the responsibility is entirely mine. While the end result remains my own interpretation I hope it may still claim to be a fair and faithful reanimation of the peculiar spirit of an age and of a group of men and women for whom I have great respect.

Theirs is only a part and only one side of the story of British colonial rule in Africa. But they have given a frank and often self-critical account of their lives, without seeking either to idealize or to patronize. As a result I, for one, have found their story all the more impressive.

*Tales from the Dark Continent* was largely inspired by Helen Fry, Chief Producer, Sound Archive Features, and producer of the BBC Radio 4 series of the same title. My special thanks are due to her and to Tony Trebble, Chief Librarian, BBC Sound Archives, without whose joint patronage and encouragement this record could never have been made. My thanks also to Connie Ross-Barnard for her assistance in producing (against all the odds) transcripts, to Diana Souhami for her picture research and to the following for their most valuable advice and assistance: Mr and Mrs J. J. Allison; Dr John Bloss; The Rt Rev. Cecil Patterson; Sir Frederick Pedlar; John

Wilkinson; D. Simpson and library staff at the Royal Commonwealth Society; the Director and staff at the Royal Geographical Society; Patricia Pugh, Archivist of the Colonial Records Project, Oxford; L. Ody, Managing Director of Walters and Co., Oxford; the United Africa Company International Ltd; Unilever Ltd; the Elder Dempster Shipping Line; the Army and Navy Stores. Finally, may I acknowledge the very special debt that I owe to my partner in work, my wife.

# INTRODUCTION

Anthony Kirk-Greene

On the eve of the Second World War Britain's Colonial Empire was made up of 45 territories, 2 million square miles and 50 million inhabitants. All but 300,000 square miles of the Empire was in tropical Africa, where there were no less than 14 territories, all of them staffed by members of the Colonial Service. A decade or so ago this Colonial Service (or Her Majesty's Overseas Civil Service, as it was by then known) followed its sister Services, the Indian Civil and Political Services and the Sudan Political Service, into extinction. This book will help to preserve the memory of what it was like, at the grass-roots level of daily routine, to live and work in Africa in the first sixty years of this century. Charles Allen has stitched together a thousand threads of narrative – memories and impressions teased out of many hours of interviews. Here is the very fabric of oral history, at once a unique testimony and an important contribution to Britain's social and Imperial history.

Having spent sixteen years in the Colonial Administrative Service in Africa, I have no difficulty in recognizing the authentic echoes of such a career in Charles Allen's rendering, though no doubt there will be some from West or East Africa who will shake their heads and lament that it was never like that for them. And while both Charles Allen and I may seem to highlight the role of the colonial administrator, no one who ever worked in the Colonial Service would wish to imply that the District Officer was the only pebble on the beach. Much of what is recalled is as true of the lives of the professional and technical officers who made up the bulk of the Colonial Service as it is of the administrators whose experiences comprise the main part of this book. Finally, the view from the *boma* is unarguably but one side of the story. What tales the African participants would have to tell – chief and clerk, peasant and politician, *askari* and *alkali*, about the Colonial Service from the receiving end!

Often alone, in no way was the District Officer in Africa lone-handed. Besides his personal staff of messengers, interpreters and a handful of

African policemen, there was the whole administrative apparatus of African chieftaincies, or Native Administrations as they came to be called, to assist in the running of the district. Moreover, in each colony there were hundreds of professional and technical officers, men and women, in the agricultural, medical, nursing, educational, police, forestry and veterinary fields; and in the Public Works Department, too – often forgotten, yet the first to come to mind when the only chair in one's mud-and-thatch rest-house lost its final leg.

Classically, the District Officer did not order, he advised; he did not rule, he administered. In practice, of course, there were good District Officers and bad District Officers, just as there were good and bad chiefs, so that 'advice' could mean anything from unambiguous instruction through tactful intervention to feet up on the office table and a sigh of 'let them ask if they want to learn'. There were always some who believed that the 'best' district was the one that gave no trouble, were rarely heard of in headquarters and never in the Colonial Office or the House of Commons. 'No progress, no palaver' ought to have been the motto of certain District Officers who would have given anything for a quiet time. Yet the principle of indirect rule, of being the whisper behind the throne, was firmly institutionalized as a tenet of Native Administration.

A lot of nonsense is talked about the colonial administration. One uninformed allegation which flies in the face of the facts is that it was only interested in law and order, never in economic or social development. The truth is that this could not be either/or; it had to be a case of first/then. Improving law and order or imposing it were understandably the first preoccupations of the earliest generation of District Officers. For all the Hollywood distortion, parts of the Sanders of the River image – of Sandi who 'sat cross-legged on his canvas chair, chewing an unsmoked cigar and drawing little patterns with his ebony stick in the sand' and whose voice when he spoke as Keeper of the King's Peace was 'bleak and cold' – do have a degree of substance. The diaries of the District Officers of the time are full of entries about installing a new chief as a break with the past, introducing a tax-gathering system, meting out what at least seemed to them to be justice, and settling fights and feuds. And what characters these first administrators were! Some had come straight in from the Boer war, men in search of the room to breathe and the chances which Africa offered. Others had transferred from the Charter Company administrations; the British Imperial East Africa Company, the Royal Niger Company and the British South Africa Company. Many were experienced administrators. A few had been adventurers; I know of one doctoral thesis on the origins of the Kenyan Service which at times reads more like fiction than fact. One recruit had been a shipwright, one an elephant hunter, another a batman to a general. A mixed bag, certainly, but those were the days when to be a character was more important than to be conventional.

After 1920, new needs called for new breeds. Now men were required who had brains in their heads as well as fire in their bellies. And from 1926 the Colonial Service reached a fresh level of professionalism, whereby every cadet underwent a year's post-graduate course at Oxford or Cambridge or later in London. More than one governor has assured me that the cream of District Officers came in two waves: one the intakes following the slump when, with the Indian Civil Service out of favour as a career abroad and with jobs at a premium at home, the Colonial Service was able to pick the very best; the other, the intakes immediately after 1946, when it recruited some of the finest officers, many with a record of war service in the Indian Army or with the King's African Rifles or Royal West African Frontier Force.

How and why did one become a District Officer? One view is expressed by a distinguished colonial administrator who admitted that the reason he applied was that, after finishing his finals at the university, he was determined never to take another examination in his life: the Colonial Service recruited on interview and references alone. Another is reflected in C. P. Snow's *The Masters*, where the Bursar ruefully explains to the Senior Tutor his doubts of his son's ability to get through his finals, adding 'He's thought to stand a chance of the Colonial Service if he can scrape a third . . . though I can't see why our colonies should need third-class men with a capacity for organized sports.' By far the most widely shared motive was, I believe, the feeling that there was an interesting, varied career in a warm climate, devoid of routine, reasonably paid, offering a real chance of creativity along with exceptional responsibilities at an early age. In the case of many of the two thousand post-war cadets, there was the additional inducement that it was an opportunity to live among peoples they had got to know and learned to like during the war or at the university.

One aspect of the Colonial Office's recruitment and posting procedures I still have not been able to have satisfactorily explained. How did the Colonial Office allocate candidates to colonies? Was a man posted to, say, Kenya, a Kenyan type (whatever that meant) before he went there, or did he become one after he had been there? Technically, we were allowed to list three choices. I put down Malaya, because I had been in India during the war and wanted to get back to South-east Asia; Hong Kong, because I had had a Chinese girl-friend and had enjoyed *The World of Suzy Wong*; and the New Hebrides, because I rather fancied my competence in French. When the telegram arrived, I was offered Nigeria: and from the moment of disembarking at Lagos I never once regretted the posting. But how they got it right when I got it wrong, I have never understood!

I have often thought that those like myself who joined the Colonial Service just after the Second World War were doubly lucky. We were in at the end of the grass-roots, out-station style of colonial administration, characterized by the firm belief that 'real' administration meant 'rural' administration. At the same time we had the opportunity to take part in a new but no less exciting and challenging aspect of colonial administration, the art not of ruling but of relinquishing an empire. Gone were the days when the District Officer could properly be termed the maid-of-all-work: treasurer, magistrate, prosecutor and defence counsel, road-builder and tax collector all rolled into one. The post-war District Officer was likely to be the leader of a District Team of professionals; in headquarters, a Permanent Secretary in one of the new ministries or private secretary to one of the new African ministers. Inevitably he became the linchpin in the new constitutional structure of elections. Though the average District Officer evinced little enthusiasm for politics in his own country, in Africa he tended to become more and more involved in the exuberant world of party political activity and, as the decade of decolonization continued, more of a bureaucrat and less of an administrator. The irony was that many of his new functions paralleled the desk-bound Whitehall career which he had consciously rejected a few years earlier in favour of the District Officer's saddle and the safari.

One of the District Officer's last functions was among the most important of all: that of training up his successors. This could take one of two forms. One was simple propinquity, in the hope that the magic of the master would wear off on his pupil – it was how the modern British colonial administrator had himself received most of his training, and it was at first thought that this would be right for the new African entry too. But a crucial point was missed. That form of training had depended upon a close and constant relationship between the District Officer and his Assistant, often on a two-men-and-a-dog out-station, and in the decade of decolonization permanent postings were very rare: early retirements, staff shortages and changing priorities resulted in a musical-chair medley of postings which could leave the pupil-cadet in charge of a division only a few weeks after his arrival.

The other way in which the new African administrative cadet was inducted into his job constituted a positive break in the tradition of Britain's Imperial Services. Institutes of Public Administration were now established in the African territories and specific training courses were mounted for Assistant District Officers. The versatile amateur, well-grounded in the classics, was giving way to the new-look administrator with his B.Sc., B.Econ. or B.A. in Public Administration.

If we ask whether – and if so where – the Colonial Administrative Service went wrong, the answer for me lies fairly and squarely in the attitude towards the admission of Africans into the Service. As late as 1938, an argument influential among colonial governments in West Africa was the 'scaffolding theory'. It would be quite wrong, the argument went, to allow Africans to become District Officers when, come Independence, the scaffolding of provincial administration would be taken down to reveal a system of self-government that was no more in need of the District Officer than the British system of local government requires a DO Fens or a PC Borders – however much some of us might sometimes feel that such a cutter-of-the-Gordian-Knot ombudsman is just what modern bureaucracy does need! Here, I believe, the Colonial Office was too lenient. Had it directed the colonial governments to embark on a positive programme of educating, training and recruiting Africans into the Administrative Service between, say, 1925 when Sir Gordon Guggisberg drew up his plan (abortive, in the event) and 1942 when Sir Alan Burns on the Gold Coast forced the issue; or had it carried through Lord Hailey's perceptive recommendation of 1941 which, sensing the appalling gap in bureaucratic competence between the European District Officer and the African first-class clerk, urged the establishment of an Intermediate Administrative Service as a training and promotion cadre for African District Officers – then, I believe, things would have gone far more smoothly when it came to the transfer of power. In addition to this neglect in training up African administrators there was also what I fear to have been the typical British administrator's attitude towards the educated élites – at least until working closely with African Members of Parliament taught him better. His often cutting contempt for them was matched only by the staunchness of his affection and admiration for the extremes of African society, the peasant and the prince – above all, for the eponymous 'Audu' in the bush at the expense of the humiliated Mister Johnsons and the much-maligned *babus* of colonial administration. Of course, one's personal relations with Africans could be a source of pleasure and pride. Often it was this which brought the greatest rewards to the routine of administration. Yet when the history of Britain's Imperial administrations comes to be written, in Asia as well as in Africa, we may well find that it was not so much race relations in general as individual social relationships which will prove to have been the Achilles' heel of the Empire.

Let me finish with an epitaph on the District Officer in Africa. It comes from the late Prime Minister of Nigeria, Sir Abubakar Tafawa Balewa. In a speech made on Independence Day in October 1960, he paid tribute to the record of the British Colonial Service. 'We are grateful to the British officers,' the Prime Minister said, 'whom we have known first as masters and then as leaders and finally as partners; but always as friends.'

# one

---

# RUNNING UP THE FLAGS

*It was very largely individuals running up flags and saying, 'We are Residents' that brought the North under administration. And it was they that really gave substance to a somewhat extravagant boast within a few years of the occupation that a virgin could walk from Lake Chad to Sokoto with a bowl of eggs on her head and neither the virgin nor the eggs would be spoiled.*

Britain's imperial rule in Africa was extraordinarily brief, as empires go. In Nigeria crown rule started in 1900 and finished in 1960, 'so that it was perfectly possible – as was, in fact, the case – for a number of old men to have lived to see the British come and go.' While collecting for Nigeria's museums at the time of Independence, Philip Allison once talked with an old chief of Benin: 'I'd called to look at some of his wood-carvings and brass castings and when I came to go he said, "I'm sorry we had to talk through an interpreter. When the British came I was out there on the Ologbo road, holding a gun for one of the chiefs when we were fighting the British. And when the British came we thought they wouldn't stay very long so none of us really bothered to learn English. I'm sorry now."' This same brief time-scale applied to almost every African territory that came under British control, with a beginning and an end within a single life-span, occupying the working lives of no more than three generations of its rulers.

But crown rule was not in itself the beginning of the British connection. In West Africa especially, British involvement went back over two centuries: 'There is a famous old quotation that "Trade follows the Flag" but in fact in West Africa and in most other parts of the Empire the reverse was true. After all, the East India Company first established British interests in India, and in Rhodesia the British South Africa Company, in East Africa it was the Imperial British East Africa Company and in Nigeria the Niger Company. These were really the first British presences.'

But long before these chartered empire-building companies there had been other interests, for 'the first signs of the white man that the African ever saw were the slave-traders and the early traders in the oil rivers; the most villainous, ghastly, dreadful people.' Relics of the trade in human lives could be found in almost every territory occupied by the British in Africa. In the West Coast it was to be seen in the big iron rings on the walls of the bank building in Bathurst where Bill Page worked as a cashier in the late 1920s and in the vast dungeons of the 'fairy-tale' Christiansborg Castle through which Gold Coast society danced congas in the 1950s. It was there in the demoralization and breakdown of tribal society and in the inter-tribal wars that were often cited as grounds for the assumption of white superiority in the early days of British rule.

In East Africa it was the flourishing traffic in slaves to the Middle East that first encouraged an active British interest in that region, while in the Islamic regions of the Sudan and Northern Nigeria the suppression of slavery was one of the declared objectives of the occupying British forces. Nor had the trade been entirely abandoned by the time that Angus Gillan came to the Sudan in 1909: 'Two or three of my servants were boys whom we managed to pick up being traded as slaves across to Jidda and Saudi Arabia. I know one little boy I had, he and his sister were being run across from some far remote part of the French Sudan and it was quite impossible to discover where one could send them back to, so one more or less had to take them on as servants.'

It was slavery and the anti-slavery movement that brought many of the early Christian missions upon the African scene. In the West Coast there was the Calabar Mission of the Church of Scotland, which had its roots in Jamaica following the emancipation of the slaves there in the 1830s:

The urge of the slave people – a great number of whom had come from Nigeria – was made very clear to the early leaders of the Calabar Mission, who raised funds to send a team of Jamaicans and Scots and Irish to Calabar and they actually arrived and set up the mission in 1846. There were no mass conversions to Christianity, but they persisted and did a remarkable job translating the Bible into the ethnic languages. And that really was a great step forward because that led them to start schools, and really the main effort of the Christian thrust was through the schools, through the children – and that persisted right through until we were absorbed into the Nigerian Church.

Although the missionaries played no official part in government there were many regions where they blazed the trail and even – in some rare cases – assisted to some degree in maintaining law and order. An outstanding example was Miss Mary Slessor of Dundee, chiefly remembered for her efforts to suppress infanticide in the Calabar region, a 'very nice old lady'. who 'had a great longing to explore and open up country further up the Cross river. Going up in canoes to Itu she started stations and collaborated very remarkably with the government District Officers of that time, who were so impressed by her influence over the chiefs that they gave her government status and she became a judge in the native courts, using a legal code that was very much her own.' When the Reverend Bob Macdonald first came out to Calabar as a missionary in 1929 Mary Slessor had been dead for fifteen years:

But of course a great number of the local people remembered her. On one occasion in a far-out village I was giving a lantern lecture, and I had a sheet up for a screen and a very doubtful kind of lantern which went on and off. But I happened to get a lot of old slides of Miss Slessor and her visitation and I showed one of this very town that I was in, and the old head chief came to me immediately afterwards and said, 'Give me that cloth, that was my friend. I want to keep it.' He had been one of her advisers and friends while she was opening up that area.

In East Africa the early pioneer whose name was best remembered was David Livingstone. Some years after the Second World War Darrell Bates was caught in heavy rain while on safari in his district of Tabora, in the middle of Tanganyika:

An old Arab asked me if I would like to come into his house to shelter from the rain, and he was very apologetic. He said, 'This is a very poor house but my house is thy house,' in the polite way that they have. And then he said, 'Many, many years ago *bwana mokolo*, the holy man, stayed here, the man that you call Livingstone. I'm an old man but I never met him of course – but my father met him, and I remember my father talking of him.' Now this was marvellous for me because Livingstone was in Tabora in 1872, I think it was, and so this went back seventy years and more. And he spoke about Livingstone as if he had met him only yesterday.

But Livingstone's main influence was concentrated further inland – in Nyasaland, which was regarded very much as Livingstone's creation:

It was he who first discovered Lake Nyasa in the late 1850s and was responsible for bringing out the University Mission to Central Africa in the 1860s, because he was quite convinced the future for Africa was to be British. It was an exclusively British dream that he had, to bring commerce and Christianity to that part of the world and he established this mission under conditions which were really almost intolerable for them to sustain, with slave-raiding going on all round them. The mission suffered disastrous casualties and had to be withdrawn after two years. The whole area was in chaos and practically depopulated by the 1870s, but the missionaries started to return and they were the first Europeans in the field. Gradually these missions developed in the 1880s, a small commercial centre grew up in Blantyre town and it was realized, with the Portuguese pressing at the southern end of the territory and the Germans in Tanganyika, that if there was to be a British presence in that part of the world, the United Kingdom Government would have to declare a Protectorate, and eventually in 1891 they did so. But all the early development and all the schools were set up by the missionaries. The Government didn't take over any responsibility for education in Nyasaland until the 1920s. The missionaries ran a great deal of the country in the early days and they were admirable people.

When Patrick Mullins came out to Nyasaland in 1952 the mission influence was still very strong: 'They lived on £30 a year and 7s. 6d. a day messing

3

allowance. They lived beside their African priests under very much the same conditions, they spoke the African languages, they understood the African better than anyone else in the country and they were entirely selfless, spending very little on themselves and devoting their lives to the people.'

But it was organized commerce rather than Christianity that really paved the way for crown rule. Here, too, the influence of the early days, the years of commercial freebooting and rivalry, continued well into the twentieth century. When Edwin Everett took up his first post at Badagri, close to Nigeria's border with Dahomey, in 1938, there was a relic of the past in the shape of the 'hulk' moored in the creek that served as both living quarters and police post. Although it was by then a two-storey structure built on a pontoon, it took its name from the days when other hulks had been moored permanently in the Badagri and other 'oil-river' creeks of Nigeria, providing homes and trading posts for the 'old coasters' and 'palm-oil ruffians' of Victorian times.

A more widespread legacy of those early trading days was the 'canteen', the up-country store operated by one or other of the many European trading companies – also known in the earlier days as 'barter-rooms' or 'factories'. Like many words in common usage in West Africa 'canteen' had its origins in the lingua franca of the coast, 'pidgin' or 'Kru-English', a basic trading language devised partly from Portuguese and partly from other sources. The spirit of nineteenth-century free enterprise also lingered on in the rival trading companies that continued to compete against one another until the economic realities of the Depression finally forced them to merge. When Donald Dunnet and Clifford Ruston came out to Nigeria after the First World War – to join rival companies which eventually became part of the United Africa Company – going into the West Africa trade was not so much a career as an adventure:

If one's health failed one was fired and that was the end of it. There was no Provident Fund and there was no superannuation – although there was free medical attention for any complaint which wasn't caused by your own indulgence. The staff were more or less expendable. This was a relic of the old sailing-ship days when you signed on as crew in a schooner and if you got back you were lucky. And while you were there you made what you could for yourself. There was more or less an understanding going back to the old sailing-ship days when the sailors up the masts, who had either to take the canvas in or put it out, had a motto: 'One hand for the owner and one hand for yourself'. And it was very much that sort of thing trading ashore – only in some cases it was two hands for yourself and nothing for the owner. There was no loyalty to the firm. They didn't deserve it.

Another feature that survived into the inter-war period was the intense

4

competition between the trading companies: 'This tradition of intense – almost insane – rivalry also dated back to the old sailing-ship days, when ships would arrive full of cargo which they were going to sell over the ship's side and buy produce to fill up the ship and sail away. And the quicker they got their business transacted and finished and got away, the less risk there was of dying. So when there were two or three ships, say, anchored in the Calabar river, there was intense competition to get away. And somehow or other that tradition had been passed on.'

West Africa's reputation as the White Man's Grave also lingered on well into the twentieth century – and with some cause. 'In the early twenties there was a great deal of illness,' recalls Clifford Ruston, 'malaria, yellow fever and blackwater fever, and the mortality was quite severe. If a man was sick and died in the early morning he was buried the same day, for obvious reasons. Seldom a month went by without our attending a funeral of some member of the European community.'

The treatment for yellow fever was particularly unpleasant: 'They stuck a needle into the stomach of the patient, pumped in a large quantity of serum, unscrewed the syringe, refilled it with the needle still in the stomach of the patient and then did a further injection.' Other unpleasantnesses abounded in the form of a wide variety of afflictions that could strike the unsuspecting. There was the *guinea* worm – 'a water-borne parasite which laid its eggs in the water and if not properly filtered or boiled – or boiled and filtered as we used to do in Nigeria – the egg hatched out inside you and the worm proceeded to wander around until it usually got stuck in one of the extremities – usually the leg, which then swelled up. Eventually the worm made a hole in the skin and the old way of getting rid of it was to wash yourself and when the tail projected you nipped it with a piece of bent straw strongly enough to prevent it drawing itself in and then each day you wound the worm out a small distance.' There was the *tumbo* fly, 'which tended to lay its eggs on wet grass or on the underside of leaves, places greatly favoured by Nigerian washerwomen for spreading clothes for drying', and whose worm manifested itself as a large boil; and the *filaria* fly, whose worms 'travelled about the body and when one got stuck in the wrist, for instance, a large bump rose up like half an orange and the fingers looked like a rubber glove that had been blown up. You also knew that if you had one you probably had lots of others and your only chance in those days of getting rid of it was if one day you suddenly began to see double, then you quickly called somebody who would look in your eye and, having seen the small worm gradually working its way across the eyeball, would pick it out with a needle or even a thorn – and that meant one worm less.'

Company rule in Nigeria – the fifteen-year administration of part of Southern Nigeria – under a royal charter by the Niger Company ended when the company's flag was hauled down at Lokoja on 31 December 1899. But there were other parts of Africa where this stage of colonial evolution continued through into the post-war period. When Bill Stubbs went out to Southern Rhodesia in 1921, that territory, as well as Northern Rhodesia, was still being governed by the British South Africa Company under a charter obtained by Cecil Rhodes in 1889: 'In fact the country was administered – and well administered – by a company and not by a crown.' Its paramilitary arm – and the service which Bill Stubbs joined – was the British South Africa Police, 'a mounted infantry regiment recruited in the first place by Cecil Rhodes or his agents in the 1890s. The advertisement used to appear in the paper – in the personal columns of *The Times*, I think it was – "Vacancies occur from time to time for the sons of gentlemen who can ride and shoot and are fond of an open-air life. Join the British South Africa Police!"'

Closely associated with Cecil Rhodes and his empire-building schemes was the Grenfell family. In 1896 Harry Grenfell's grandfather, Lord Grey, was appointed Administrator of Southern Rhodesia and brought his wife and daughter approximately a thousand miles in an ox-wagon from the railhead at Mafeking to Bulawayo: 'The result was that in August 1896 my grandfather, my grandmother and my mother were living in Government House at Bulawayo, a simple building built on the site of the *kraal* which had been occupied by Lobengula, who had been king of the Matabele before the pioneers entered Rhodesia with C. J. Rhodes.' In that same year the Matabele Uprising took place – the last, unsuccessful stand against the white settlement of Southern Rhodesia: 'As a girl of seventeen my mother rode on to the Matopo hills with C. J. Rhodes at one of the meetings which led to the making of peace with the Matabele.'

The other territory in which white settlement was promoted was Kenya and it was while serving there with the King's African Rifles in 1924 that Anthony Lytton took part in what may well have been the last great *vortrek* by covered wagon into the African interior:

Part of my task was to arrange for a boat to be despatched on ox-wagons in pieces together with four Indian carpenters, who were to put it together on the very unfriendly shores of Lake Rudolf. In order that matters should be properly done, we had imported a South African who was called a conductor, John Muller, a truly magnificent type of man who knew every one of his five or six hundred beasts and who himself, at night, in areas infested with tsetse fly, took through the *drifts* – that is to say, the river-beds – every single wagon. Now the wagons were relatively small affairs and there were nine yoke of oxen – that's eighteen in each of thirty wagons. Therefore a very considerable herd of animals and a very considerable cloud of dust and a very considerable journey stretching out over an area that had no proper road at all. The safari took place from six to ten in the morning, when we did eight miles;

two miles an hour. Then we *outspanned*, that is to say we stopped in a place preferably with water and grazing. From four to six we went another four miles – a total of twelve miles a day, and therefore a very slow progress, with plenty of time to wander about the country and inspect the game.

Anthony Lytton was then on his way to take over a district 'about one-fifth the size of England' as its military Officer-in-Charge, a curious and possibly unique anomaly created by special circumstances – but one that harked back directly to the era of pacification, the period round about the turn of the century when a number of territories had been occupied by military force and governed by a military administration. So it was that in 1924 Anthony Lytton found himself acting very much as his military predecessors had done a quarter of a century earlier in such territories as Northern Nigeria and Uganda:

All powers connected with administration were vested in the one white officer in any single post, such as the post I first went to at a place called Barseloy. All powers – of every sort – whether educational, medical, religious or anything else; they were all nominally vested in the Officer-in-Charge. As regards court matters and malefactors, I was a second class magistrate with power to imprison for up to two years. I rather think that in the period of fourteen or eighteen months that I was with the Samburu I dealt with no case at all – no case was brought before me; there was no crime. The chiefs were there and I suppose they exercised a certain amount of discipline. But there wasn't a civil administration at all, until – with the end of my time there – District Commissioners came and took over in the usual way.

In fact, he was governing in very much the manner instituted by the father of the King's African Rifles, Frederick Lugard – who first came to that region in 1890 with his own military force of fifty Somalis and fifty Sudanese. It was Lord Lugard, more than any other single individual, who set the style for future crown rule throughout the British territories in Africa. In particular, he was the architect of indirect rule, the system of dual government which 'came about partly because in various parts of Africa we'd bitten off more than we could chew. We couldn't possibly administer all these people and these vast territories closely. So our policy always was to leave as much as possible to the people themselves and not to interfere with their lives unless it was obvious that what they were doing was wrong. If they could settle their own quarrels, so much the better.'

The classic example of the application of the dual mandate was in Northern Nigeria, where political officers, drawn initially from Lord Lugard's occupying forces, left the running of local affairs very much in the hands of the local emirs. As a result there arose a marked division in the style of government between North and South: 'In the South it was direct rule and the District Commissioner really ran the show, whereas in the North the chiefs ran it under the supervision of the district staff.' Under Lord Lugard's direction these two separate territories were eventually brought together as the two provinces of the Protectorate of Nigeria, together with a small area round Lagos that was known as the Colony of Nigeria: 'So we talked of the Colony and Protectorate of Nigeria.'

One territory that was neither colony nor protectorate was the Condominium of the Sudan, where the flags of Great Britain and Egypt flew side by side outside every government building. Although it continued to be administered by a political service rather than a colonial service, its military administrators had departed by the time that James Robertson came out in 1922. But there were still plenty of reminders of the past:

At Omdurman the Mahdi's tomb was still unrepaired and there was a hole in the roof where a shell had gone through when one of Kitchener's gun-boats had shelled it. One of the things I did later in 1946 or '47 was to allow the Mahdi's son to rebuild his tomb. Quite a lot of the old men we met in these early days were people who had actually fought at the battle of Omdurman when Kitchener defeated the Khalifa's troops. There was one old gentleman in Western Kordofan who at the least provocation would pull up his pants and show you a hole in his leg which, he said, had been done by one of those 'Englezi' bullets; and there was an old gentleman called Ali Gula who used to tell me about Gordon and when Gordon used to ride through the country. Gordon was still quite a name in parts of Western Sudan.

The first generation of British administrators was drawn very largely from the ranks of the army or from such local paramilitary forces as the Royal Niger Constabulary or the British South Africa Police. One of the last to make this transition was Bill Stubbs, who transferred first to the Northern Rhodesia Police in 1924, just after that territory had been handed over to the Crown by the British South Africa Company, and then – with a little help from an influential uncle – into the civil administration:

Nobody else was appointed in such a way after me until the end of the Second World War when recruiting became a slightly different matter. But the earliest native commissioners and magistrates were men of very varied abilities and experience, some had been soldiers and some had been more or less adventurers who had fitted into the local pattern and were taken on. Some of our more outstanding early native commissioners came in by this route. Characters like Bobo Young, for example, a famous man in the early pioneer days who had started life as a pastry cook and then joined the army and saw service with the British Central Africa Company. All this, however, finished in about 1912 when the first batch of recruits came out direct from university.

Not all these early administrators were models of probity – as became apparent to Gerald Reece when he first came out to Kenya in 1925:

I'm afraid at the beginning I got a rather poor opinion of some of the older men. Their attitude to their job seemed to be different to those who'd just come out. For example, when they travelled – which they didn't do a very great deal – they would set up a Union Jack in their camp and rather tend to try and impress the natives with what wonderful things the British were doing for them; the whole idea of the White Man's Burden. I remember one of these old soldiers who, when he travelled north into the country of the Nilotic people, where the men are completely naked, always took with him an Indian trader with a large supply of khaki shorts, which he more or less forced the people to buy from the Indian by selling their goats. Now I thought that was a particularly bad thing to do because the Nilotic people have always been naked and are really very clean and, in their own way, a model people. But as soon as they put on khaki shorts, which were impossible for them to keep very clean, it was far less hygienic and healthy.

## The Surest Protector of Health & Comfort in Tropical Countries

Wherever the Britisher pioneers or settles, Burberry Kit provides the most comfortable and protective equipment— dress that proves a standby for years against rough usage, hard wear and extreme climates.

Advertisement for colonial wear 1931, its two illustrations representing the *beau ideals* of the soldier-pioneer and the civil administrator.

An equally unattractive manifestation not so much of the White Man's Burden as of the Black Man's Burden could still be observed in Zanzibar when William Addis first came there in 1925: 'If you were riding along and a man – even a long way off – saw you, he'd kneel down and start clapping and he'd go on doing this until you passed him. And if they came into the office the first thing they did was to kneel down and clap. They thought every white man was just perfect – and I never felt more like a tin god.'

Nevertheless, it was this early pioneer generation of administrators – the true contemporaries of Edgar Wallace's fictional character Sanders of the River – that created the legends which their successors savoured and enjoyed. One of the great characters of the pre-war period in Nigeria, about whom stories were still being told half a century later, was a man named Cockburn, known – no doubt for some sound reason – as Rustybuckle:

Many amusing stories are told about him and one of the best is that he was on the river steamer when the Governor, Sir Walter Edgerton, came up the river on a tour of inspection. He had to reprimand Rustybuckle for one of his various crimes and Rustybuckle listened for a while and then suddenly said, 'I can't stand this any longer,' and dived over the side. Everyone rushed to the side that he had gone over and a boat was lowered and the Governor himself was very upset by this and said that he would never have spoken to Rustybuckle in that way if he had known that it would have this result. In the meantime Rustybuckle, who was a very fine swimmer, had dived under the ship and come up on the other side, and he came up behind the Governor and said, 'I beg your pardon for interrupting you, sir.'

Survivors from this generation could still be found in nearly every territory in the inter-war period. In Somaliland there was the somewhat pompous governor who, when he got back from leave and landed at Berbera, 'got his house-boy to go down to the quay with an old gramophone to play "God Save the King" as he stepped ashore.' In Tanganyika there was the District Officer who 'woke up one morning to find an ant-hill beside his bed, lopped the top off with a *panga*, poured some paraffin over it and used it as a bedside table.' In the Northern Province of Uganda there was a well-known Provincial Commissioner who was said to wear his dinner jacket while out on safari. Dick Stone met him in 1937 shortly before his retirement: 'He always used to say – and he said this to me – "My boy, you must never have more than one drink in the evening." And I thought this seemed a bit extraordinary until I actually saw what he poured into his glass. He filled his glass half full of whisky and then added a touch of water – and that was his one drink.' Dick Stone's own father had himself acquired some local notoriety as a District Commissioner across the border in Kenya: 'When he was DC of Embu and people wanted to see him on what was called *shauri* – business of some kind – he made them walk up the hill where his office was with a large stone on their heads, and with these stones – after several thousand had been collected – he started building the *boma*, which became the district office.'

Eccentricity and foibles of character were qualities as much appreciated by Africans as by Europeans. Donald Dunnet recalls how in his early days in Nigeria 'it was common practice to give Europeans nicknames if they'd been long enough in the community to get reasonably well known. For example, we had one young chap who was very good-looking and he was known as *Ezecolobia*, which in Ibo is "king of the young men". There was another trading chap who had very slim hips and he was known as *Weng-wela*, which means "lizard". The African women in that area had a custom of wearing strings of beads round their waists which protruded underneath their cloth and gave them a sort of bustle appearance. Well, one of our chaps had a bottom that stuck out like that so he was known as *Jigada*, which is the name for these beads. Knowing that so many people had got nicknames, I made enquiries about my own and I was rather sorry I did because I was particularly corpulent at that time and my native name turned out to be *Miliafu*, which is "waterbelly".'

Undoubtedly one factor in exaggerating personality traits or behaviour was the extreme living and working conditions that many of these early pioneers had to endure. These conditions varied very greatly both from one territory to another and within each territory. Viewed from a strictly Western point of view, social development was equally varied. From a very early date it was possible to find in Bathurst, the capital of the Gambia, a black African society 'long accustomed to very easy social equality with their European counterparts in office' – whereas on the other side of Africa the social gulf between the races remained fixed for years to come. Coming out to Africa in 1932 as the wife of the new Governor of Uganda, having spent many years in India and Iraq, Violet Bourdillon was 'terribly depressed' by what she found:

I remember a friend coming to stay with me from India. We went on tour and she said, 'Oh, do take me out and show me their things, their carpets and so on.' I said, 'What things? They haven't got any things. They haven't even got the wheel. They don't make their own pottery. They've got some straw mats but I can't show you anything.' And I remember saying to one of the officials, 'I wish I could see something old' – because we'd just come from Ur of the Chaldees, you see – and the official said, 'Oh, but you are going to.' I said, 'How delightful! What are we going to see?' and he said, 'You are going to see a very ancient fort.' And I said, 'Yes, and who built it?' and he said, 'Lord Lugard'.

The contrast between British Uganda and British India was particularly marked: 'There was no comparison at all. In India even in our junior days

# TENTS

## FOR THE COLONIES.

### Fitted with VERANDAH, BATHROOM, &c.

As used by most eminent Travellers, and supplied to H.M. Government for East, West, Central, and South Africa, &c.

### SPECIAL TENTS FOR EXPLORERS & MOUNTAINEERING

# COMPLETE EQUIPMENT.

### CAMP FURNITURE WITH LATEST IMPROVEMENTS.
### AIR AND WATERTIGHT TRUNKS.
### UNIFORMS AND CLOTHING OF ALL KINDS.

"Consult with Messrs. Silver & Co., who know exactly what is needed for every part of the Globe."—*Extract from " Notes on Outfit," by the Royal Geographical Society.*

Advertisement from the Colonial Office List Advertiser

we toured far better than in Uganda. We travelled with an entourage of elephants and goodness knows what. But as a governor's wife I marched every bit of Uganda; we had two fly-tents that we slept under and everything was portered and done on the march.'

In 1935 when she and her husband moved on to Nigeria, Violet Bourdillon found Nigerian society very different. But even in West Africa, where colonial governors might reasonably have expected a certain standard of creature comforts, there were still surprising shortcomings. As late as 1941, when Alan Burns took over as Governor of the Gold Coast and moved into Christiansborg Castle, he found to his considerable astonishment that there was no plumbing. Indeed, the developing Colonial Service was 'a very austere service indeed' by comparison with the Indian Civil Service: 'All our colonial territories were hard up and there was none of the panoply of the Raj that had been accumulated over centuries in India against what had been basically a pretty wealthy background. None of this applied for us. The countries were wretchedly poor and the service, of course, was equally very poorly paid and poorly treated, by comparison with the ICS – all arising out of the financial circumstances which prevailed.'

Another obvious difference between India and Africa lay in communications. Even in 1927, when Martin Lindsay came out on attachment to the Nigeria Regiment, he found Nigeria to be 'a very primitive country' in this respect: 'There was only one railway line, from Lagos in the south to Kano in the north and, if you were stationed at one of the outposts like Sokoto in the north-west or Maiduguri in the north-east, from the moment you left the railhead you walked. You walked for three weeks to get to your post, with sixteen or twenty bearers carrying your kit on their heads, and then when you were due to go on leave you walked for another three weeks back to the railhead to take the train back again.'

In East or Central Africa the position was, if anything, worse. When an officer of the King's African Rifles was posted to a remote detachment like Wajir in Kenya's Northern Frontier District he had to take with him, as Brian Montgomery did in 1928, one year's supply of tinned food and other commodities:

No facilities existed there and you couldn't buy anything at all in terms of tinned food and the like. So I went to the firm of Jacobs in Nairobi, the only departmental store of any size there at that time, and I purchased a year's supply of tinned food. I have the bill still, and looking through it I see that this included thirty-six tins of sausages, twenty-one pairs of socks, a plentiful supply of Eno's Fruit Salts, one table lamp, one iron kettle and things of that kind. The bill came to £175 for which I got an advance of pay, and it did not take long to pay that back, as up in the Northern Frontier District there was nothing whatever to spend one's pay on except the wages of one's boy or servant at 20s. a month, the cook at 30s. a month and his *mtoto* at 10s. a month.

Given such conditions it was inevitable that many territories remained very much 'a man's world', placed virtually out of bounds for European women for many years to come. 'I think in the whole of my eighteen months I only spoke to a white woman about three times,' declares Martin Lindsay, 'probably just to say good afternoon when she came to watch a polo game, and nothing more than that. No white woman spent more than nine months at a time there and, of course, there wasn't a single white child in the whole of the country.' The consequences of this shortage of European female company were predictable. 'There was one custom that I came across in Wajir which at the age of twenty-three I found rather strange,' recalls Brian Montgomery. 'Shortly after I'd joined, the officer commanding the detachment and the DC came up to me and said would I like them to provide me with a *bibi*? I was not entirely clear what they meant but it soon became apparent they were referring to the services of a Somali girl-friend or sleeping partner.' In East Africa it was generally believed that 'East African officers as a whole maintained a very much stricter code in the matter of sleeping with African women' – sometimes referred to as 'sleeping dictionaries', from their obvious advantages as language instructors – than did their fellow-officers in West Africa. No doubt those in West Africa thought the reverse. 'The convention was abstinence for most people for most of their tour,' asserts Martin Lindsay, 'and that was the position in the central stations like mine, but I think that in the outposts most people probably had an African girl living with them. She wouldn't have her meals with the officer, and she wouldn't be seen in the house. She would merely have her own house behind, along with his servants and his servants' wives, and she'd only come into the house after dark. That was the life of most lonely men in the lonely stations and, of course, they did learn to speak the language far better than those of us who lived a life of abstinence.'

One result of this early fraternization was the notorious affair of the Secret Circulars A and B, issued by the Secretary of State for the Colonies in 1909: The first declared that "It had come to His Honour's attention that a certain number of government officials were living in a state of concubinage with native women and a very serious view would be taken of people living under these circumstances." Whereupon all sorts of unpleasantnesses beset the whole of the government service and a hurried Circular B was sent round saying that "With regard to my last Secret Circular A, it now appears that *not* such a serious view will be taken of government officers living in a state of concubinage with native women."

For District Officers like Nigel Cooke who followed this first generation, these early administrators laid up 'a capital of prestige and goodwill. One was very conscious all the time that in most places the British administrators were there and the people wanted them to be there because there was a need for law and order. And it was this capital on which my generation could draw and hopefully add to.'

Airylight, yet strong and durable, Burberry Kit withstands the roughest wear, and is so closely-woven that even the dreaded wachteen-beetje thorns and spear-grass cannot penetrate its thin and flexible texture.

A curious advertisement that appeared in 1931, seeming to suggest that the advertised material withstood spears as well as *wachteen-beetje* thorns and spear-grass.

# two

# WHITE MAN'S BURDEN; WHITE MAN'S GRAVE

*Beware, take care of the Bight of Benin;*
*One comes out though forty go in.*

From an early age historical events impelled Angus Gillan towards a life of service in the Sudan:

The name of Gordon was still very familiar to us in the nursery and in our schooldays; the Kitchener expedition, of course, occurred while I was still at school and there was something which appealed to us rather directly. We had been mixed up in it and we felt, I think, that we owed something to Gordon. Then when I went up to Oxford and started really thinking about what I was going to do I was attracted by some form of life in what one is not ashamed to call the Empire – though, of course, strictly speaking the Sudan didn't belong to the Empire.

In 1908 he applied to join the Sudan Political Service, then the best paid of all the Imperial Services, with a starting salary of £420 per annum:

I have got to say that the Sudan appealed to one because there was no competitive examination. There was a current phrase – I think it originated from the Warden of New College – that the Sudan was a country of blacks ruled by blues and there was just that essence of truth in it that these little stories convey. They wanted people who had had a share of responsibility, which I suppose comes to one if one is lucky enough to get on in the athletic world, and that is what Lord Cromer, who was the originator of the Sudan Political Service, really seemed to want – and I venture to think it worked reasonably well.

Angus Gillan himself was a notable oarsman who took time off during his third year in the Sudan to row in the 1912 Olympics. The same sporting prowess was evident in his fellow recruits:

Four of us went out together: two – myself and one other, Charles Dupuis, – from Oxford, and Robin Baily from Cambridge and Geoffrey Sarsfield-Hall from Trinity College, Dublin. I happened to have gained a certain notoriety in rowing, Charles Dupuis had rowed for his college and was a thoroughly all-round chap – I think he was president of his common room – Robin Baily was one of the best wicket-keepers Cambridge had produced up to that time and Sarsfield-Hall took a blue for hockey. So that we had a certain amount of athletic prowess between us, and I think our degrees varied between seconds and thirds.

After completing an additional year of training at Oxford, he and the other three probationer Deputy-Inspectors signed contracts, which laid down that 'we couldn't get married until we were taken on to pension, which roughly meant two years', and sailed to Alexandria. From there they proceeded to Cairo, where they brought themselves *tarboshes*:

In those days it was part of the office kit, I don't say we liked them very much but there it was. Of course, outside one wore a pith helmet or something of that sort until, say, three o'clock in the afternoon, and then probably a homburg hat until sunset. There were a couple of chaps who in my day used to go about without helmets; one looked on them both as rather mad, but whether they were mad because they didn't wear helmets or whether they didn't wear helmets because they were mad I really wouldn't know.

Proceeding up the Nile by rail and steamer they finally reached Khartoum, which was just beginning to take shape as a modern town:

In fact the river frontage was a very civilized-looking place; nice houses, gardens and all the rest of it, with the native population by and large living across the White Nile in Omdurman. But Khartoum itself was being built on Western lines – though not on the same lines as I've heard of anywhere else – because Kitchener laid down that it should be built in the form of a Union Jack, and for quite a long time they did stick to that form, until gradually it proved to be impossible and you got funny rows of houses cutting across at angles which did not appear on the Union Jack. But that was the original idea.

Society ran on rather different lines to what it did twenty or thirty years later, naturally. The people in high office were very often the people who had come up with Kitchener on the expedition and it was still very much a military administration. Some of them looked on us rather as a new type of young man that they didn't approve of. There were very few women there. It was very much a club life in those days and it took some courage after lunch to walk around the verandah of the club with all those old men sitting with newspapers in front of them and some of them looking over the top; you almost heard them saying, 'Who's that blanketty civilian, eh?'

It was also a very much noisier place than it became even in the days of the motor-car because everyone had a donkey in one's yard. The high and mighty had their own traps with ponies and a lot of people had riding ponies, but most of us had a donkey to take us to the office – and when one donkey started roaring, every donkey in the neighbourhood took it up and one was awakened in the middle of the night two or three times usually by a concerted choir of donkeys.

His first three months Angus Gillan spent at headquarters in Khartoum and across the river at Omdurman where 'one still felt the influence of previous history under the Mahdi and the Khalifa's reign. Slattin, of course, was a power in the land. He kindly asked the four of us to dinner one night and his reminiscences were extraordinarily interesting. He had been a prisoner of the Mahdi and became a Moslem not, I think, to save himself, but for the benefit of his own people. But he was wonderfully little embittered.' After spending a month in the Khalifa's old house under the charge of the Inspector of the District he began to go further afield. He learnt that Sudan was really made up of two very different regions:

The North was entirely Moslem, Arabic-speaking nearly everywhere except in the Red Sea hills where the Beggara tribes talked their own languages – the Beggaras being the fuzzy-wuzzies, the 'big, black bounding beggar that broke a British square' – but apart from that all Arabic-speaking and mostly Arab with a good deal of dark blood in them. And desert almost entirely, except for the narrow Nile valley. Then the South, beyond latitude 12, roughly, where you came into entirely different country, a country of black tribes, generations behind in what we call civilization, from the six-foot-six Nilotic Nuer to the squat forest people, pagan except where Christian missions had made their influence felt – and talking dozens of different languages. There were many parts where one was still called a Turk, because they and the Egyptians were the only whitish people they'd seen – and one didn't like the name of Turk because it did seem at that time to have connotations of slavery.

In due course Angus Gillan was posted to his first station, the headquarters of Kordofan Province at El Obeid:

I was dumped at Duein on the White Nile and there was allotted a number of hard camels to take me out to El Obeid, about five or six days journey. A good riding camel is one of the most comfortable means of locomotion I can possibly imagine; on the other hand a bad camel can make every bone of your body ache. So the ordinary hard handler was not a thing one would encourage, but still, it was the only thing one could get. From Duein to El Obeid it is typical scrub country; gum trees, various sorts of acacias – attractive country at sunset and sunrise, but it loses a good deal of its charm when the sun is beating down on your head. I was lucky enough to shoot a gazelle or two, which apart from being good for the pot made one feel that one really was going to be a game hunter. And I got up to El Obeid where I was welcomed by a very nice lot of chaps, mostly military.

Social life on what was still an entirely all-male station revolved around the mess, a simple rest-house where officers met for meals and drinks in the evening: 'Like all newly joined people, I was immediately made mess

MENU

EL OBEID, KORDOFAN.

Feb. 27th 1912

CAVIAR RUSSE

CONSOMMÉ AUX POINTES D'ASPERGES

SOUFFLÉS DE SAUMON

FOIE GRAS EN ASPIC

COTELETTES DE MOUTON

DINDON FARCI, LÉGUMES

MACÉDOINE DE FRUITS

CRÈME AUX CERISES

SCOTCH WOODCOCK

The menu commemorates the completion of the new railway line from Khartoum to El Obeid in 1912, formally declared open by Lord Kitchener of Khartoum himself. From the album of Sir Angus Gillan.

president, which meant that one did the donkey work.' Here he made the acquaintance of Uncle Zaid, the head waiter, who was many years later to become his personal servant – 'a grand old man and the best servant I ever had'. Uncle Zaid had been captured as a boy of seventeen at the Battle of Atbarah and had been with British officers ever since:

He had, like all of them, his eccentricities. You could bring anybody you liked to breakfast, lunch, dinner, it didn't matter, nor did it to the cook – somehow there was always something – but if I brought in anyone to tea he'd duly serve it but afterwards he'd come up and say, 'Mr So and So came to tea, I was not informed.' By and large one preferred servants who couldn't speak English – or who one thought couldn't speak English. This dear old Uncle Zaid never spoke to me in English at all, but he understood it all right. I remember once at some dinner party that the talk got on to some trouble in the Nuba mountains many years before and somebody said it was in such and such a month – 'Oh no, it couldn't have been because someone was on leave' – and so the talk went on with the usual chatter. Finally Uncle Zaid could bear it no longer. He bent down to my ear and said, 'It was 11 September 1904.'

As a Deputy-Inspector in a station like El Obeid, Gillan found himself called upon to be a jack of all trades:

There was the Provincial Governor and then there were a few Inspectors and they looked after the executive staff who were mostly Egyptian, and gradually the Inspector assumed the more permanent duties of the District Commissioner – as he eventually became even in title. You had all sorts of jobs thrust on you. You were of course responsible for the taxation and you were a magistrate and in El Obeid you had to go around with a theodolite marking out people's homes for them – the sort of thing a survey department, a public works department and a land office would have to combine to do. In a rough and ready way the Inspector had to do the whole thing.

A good part of his time was taken up with touring the district:

There was a tremendous lot to be said for the old slow touring on a pony or on a camel. You could keep in much closer touch with the people. Usually some sheikh or a man of importance would be riding along with you and in ordinary chat one learnt a great deal more than you could however much you trekked around in a car.

One of the rather happy incidents which often happened when one was touring round, was that you'd go into a village and somebody would come up to you, shake you warmly by the hand and ask how you were. And often one didn't recognize them straight away and you'd say, 'When did we meet last?' 'Oh, don't you remember? You sentenced me to six months in prison in your jail.'

Of course travelling around in those days, and even living in one's own house, might well be pretty primitive. One depended very largely for light on what we called *shamardans* – rather on the lines of the old carriage lamp, with a spring to keep the candle up and a globe which withstood a great deal of wind. They've given place, of course first to the pressure lamp and then to electricity. All one's kit was simple; a camp bath, camp chairs and, of course, if one was going to visit anyone, one took one's bed with one, which was considered in a later period as rather insulting to one's host.

In 1916 Angus Gillan became a central participant in events that led to the last major annexation of territory of the period of pacification:

At the beginning of 1913 I was transferred from El Obeid to Nahud, the most western district of Kordofan and of the Sudan. Bordering on it was Darfur, which was originally part of the Sudan under Slattin, previous to the Mahdi. On the reoccupation of Sudan, Darfur was really too big a nut to crack and the effective government boundary ended at the Nahud District. Beyond that the Sultan, Ali Dinar, paid a nominal tribute to the Sudan but nobody ever went across the border.

Soon after the outbreak of the First World War the Sultan stopped paying his tribute and announced that he wasn't going to pay any more: 'In January 1916 I was sitting in my office one morning when two obviously terrified men came crawling into the office – which was not the usual form for our petitioners to adopt – and handed over my desk two spears and two throwing-sticks engraved with texts from the Koran about the fate to be suffered by infidels – the obvious implication being a declaration of war.'

After unsuccessful attempts by the Sudan Government to defuse the situation, an expeditionary force was sent in to Darfur. After a one-sided engagement outside El Fasher the Sultan fled south with the remains of his army. A small force of mounted infantry was sent after him, which Angus Gillan accompanied as Political Officer:

We found the camp in which he'd been hiding for the last two or three months empty – but the pots were still boiling and we collected a very large number of rifles and such like. We were sitting at the next halt in the evening when two people came in who, I discovered, were Ali Dinar's spies, sent out to see where we were. Perhaps wisely they turned coat and told us where he was. So we set off that evening and at almost seven in the morning we found his camp and the machine-gun was playing on his camp before they had realized we were there. Off they scampered and off we scampered behind them from one little prominence to another. There was a series of little battles and at the site of the second or third we came across the body of a man, which was Ali Dinar with a bullet through his head. So the old gentleman eventually died in the field of battle, as I have no doubt he would have wished, and that finished the show. It took some time to get things settled down but on 1 January 1917, Darfur was declared to be an ordinary province of the Sudan.

Alan Burns came out to Nigeria in 1912, the same year in which Sir Frederick Lugard returned to unite the two separate regions of Northern and Southern Nigeria into the Protectorate of Nigeria. His background was rather exceptional:

I was born in the West Indies – and practically into the Colonial Service, as my grandfather had been Auditor-General of the Leeward Islands and my father was Treasurer of St Kitts. I also had an elder brother who was in the Colonial Service. My father's friends were all members of the civil service and it seemed to me the natural career for any young man.

After working in the local civil service for several years and seeing few prospects of advancement, he applied for promotion to the West Africa Service at a salary of £300 a year:

When I received my offer of an appointment to Nigeria, all my friends in the West Indies advised me strongly not to go there as it was almost certain death; West Africa was regarded as a White Man's Grave. However, I was determined to chance my arm and I went. Casualties *were* pretty heavy there and a lot of the men that went out at the same time as I did didn't survive; either they died or were invalided out of the service.

Arriving off Lagos in 1912, Burns was surprised to find that the entrance to the harbour was too shallow to allow steamers to enter. Instead passengers were lowered into surf-boats in what were known as '*mammy*-chairs' – 'a wooden box suspended by a chain from the derrick on the steamer's deck'. After being transferred from the surf-boats to a tender, passengers were brought alongside the Customs wharf: 'I landed from the tender and I saw a white man. I went up to him and I said, "Can you tell me where I have to go and how to get there?" And he said, "Where have you come from?" So I said, "I've just come from England." He said, "Well, why don't you go back there?"'

As in the Sudan, Nigeria was divided both geographically and culturally into two distinct regions:

Along the coast were the mangrove swamps, including the Niger Delta which covered a considerable area, and behind the mangrove swamps were the tropical forests and behind that again a savannah area until you got up to the north of Northern Nigeria where you come on to the Sahara Desert. The main communications in those days were along the rivers and creeks. There's a continual line of creeks all the way along the coast from Lagos to the far east of Nigeria and you could go by canoe or launch the whole distance without seeing the sea at all. There was also a railway which went up to Kano, and there were a few roads, but in those days

23

the main means of communications were by river or creek in launches or canoes and, on the main rivers, the sternwheelers, which had engines heated by wood cut along the banks of the river and taken on board at various stopping places.

Lagos itself was still a comparatively small town:

The Europeans lived, as a rule, round the race course at one end of the town, and the African quarter was a huddle of buildings, with very few good streets and practically no amenities. But there was electricity, which was surprising to me. There were a number of bungalows, but I was living in a building called the 'chest of drawers' which consisted of six quarters, each of them having a bedroom and a verandah, and a common dining-room which very few of us used. There was a men's club, called the Gin Palace, which was a very popular resort of the white men in Lagos and also included three or four Africans – but there were no ladies admitted and it was really too expensive for the junior people to join. I remember a man from one of the outside provinces coming to Lagos and noticing there were several wives there as well as nursing sisters and remarking that Lagos was simply crawling with women.

Here, too, there were strong opinions about the best ways of keeping healthy: 'The principal danger was malaria and sunstroke. One thing that was compulsory was the taking of five grains of quinine a day, taken with a drink at midday just before lunch. And if you didn't take it and you got ill your salary was liable to be stopped.' It was also virtually compulsory to wear a helmet if you went out into the sun:

I remember one of the very early rebukes I received was because I walked for a few yards in the open air without my helmet and a messenger arrived from the Colonial Secretary to say that he wished to see me. I went trembling into the presence and, in a very rough voice, he said to me that it didn't matter very much whether I died or not but think of the trouble it would be to bury me and get another man out from England to take my place! We all had to wear, as well, a spine-pad on the back of our shirts, a thick material buttoned on to the back of one's bush shirt. And the women all had to wear double-*terais* and a veil hanging down the back of their necks.

After several months in Lagos, Alan Burns was posted to a Customs station at Kokotown on the Benue river:

I went through the creeks from Lagos to Kokotown by launch and when I got to Kokotown I saw a white man on the wharf – the man I was supposed to be relieving. When I had handed him my letter of introduction he read it and put it in his pocket and I said, 'Well, then, will it please you to hand over to me?' He said, 'Who are you?' I said, 'My name is Burns. I'm the man referred to in that letter.' He said, 'Burns was referred to in the letter, but I don't know that you are Burns.' I then

'Dressing is a regular battle' – a light-hearted sketch from Capt A. J. N. Tremearne's *Notes and Anecdotes* written in 1910, showing something of the style of living in the Nigerian bush at that time. The collapsible camp bath continued to be of service for another half century.

said, 'Well, look at my luggage, it's all marked Burns.' He said, 'Yes, I can see that, but it doesn't follow that it's your luggage.' I think the most charitable way to describe it is to say that he was mentally disturbed.

Having successfully relieved his fellow-officer of his post, Alan Burns settled down to his new job:

Kokotown at that time was a big trading centre and people spoke English of a sort, but generally pidgin English, which is a terrible language – but this was an old tradition from the sailing-ship days. It had curious words like 'live' that were used for everything. Instead of saying, 'That book is on the table' you'd say, 'That book live for table' and, instead of 'A man is dying', 'live for dying'!

My bungalow at Kokotown consisted of a bedroom and a sitting-room, and a wide verandah which in fact was used more than anything else. There was a store-room but there was no bathroom. I had my bath on the verandah in the evening and there was nobody there to see me because the bungalow stood in its own grounds on the banks of the river – and it was nothing unusual to see a crocodile perched on the bank sunning itself. There was no electric light in the bungalow. We had oil lamps, *punkah* lamps with a fan instead of a chimney.

Whenever the opportunity arose Alan Burns went up-river to the district headquarters at Sapele, where white officials gathered at what was known as the 'Scotch club': 'We used to meet every evening after tennis on the banks of the river and our boys would bring out our own chairs and our own whisky and our own lamps and everything and we'd sit there and talk, generally about the work.' Kokotown itself had few social attractions:

There was nothing to do in the place, so some of the time I spent settling a land dispute for the District Commissioner with the chief, Nana, who was a very intelligent and pleasant man. In the old days he had been a principal slave-dealer in that part of the world and his town had only been captured after a considerable fight between four British cruisers and his own people. He was then tried and sentenced to deportation to Accra where he went for some time, and when he came back he settled in a town just below Kokotown, which he called America. When I went down to see him he invariably treated me to hot champagne.

This first 'tour of duty' lasted just one year, with very generous leave conditions 'due, very largely, to the health conditions in the colony. You got leave then of two weeks each way on a steamer going to and from England and four months in England.' After returning from leave Alan Burns was posted to the Chief Secretary's Office in the Secretariat Building in Lagos where 'they expected me to work very hard and we did work hard. But everybody was very willing to do it.' Here his duties brought him into contact with the Governor, Lord Lugard, who later invited him to become his aide-de-camp and part-time private secretary:

He was a tremendous worker, he'd work for hours in his office and very often until two or three in the morning. But his one fault, as I could see it, was that he would never depute anything to anyone else. He loved working and he hated anyone else doing the work that he himself could do. I remember once going into his office and seeing him checking a proof and I offered to do it myself for him. He turned to me with his usual sweet smile and said, 'My dear Burns, you could probably do it better than I can, but then, I like doing it' – and that was the end of that. On one occasion the doctor advised him to take more exercise and to play tennis so I fixed up a game for him and he was to play for an hour. He arrived at five o'clock and at six o'clock he put down his racquet in the middle of the game and went in back to his work. He was a very great man and in Nigeria at that time was regarded as really the creator of the country – and everybody admired him immensely.

Lord Lugard's retirement in 1918 marked the end of the era of pacification. Among the many whose lives he influenced to a marked degree was Sylvia Leith-Ross. When she first met her future husband, Captain Arthur Leith-Ross, he was serving with Lugard's West Africa Frontier Force in

Northern Nigeria. But there was already in her family a remarkable association with West Africa:

My father had been in command of the sloop *Pandora* on the West Africa Station and had been at the taking of Lagos – and he had also captured the last Portuguese slaver. I still remember his description of what that slaver was like when his own people boarded it. There was one occasion when he must have gone up the Cross river to rescue some German traders who were trapped amongst very warlike natives and he went up and rescued them and they didn't even thank him – they didn't even give him a bottle of beer!

Her brother had also gone out to Nigeria, first with the Royal Niger Constabulary in 1898 and then as one of Lugard's administrators: 'My brother had met my husband out in Nigeria and had decided at once that he was the man that his little sister ought to marry. Both were having their leaves at the same time and so my brother brought him back with him and he stayed with us in our Sussex home.'

At that time wives were not allowed up to Northern Nigeria without the express permission of the then Sir Frederick Lugard:

Fortunately I passed all right. But as far as I can remember there were only three wives out in Northern Nigeria at that time. Nigeria was definitely known as a White Man's Grave – and actually it was. The mortality rate was very severe. Official statistics stated that one in five were either invalided or dead within a year. Yet somehow we went out quite carefree and it seemed somehow worthwhile to run the risk. My husband had a job there, I loved my husband and I followed him.

In the late summer of 1907 Mrs Leith-Ross sailed out to Nigeria with her husband on one of the passenger steamers of the Elder Dempster Line:

I remember that we had to take absolutely everything with us, all clothing, all drink, all food and almost all furniture. But the bulk of our luggage consisted I suppose of the *chop* boxes containing food for eighteen months. These were generally packed by wonderful firms like Whale and Co. or Griffiths McAllister, or the Army and Navy Stores. An officer was entitled to eighty carriers for his tour of eighteen months, eighty loads of fifty-six pounds, because fifty-six pounds was supposed to be the normal weight that a native carrier could carry with ease – although very often they carried a good deal more without a word of complaint. We had camp equipment, of course, which included things like a camp chair and a camp stool, and a camp bed with a cork mattress, and a bath – a tin bath with a cover and a wickerwork lining into which you packed all your toilet necessities. Of course, one had to take one's own lamps, too, especially the marvellous Lord's lamp, which was a kerosene lamp mounted upon four legs which could be set up on a sandbank, or on a rock, or in the middle of a river – wherever one wanted it. Mosquito nets, of course, had to be used everywhere and it was quite fatal not to do so.

We had as additional baggage an elegant, high-sprung dog-cart for which my husband hoped he would be able to train one of the native ponies. It was very elegant but on the whole rather useless as there wasn't a single road in the whole of Northern Nigeria. There were only carriers or camels or canoes or bullocks, or ponies or chiefly the human being, the marvellous Nigerian carrier.

The voyage out took three weeks, with the steamers then sailing nearer to the coast and calling at more ports.

Our fellow-passengers were nearly all government servants, a few agents going out for the trading firms and a missionary or two, that was all. But there was a very

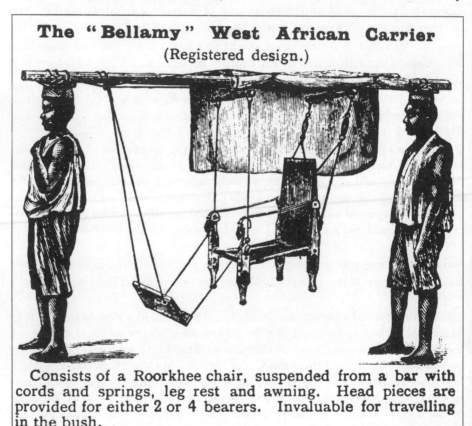

## The "Bellamy" West African Carrier
### (Registered design.)

Consists of a Roorkhee chair, suspended from a bar with cords and springs, leg rest and awning. Head pieces are provided for either 2 or 4 bearers. Invaluable for travelling in the bush.

Each ........................................................ £5  15  0

From the Army and Navy Catalogue 1905. Not a standard item of equipment but no doubt invaluable if the occupant happened to be suffering from malaria or some other illness.

curious division among the passengers which even the ship's officers recognized. The purser would never have put at the same table officials going to Northern Nigeria and those going to Southern Nigeria. In fact we never spoke to each other. We looked upon each other with equal contempt, I think. We somehow took it for granted that all Southern officials were rather fat, rather flabby and that they started drinking at six o'clock while we never started before six-thirty. In the North you rode on horses, in the South they walked and, it is said, some officials were even carried in hammocks!

The approach to West Africa made itself felt by an extraordinary smell of swamp, hot and humid. We in the North did not land in Lagos, we stayed on board and transhipped into a sternwheeler which was to take us up the Niger. The transfer was done in the midst of shrieks and yells and a welter of luggage thrown in every direction, but somehow it all sorted itself out and eventually – there were only five of us by that time – we were more or less installed. The sternwheeler took a week to get up to Lokoja. It was an extraordinary craft, flat-bottomed, two decks and on the top deck there were, I think, three cabins which were just three boxes with no furniture at all. So your own camp furniture had to be put up. On the lower deck huddled African passengers, one's own servants and one's own cooks, and men and women and children and chickens and goats and great piles of foodstuffs. The captains of these sternwheelers were generally very aloof and there was a legend that they were all Swedish counts.

This first journey was a wonderful introduction to Nigeria; the sternwheeler progressed very slowly up the steaming river, high banks of copper-coloured vegetation cut off all view at the sides and and for three or four days one saw nothing at all except the forest, a few sandbanks, a few crocodiles. And of course, we anchored at night. We drew in close to the bank, the engines stopped and an anchor or two was let down. Then the forest thinned and we came to more open country. Small villages appeared on the banks of the river and after eight days we reached Lokoja, which is at the junction of the Benue and the Niger river. A little further on we transhipped into native canoes to go up the Kaduna river. A little short of Zungeru the river narrowed and we disembarked and took an extraordinary little train which was really more like a tramway, for a few miles to Zungeru itself, which was the headquarters at that time of Northern Nigeria and consisted chiefly of the military barracks and a few bungalows. There was a small hospital, a fairly large cemetery, and Government House was nothing but a rather large bungalow, really not much better than those of the ordinary officials.

All these bungalows had been shipped out from England and erected by the Public Works Department using local labour. And they were all of one type:

One could find them anywhere with exactly the same lack of amenities. They consisted of three rooms and a wide verandah all round. I had realized exactly what the bungalows would be like so it seemed perfectly natural to me, but they were even uglier than I thought they would be, and devoid of any furniture except some large and heavy tables and a *punkah*, which was, so to speak, a petticoat attached to a long parallel pole which was swung back and forth by a small boy sitting on the verandah.

Mrs Leith-Ross's arrival in Zungeru caused something of a stir:

There were no wives there at all at that moment. There were two nursing sisters and the warden of a freed slaves home. I was the only wife. In fact, I think the officials were astonished to see that any white wife was allowed out, as I think there were only three others in the whole country. The white officials of course were few and far between themselves; I think I'm right in saying that there were altogether at that time forty administrative officers for the whole of Nigeria.

From the domestic point of view there were very few amenities to be found in Zungeru. But there were the servants:

Fortunately, my husband didn't lose his servants as sometimes happened when they saw a white woman coming – they stayed. The cook was a coast man – they came from Accra and were supposed to be the best ones – and my husband had a devoted steward for himself – although somehow the custom had grown up that all servants were called boy, no matter what their age was. Later they became a little more sophisticated and those who'd had a certain amount of training wished to be called steward. In addition to the boy there was the 'small boy' and the 'small-small boy'. And generally there was a gardener and, of course, the horse-boys. The water was brought by prisoners from some distance away but had, of course, to be boiled and filtered. It was kept cool to a certain degree in great earthenware jars which were stood on the verandahs and these coolers also served as our refrigerators, so boxes of any tinned butter or any drinks were floated in the coolers. Meat had to be eaten almost at once, although the Public Works Department provided a meat safe, which was a large box with muslin sides hung from the ceiling.

Something that always surprised the newcomer was the variety of insect life, which Sylvia Leith-Ross found quite amazing:

From the point of view of the housewife I think the ants were the worst enemies. They managed to damage almost everything, they even seemed able to eat through a tin, because all our groceries had to come out in tins. Anything you put on the table was immediately covered in ants, so everything had to be either kept in a firmly closed tin or set in a receptacle placed in a bowl of water.

Of course the evenings were the worst time because mosquitoes and flies of every description gathered round the lamps. And in the evening everybody dressed for dinner, whether you were at home or went out; you wouldn't dream of doing otherwise. I remember very well having a bath towel put over my side-saddle and riding off to dine in a long, low-necked dress. Of course, the conversation was almost entirely shop, but, all the same, of a high order; it wasn't only about who was

itish society in Sierra Leone gathered to welcome the arrival of the Duke and Duchess of
nnaught in Freetown in 1910; a far from typical picture of colonial life. Although not the
lest British possession in West Africa, Sierra Leone had been a crown colony since 1807,
lowing the abolition of the slave trade.

Kitting-up for Africa; drays collecting chop-boxes and baggage from Walters of Oxford in the 1920s. Walters and Co. was only one of a number of tropical outfitters that specialized in supplying colonial officials with all their requirements prior to their departure for the colonies.

The gateway to Uganda, *c.* 1910; travellers from Kenya and Tanganyika were ferried across Lake Victoria by wood-fired steamers to the mole at Entebbe.

*Above* Trade before the flag; the interior of one of the many 'canteens' or 'barter rooms' established by rival trading companies on the West African coast in the nineteenth century, Liberia *c.* 1920.

*Left* White ducks and 'Bombay bowlers', Lagos 1919; the newly-arrived 'first tour' man (Clifford Ruston, second from right) with other assistants of the Lagos Stores Ltd.

The opening-up of the African interior; a survey party complete with plane-table, drummers and armed *askaris* sets off on safari, Uganda *c.* 1907.

'Blues ruling blacks'; The newly appointed Deputy-Inspector (Angus Gillan, centre) with colleagues of the Sudan Political Service, a *corps d'élite* of some 100 officers who administered one million square miles of Sudanese territory in nominal partnership with Egypt, 1910.

going to get promotion or who was going on leave. It was nearly always in some form or other about the good of the country at large. Their minds seemed to be really full of their work, of what they were actually doing and what they meant to do. But really, not much entertaining was done. For one thing there were so few women and at the end of the day everyone was very tired. The climate was abominable, the heat intense, the glare was constant.

Ever since her arrival in Nigeria, Sylvia Leith-Ross had carried with her a premonition of tragedy: 'In the beginning it was not quite fear; although I had no fear for myself I had always the feeling of an impending disaster and I could not get rid of it, therefore I dreaded Nigeria in an almost impersonal way.' Finally, when she and her husband had been in Zungeru for just one year disaster came:

My husband had had blackwater once before and had somehow survived, although he'd been completely alone. The second time it happened in Zungeru; one doesn't know why, it was just an infection, but at the time there was no known cure. He was at once taken to the small hospital and two doctors stayed with him day and night for two days, but he grew weaker and weaker and died within three days.

Of course, death was accepted as part of the day's work, but he had been so much liked that the whole of his colleagues and even the black clerks and the transport boys were all shocked deeply and were, in a way, not so sorry for me as sorry for themselves in that they'd lost a friend and an example. Everybody was kindness itself to me but the only thing to do was for me to go home. And when I left I found that of the five of us who had started for Northern Nigeria, I was the only one to return to England. The others were all dead.

This was only the beginning of Sylvia Leith-Ross's life in Nigeria, for 'it was only when she had done her worst that I realized how much I loved her.' She resolved to return and in due course she found a means to do so:

Quite suddenly I remembered a day when my husband and I had been riding out together and we passed a camp of Fulani herdsmen. The men were away but the women came out of their little house and looked at us very shyly, then they came a little nearer to me and smiled at me and I smiled back. It was dusk and the cattle were just coming home, with their wide horns and their great white flanks. We stayed a few moments amongst them and then rode away, but one Fulani woman must have known a few words in Hausa because she called out, 'Come back, come back again.' And I remembered their voices and the lilt of their lovely language and I suddenly thought I'll go back and study the Fulani language.

With Lord Lugard's permission Sylvia Leith-Ross eventually returned to Nigeria to begin a pioneer study of the Fulani language and culture that was to take her many years. In 1926 she became Nigeria's first Lady Superintendent of Education.

The Great War effectively brought to an end an era that had been characterized by supreme self-confidence. 'I don't know really how far one looked ahead,' acknowledges Angus Gillan. 'It was in the days when the Empire was, shall we say, cock of the world? And at that stage of one's career I don't think the young man thought a great deal as to when – even as to whether – the Sudan or an Indian state or Nigeria or whatever it might be would begin to demand Independence. It was only really after the First World War I think that one began seriously to consider these things.'

## three

# TO AFRICA

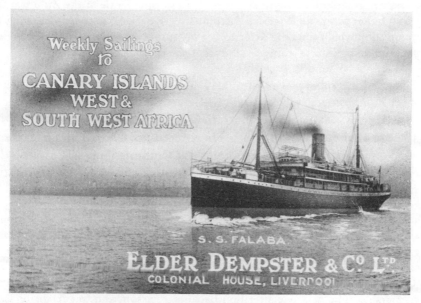

The young men who went out between the wars to serve in the colonial administration or in the military services shared a common background. They were drawn from the middle classes and the great majority had been brought up in the 'British tradition of service' that was part and parcel of prep and public school education: 'One didn't go out carrying the banner of Wellington, but one did go out imbued with certain standards.' Chris Farmer, who joined the Administrative Service in Nigeria, saw himself as a typical product of 'the much-maligned public school system which, whatever you may say against it, did inculcate a sense of responsibility. I was head of my house, I was deputy head of the school, captain of rugger, and company sergeant-major in the Officer Training Corps, exercising responsibility and learning to use the authority which went with the responsibility, so that when eventually I found myself out in the bush in Nigeria on my own I wasn't worried about it in the slightest way.'

Only slightly less dominant a force was the tradition of family service that made a career in one or other of the Imperial Services almost inevitable. In some families this tradition flourished to a remarkable degree, as in Charles Meek's family:

The whole of my family, like so many British middle-class families in the nineteenth century, was very strongly connected with the forces and with Imperial administration in one form or another. My great-grandfather was General Sir Thomas Gordon, who was a notable figure in Indian administration, and was one of a remarkable pair of twin generals; they both took all their steps in the army on the same day, and ended up as generals on the same day and were knighted on the same day. I also had an uncle in India with a long connection with the Indian political service, my grandfather fought at Ulundi, the closing battle of the Zulu war, and my own father was in the Nigerian Administrative Service, so there's this long web of connection which certainly determined my future career. I never had any other thought of going into anything at all except the colonial civil service.

Brian Montgomery was similarly influenced: 'My grandfather, Sir Robert Montgomery, was Lieutenant-Governor of the Punjab, just after the Indian Mutiny. My father was born in Cawnpore and spent his boyhood up to the age of about eight in India. He entered the Church and became the Bishop of Tasmania. One of my uncles was Commissioner of Rawalpindi in India, and another was a Commissioner in Kenya.' As far as his own generation was concerned:

There was never any question but that most of us would have some connections in their professions with the British Empire. My eldest brother became a constable in the British South Africa Police, from which he gravitated up to Kenya and finished up as Chief Native Commissioner there. His younger brother next to him went out to Canada. My next brother to him was the one who served in India and became field-marshal. The next one after him became a parson, and was rector of Lady-smith in South Africa and later on a canon in the Arctic. It followed that when my time came – and I was the last of nine children – I should join the army. I joined the King's African Rifles and later on transferred to the Indian Army.

In the nineteenth century and up to the outbreak of the First World War the main attraction for those seeking a colonial career was to be found in India, where the most prestigious position was occupied by the Indian Civil Service. But as demands for home rule in Indian grew, so its attraction diminished: 'My grandfather and my father served in India; they were merchants in Calcutta,' recalls James Robertson:

So all my young life I was brought up to think of carrying on the tradition of going to India. My father had a great admiration for the Indian Civil Service and the idea was that when I had got my degree at Oxford I should go there. Well, of course, in 1921–2 conditions in India were a bit difficult. There were bandits, massacres and so forth. Meanwhile friends of mine had gone into the Colonial Service and into the Sudan Political Service and I heard quite a lot about that. Well, at the end of my academic time at Oxford I put my name in for the whole three and, in fact, the Sudan interview came off first and they took me.

For Darrell Bates, too, a career in the Indian Civil Service had been a boyhood ambition: 'But while I was at Oxford I came across people whose parents lived in India or who had an Indian background, and they gradually convinced me that India would become independent fairly soon and that if I went there I might well find myself out of a job. And at that time the Sudan Political Service and the Colonial Service were becoming careers of tremendous interest to people at university who affected a sort of balance between brain and brawn – an intelligent man's outdoor life – and so I switched.'

Although the British colonization of Africa was still in the twenties and thirties too recent a phenomenon to have allowed any widespread ancestral pattern of son following father to have developed – as was the case in India – there were indeed some young men going out to territories where their fathers had been before them. Nigel Cooke's father had been in mining in Northern Nigeria since 1910 and Dick Symes-Thompson had been born in Kenya, where his father had bought a coffee plantation and settled in 1913: 'My mother also had African connections as she had been born in Basutoland where her father was a Resident, and for this reason I had always considered a job in Africa, possibly in the administration.' In Harry Grenfell's case the connection with Africa went back even further, to his grandfather's friendship with Cecil Rhodes and the white settlement of Rhodesia in the 1890s.

But there were many who had no such connections. Some of them, like Frank Loyd, joined simply because it had been their childhood ambition to do so: 'From an early age I had thought in terms of joining the Colonial Service, even when I was still at prep school – and for some reason or other it stuck.' Many others had no such early ambitions and, like Anthony Kirk-Greene, who joined the Nigerian Administrative Service after the Second World War, knew virtually nothing about the Colonial Service: 'I even remember going out in the troop-ship during the war and being given a paperback which was called *Diary of a District Officer*. I had no idea what a District Officer was – if I thought of it at all it was as a sort of male variant of the district nurse – that was how ignorant I was.'

Although it was not published until 1942, Kenneth Bradley's *Diary of a District Officer* did, in fact, have a strong influence on a later generation of recruits. Earlier generations had to rely on Allan Quatermain and Edgar Wallace for their African reading.

Two other factors played a major part in shaping the decisions of those who were to go out to Africa. The first was the obvious attraction of an outdoor life, one that combined travel with sunshine and a strong element of human interest – and which was far removed from the 'rather stuffy, formal career structure' which most other young graduates would be doomed to

35

follow. The second factor was rather more practical; the need to find a good job at a time when job prospects were far from secure, something that Nigel Cooke was very aware of in 1934: 'Going up to Cambridge at a time when the slump was very fresh in people's minds I was conscious all the time of the danger of arriving at the other end without a job, and in fact the salary that was offered to colonial cadets was very good indeed when you think that a schoolmaster was lucky to get £200, and we were on the princely sum of £400 a year.'

One of those young men who did arrive at the other end of his degree course without finding a job was Richard Turnbull who, by his own admission, joined the Colonial Service more or less by chance:

I'd taken my degree as a physical chemist and I'd hoped to get into industry but I failed to get a first; I was too interested in rowing and listening to music and making merry and I only got a second. Had I got a first I should almost certainly have been accepted by ICI and gone to the north country. As it was, I had to look for a job and there were thousands of us in 1929 looking for jobs and there were three million unemployed. Well, in the month of July I was walking down Whitehall on my way to the Abbey to hear a chorale that was being sung that day and I saw the name Richmond Terrace. And I knew I'd read it somewhere so I walked round Richmond Terrace and I came across the Colonial Office Appointments Board. And I banged on the door, walked in and the commissionaire said, 'If you're expecting to be appointed this year you're three months too late.' All the same, I got a collection of application forms, filled them in and presented them. Very much to my surprise, I was called up for an interview.

There were others who were also swayed by pressing financial needs, particularly in the army: 'Quite frankly, the reason why most army officers fifty years ago decided to serve in Africa was nearly always because they were in debt. No doubt there were cases where they were crossed in love or wanted adventure, but army officers were very badly paid in those days and it was very easy to get into debt – the debt usually taking the form of getting well behindhand with their payments to their tailor, because in those days regimental tailors gave officers unlimited credit – or else they had an overdraft at the bank.'

One such officer who found it impossible to live on his pay was Brian Montgomery, who applied for secondment to the King's African Rifles in 1927:

In the British Army of those days, and particularly in the infantry regiments of the line – what were called the unfashionable regiments – none of the officers, or very few, had any private means and therefore when the time came to compete with marriage, for instance, or other expenses, it was not possible to survive in England.

And therefore many officers volunteered to join any of the colonial forces, which were paid for by the governments of those territories and provided much better pay. As my eldest brother was already Commissioner in Kenya it seemed quite natural that I should join the King's African Rifles, where the pay was £500 a year, which seemed a princely sum in those days, being in fact more than double the pay of a subaltern in the British Army in the UK.

It was the same basic reason that brought twenty-year-old Donald Dunnet into the West Africa trade:

I was on leave as a young soldier immediately after the armistice and I met a man who was working in Nigeria and was home on leave, and apparently it was quite a rewarding sort of job. There had been a boom in the West African trade just after the end of the war and he had earned very considerable commissions, and although I realized that working conditions in West Africa were supposed to be very bad, I couldn't imagine that they were as bad as some of the foxholes around Mount Kemel and the money was certainly better – and I was rather attracted to the romance of mercantile commerce. So I applied for a job with the people with whom he was employed.

An escape, even if only a temporary one ('West Africa was not a place where you went for a lifetime. You went there for your tour or tours, and then you came back'), was what a job as a cashier with the Bank of British West Africa offered Bill Page in 1926 – as well as the opportunity to better himself:

I'd been working in Lloyds Bank for something like four years and although I was no longer the junior junior but the senior junior I found that the work was frightfully unedifying, just listing cheques and adding them up, being everybody's dogsbody. So I began thinking of a change – and the colonies and India did afford an escape from the constricting circumstances at home. And then there was the money; I'd been working for four years and still getting about £2 a week – well, you couldn't take your girl-friend to the pictures on that! So I wrote to a firm in London that catered for people like me who wanted jobs abroad and they sent me a number of forms to fill in. I think I filled in a couple for India and then one came for the Bank of British West Africa. Well, that sounded more romantic. I'd just been to the Wembley Empire Exhibition and there was a living model of an African village, all hot and tropical and brown and that seemed to indicate that West Africa wouldn't be a bad place, so I applied and had an interview and got the job.

There was also a sizable body of young men – and women – for whom Africa offered rewards that were anything but financial. In 1929 Robert Macdonald became a member of this dedicated band:

Although we were very much attached to the Church there was no tradition of missionary work in my family. But there was a missionary in the South Seas, Chalmers of New Guinea, a Scotsman whose life had fascinated me as a young boy. He was actually murdered and eaten, I believe, but that didn't deflect me from the idea. I'd wanted to be a missionary for as long as I can remember, but I was drawn to Africa because my cousin was already there doing interesting and exciting medical work, and two of my college colleagues were already there, and their letters and meeting them on leave confirmed my desire to make it the Calabar Mission in south-eastern Nigeria rather than anywhere else.

For some the process of selection seemed arbitrary, as Donald Dunnet found when he applied to the trading company of Miller Brothers of Liverpool: 'I don't think they were having too many applicants for the job because all they seemed to want to know about me was the size of my neck, as they were going to buy me some shirts – on a buy now, pay later sort of thing.' And when Clifford Ruston applied to join the Lagos Stores trading company in 1919 what his future employers seemed chiefly interested in was his sobriety: 'One of the clauses in the agreement for two years' service that I signed was that the clerk – I was always referred to as the clerk – would not indulge in alcoholic liquor save at meals or with the express written permission of the company's medical attendant. I may say that when I got to Lagos I found that this clause wasn't strictly adhered to.' But for those hoping to join the Colonial Administrative Service the selection process was anything but rudimentary. It began with references – from headmasters, commanding officers, college tutors, heads of houses – and a good, but not too good, degree: 'The standard laid down was that you had to have at least a second class honours degree or show (in the immediate post-war period) that had you gone to university you would have had second class honours.'

After the references there were the interviews. Here, as in every stage of the selection process, was to be found presiding the Patronage Secretary, Major – later Sir – Ralph Furse, who held the post for almost as long as anyone could remember. By the time that Kenneth Smith came to join his Appointments Department in 1945, Furse was practically stone deaf; but he was still very much an elder statesman – and his influence was still paramount:

He had been since 1911, I think, head of that branch of the service as, in the first place, Patronage Secretary to the Secretary of State. He'd continued all through the post-war period of the construction of the Colonial Service – rather nicely, he had been joined by his brother-in-law, Captain Newbolt, the son of the poet, and it was these two who between them can be said to be responsible for creating a unified service for the administration of the Colonial Empire and the manner in which candidates for it were selected and trained.

38

Furse himself personally vetted thousands of young men in their first informal interviews before they faced the final interview board. Robin Short came up before him in 1949: 'I remember Sir Ralph Furse as a very benevolent old gentleman, asking me the time-honoured question, "Do you play cricket?" to which I am glad to say I was able to answer that I did. He also asked me, even in 1949, whether I would be prepared to ask Africans into my home, and I had, of course, to say, "Yes, I should be delighted, if they were friends of mine."

It could well have been Furse who interviewed Richard Turnbull when he presented himself at the Colonial Office twenty years earlier and was questioned by 'a very charming and, I realize now, a very astute fellow. He asked any number of questions, most of which seemed to be pretty irrelevant. One I do remember was this: he said to me, "Do you think you could tell a smoking-room story to an African elder?" I said I was quite certain I could. It seemed to me at the time a ridiculous question but, of course, it wasn't. When I look back and think of the hours and hours I spent with dear old men swapping off-colour stories and both of us laughing ourselves silly and enjoying it immensely, I realize what a very, very profound chap my interviewer was.'

The final interview was usually a very formal affair. Darrell Bates recalls how 'I found myself one hot summer afternoon at Burlington House, and there on the other side of the table was a really alarming number of distinguished faces. None of them smiled when I came in and while I stood there waiting for someone to speak to me I felt as if they were taking my clothes off one by one and pricing them and having a look at how recently I had cut my hair and cut my fingernails. But once they started on the questions they were for the most part thoughtful and kind and wise.'

There was one particular line of questioning that remained as pertinent in the 1950s as it had been fifty years earlier: how would you really cope with what was likely to be a pretty lonely life? Questions about ultimate self-determination for the colonies regularly came up, but what was not considered, even as late as 1949, when Anthony Kirk-Greene faced his selection board, was the possibility that entrants to the Colonial Service might be embarking on a short-term career: 'If we had thought this our minds were very quickly put to rest by the selection board. Indeed the Governor of Nigeria two years later greeted one of his cadets by saying, "And how long do you think you'll be here?" The cadet, an extremely bright person, said, "Well, I suppose half a dozen years." And Governor MacPherson patted him on the knee and said, "Don't you worry, my boy, my son is just going into the Colonial Service and he has a career in front of him."'

This optimism about their career prospects was shared by the great majority of successful applicants as they began their year of training at either Oxford or Cambridge: 'Few if any of us on the Colonial Service Course at Oxford in 1935–6 thought that we should run out of time,' recalls George Sinclair. 'Most of us were so entranced by the idea of the job ahead and the opportunities and responsibilities that I doubt whether many of us thought much about the time-scale.'

By the time their courses had begun the ultimate destination of the newly appointed cadet probationers had been determined. Each applicant had listed his preferences, which had certainly been considered – even if they could not always be met: 'There was no specific purpose or method behind Colonial Office posting as far as we could see. A certain number of cadets were needed each year for each colony, and unless one had special connections in one colony or another I think somebody simply took a pin and selected one's name and sent one to that colony.'

Some had no preference, and were content to be sent wherever the Colonial Office decided. Others had preferences that were largely determined by the duration of the tour of duty, which varied greatly from one territory to another. It could be as short as twelve months in West Africa and as long as four years in the more temperate regions. This was certainly one of the reasons that prompted Frank Loyd to put Uganda down as his first choice rather than Kenya, 'because Uganda only had a two-and-a-half or perhaps a two-year tour, whereas Kenya had four, and for someone like myself the prospect of being away from England for as long as four years was rather awful. So I opted for the one with the briefest tour, which just shows how little I knew about Africa as a whole and East Africa in particular. I was, in fact, sent to Kenya, so the gods were with me.'

After the Indian Civil Service and the Sudan Political Service, Northern Nigeria probably occupied the most prestigious position on the Imperial list – although such a claim would be fiercely disputed by colonial officers whose loyalties lay elsewhere. But the fact that Nigeria was always the most popular choice among recruits was due as much to the fact of its being one of the largest and the best known of the colonial territories as it was to anything else.

What had earlier been called the Tropical African Service Course and had been held at the Imperial Institute in London had expanded in the mid-twenties from a somewhat rudimentary training course into a well-organized Colonial Service Course run jointly at the two leading universities and embracing a wide variety of subjects. Other 'support' services and departments such as the Agricultural and Forest Services or the Colonial Police also ran their own specialized courses. For Darrell Bates, as for many others, this was a year of total freedom from responsibility:

One had all the excitement of being at Oxford without having the pressure of an exam and one had all the joys of an Oxford which one had got to know without the constant worry about whether you would get a job at the end of it. And now they were actually paying me to take a course, so it was tremendous fun. But the course itself was designed perhaps to produce a whole set of poobahs. One had a tremendous variety of function and one got to know a little about a lot of things and not very much about anything in particular.

Part of the training was practical, 'designed to teach you rural agriculture, anti-erosion techniques, rural hygiene and elementary public engineering', but there was also training that 'took you through the rules of law and evidence, with a view to your being able to sit in a court from the day of your arrival.' Then there was a part of the course that was related directly to the region to which the cadet would be sent. George Sinclair, expecting to be sent to Ashanti, considered himself to be particularly fortunate to have as his tutor Captain R. S. Rattray, one of the great characters of West Africa:

Rattray had been in West Africa since he was about seventeen or eighteen. He had left school in Scotland to serve in the South African war. After that he became an elephant hunter and as he moved northwards through Africa he recorded languages and folklore on his way. Finally he came in to the northern territories of the Gold Coast where he became a District Commissioner, later a Provincial Commissioner and then a government anthropologist. He then began to publish his books about the laws, religion, customs, folk-stories and proverbs of the Ashanti people — to whom he was known as *mako*, which means 'pepper', because he was so quick. I spent a year with him and was completely entranced with his approach to people as individuals and his respect for the people amongst whom he worked.

Behind the language courses and the law studies and the practical training there was also a clear-cut philosophy that was symbolized by the required reading of Lord Lugard's *Dual Mandate*. Its general tenor was that 'your job is to learn how they govern themselves and assist that process. You'll be there for a very long time, you're there to give support to existing native structures, to enable them to evolve naturally – and there is no immediate necessity either to understand urban politics or transpose Westminster models of government.'

Although it was enjoyed, this year of training was not always considered useful either by those who received it or by those for whom they worked, as Anthony Kirk-Greene found when it came to putting theory into practice:

Looking through my notebooks I see that on the administrative and political side, what I learnt would have been useful if I'd been appointed governor straight away rather than a mere Assistant District Officer – and my superiors didn't hesitate to point this out to me pretty quickly. My first Resident said to me. 'I suppose you, too, have wasted this year at Cambridge.' He didn't really mean this because I was wearing a Hawks tie, having got a blue, and he, too, was wearing the same tie, but I asked him, 'Well, what would have been useful?' and he said, 'There are only two things needed to make that course worthwhile; if you can do native treasury accounts and if you can type. Anything else – you've wasted your time!'

Once the course was completed the cadets had a few weeks leave in which to prepare themselves for departure. For those uncertain as to how to equip themselves there were the services of such rival firms of colonial outfitters as Griffiths McAllister of Regent Street, Messrs F. P. Baker of Golden Square and in Oxford, Walters and Co. of 10 The Turl, who descended upon all colonial appointees, offering exceptionally generous terms of credit that could be spread over the first tour of service or even longer. Although the days of *chop* boxes and self-sufficiency had largely ended, there was still a tendency among those outfitters to over-supply and to think in somewhat old-fashioned terms. 'Tropical outfitters were very keen on nineteenth-century pith helmets,' recalls Darrell Bates. 'They had a tremendous variety of 'Bombay bowlers' and there was one I remember with a flap at the back like the thing that a tortoise has. So, of course, when I got to Africa I arrived fully equipped with Bombay bowlers and pith helmets. In the end I gave them all away and bought a panama.'

Two other relics of the past that were still being supplied well into the inter-war period were the cholera-belt and the spine-pad, the latter an ominously coffin-shaped piece of cloth fitted with buttons and worn down the back. The position had scarcely changed even when Charles Meek went along with his father to buy his kit from F. P. Baker in wartime London in 1941:

My father had retired from Nigeria in 1932 and it was at once apparent to me how very old-fashioned his ideas were as he tried to persuade me to buy spine-pads, red flannel and all that kind of thing. And I was very successful in rejecting his advice until he scored one notable triumph with the help of Baker's assistant. This was in the form of a portable lavatory seat, which I felt must be a very old-fashioned bit of equipment and certainly not needed in these modern days – and I resisted very strongly until the shop assistant trumped my ace by saying, 'Look here, sir, I'll put it up for you.' And as a young man of twenty I was so abashed and red in the face at the very thought of this lavatory seat being erected in the middle of Baker's emporium that I said, 'No, no, I'll take it.' And in the end I'm bound to confess that it was one of the most splendid bits of safari equipment I ever had.

Other apparently outmoded pieces of equipment similarly turned out to be invaluable in the field: mosquito boots made of leather or white canvas

## SPECIMEN OUTFIT AS SUPPLIED TO CLIENTS
### GOING TO TANGANYIKA TERRITORY
### COLONIAL SERVICE.
#### December, 1925.

2 Khaki Drill Tunics.
2 Pairs Cotton Bedford Cord Breeches.
Tropical Weight Dress Coat.
Blue Flannel Blazer.
3 Pairs White Flannel Trousers.
1 Pair Light Grey ditto.
College Wire Crest for Blazer.
Light Weight Cotton Dressing Gown.
6 Dress Collars.
9 Khaki Ties.
Special All Wool Solaro Bush Shirt.
2 Khaki Cotton Shirts.
Spine pads to ditto.
Jaegar Cholera Belt.
Sweater, light wool.
2 Pairs Fox's Tropical Puttees.
White Cashmere Square.
2 Pairs Mosquito Boots.
Pair Bush Boots.
Pair Leather Leggings.
'X' Chair Green Canvas Deck Chair with leg rests.
Green Canvas Valise.
Green Canvas Bucket.
'X' Chair Bath and Washstand complete in bag.
3 Steel Japanned Cases, 25 in., with wooden bottoms.
Steel Helmet Case for 2 Helmets.
2 Hurricane Lamps.
Special Cook's Case, fitted.
2 Sporting Guns and all accessories.
Khaki Wolseley Helmet.
White ditto and badge.
2 Waterproof Cases for same.

A specimen list from *Suggestions for Tropical Outfit and Equipment* as
supplied by Walters and Co. to newly-appointed Cadets, 1925.

and worn in the evenings to protect ankles and calves, and what was known in East Africa as the *jilumchi* or *chilumchi* – 'a most extraordinary thing, an ordinary tin basin with a canvas cover which was strapped down over the top and in that you kept all your washing kit and your sponges and razors and also pyjamas, so that when you travelled light you had no other piece of luggage, apart from your bedding roll, and you required nothing else.' There was also a larger version of the *jilumchi*, a tin bath with 'a very splendid wicker basket affair that went inside and was meant to contain all one's dirty clothes'.

Then there was the problem of what the well-dressed colonial official ought to wear. 'I remember having anxious moments looking at photographs in old books of District Officers,' says Anthony Kirk-Greene. 'Did one wear a uniform? Did one wear short or long stockings? Did one wear very long shorts? Could you wear an open-necked shirt? Did you have a tie? I remember going through all sorts of advertisements and brochures from the Colonial Office about our man in so-and-so, trying to work this out.' There was indeed an Administrative Service uniform – a white one with gold buttons and a Wolseley helmet to match, to be worn on 'splendid occasions' but otherwise to be avoided: 'Uniforms in tropical Africa are not the ideal way of being comfortable and although for the Africans a uniform is a splendid thing and something they quite rightly enjoy and admire, for ourselves we would only wear these things when we had to and were much happier dressed as ordinary members of the public.' Officers in the Sudan and in Kenya stuck to a khaki uniform – in Kenya they had their own idiosyncratic system of rings worn on the sleeve which was said to go back to some obscure naval connection – but for the most part District Officers preferred to go about in khaki shorts with stockings up to the knee, worn with an open-necked bush shirt.

The traditional port of embarkation for Africa was Liverpool. It was from here that the ships of the Elder Dempster fleet sailed on alternate Wednesdays for the West Africa Coast, leaving the British India and the Union Castle lines, departing from Tilbury, to serve the East Coast. Elder Dempster was a major institution on the coast, the 'big canoe man pass all', celebrated in the working songs of the Kru boatmen from Cape Coast Castle to Calabar, but as passenger liners went Elder Dempster ships were modest in size and far from luxurious in their fittings, reflecting the fact that their passenger lists were made up very largely of government servants, traders and missionaries – nearly all of whom travelled saloon or first class, leaving the second class to B class officials and the third class to Africans.

Donald Dunnet sailed for Nigeria aboard the Elder Dempster mail steamer the S.S. *Obinsee* in June 1920, after being given a brief once-over by his employers, which was done 'just to see that the men were sober before they actually sailed, because there were cases when people had turned up very drunk and the sailing had been cancelled on the spot'. He had brought himself a dinner suit 'because I understood it to be *de rigueur* to wear one on board, and I was very anxious to put this on. But as time came on for dinner I looked round anxiously and I couldn't see anybody wearing one so I thought, well, perhaps you don't do it on the first night – and that turned out to be the case.' On subsequent nights everybody in the first class dressed for dinner, the men wearing dinner suits or – in the thirties – white shell jackets, with those in the Administrative Service sporting cummerbunds of different colours – green for Nigeria, red for Sierra Leone and, of course, gold for the Gold Coast.

Although the different professions tended to seek out each other's company, perhaps the strongest division was between 'old coasters' and 'first-timers' or 'first-tour men'. Seated among old coasters at the Purser's table, Donald Dunnet felt himself to be very insignificant: 'The Purser was a great big chap, a pretty imposing figure, who had a pint of cold lager with his breakfast, and he strode round the deck looking very, very important, and he was very patronizing and made me feel very humble. In an endeavour to make up some conversation I asked him about the native quarter in Lagos, and he looked very superciliously at me and said, "Well, it's all native quarter in Lagos." So I didn't get very far with the conversation.'

It was almost a tradition that old coasters regaled newcomers during the two-week run across the 'Elder Dempster boneyard' with tall tales about the White Man's Grave, designed, as George Sinclair states, 'partly as lessons but mainly to horrify us with the prospect ahead. These stories were highlighted when we reached Sierra Leone and somebody came on board to meet Sierra Leone officers. The conversation ran like this: "Poor old Cocky." "Yes, indeed, poor old Cocky. Snake-bite, wasn't it?" We turned round and sought the bar.'

It was at the ship's bar, bound for Mombasa via the Suez Canal, that Captain Montgomery – and no doubt many other young gentlemen – first made the acquaintance of pink gin, as well as of the practice of signing chits rather than paying up on the spot, a dangerous custom as some found to their cost at the end of the voyage. David Allen was on board the steamship *Accra* when it was torpedoed in 1940. The morale of the passengers received a mighty boost when they observed the chief steward standing on the bridge: 'He shouted to us all and then out of his pocket he took all the chits that we'd signed, and he held them up and he tore them up in his hand and threw them into the sea!'

The first port of call on the African mainland was generally Freetown, first visited by Hugh Moresby-White in 1915:

Looking at it through the porthole of my cabin I thought what a lovely little place it was, with its picturesque little harbour – though it was very, very hot. And I remember a wreck, an old slaver, stranded on a rock at the entrance to the harbour. It was there for years. And there was a familiar figure, too, in the harbour – an African in a canoe wearing just a loin-cloth round his middle and a battered top hat on his head. He would sing English popular songs – a very cheerful chap, as Africans are – and the passengers would be leaning over the rail looking down at him and what he was waiting for was for coins to be thrown overboard. When the coin was thrown into the water he'd take his hat off and put it down in the canoe and dive down and collect the penny before it had gone very far. He was always there – for years and years.

Very much the same sight met Philip Allison as his ship lay off Freetown in 1931. 'There were a lot of locals in canoes playing about down below and diving for pennies and so on, and I was on one of the upper decks and I leant out of the shadow of the deck above and stuck my head out into the sun, and an old missionary lady tapped me on the shoulder and said, "You must be careful. You are in the tropics now, young man!"'

On the East African Coast, as the British India and Union Castle steamers sailed on down past Mombasa, the approach to the island of Zanzibar was heralded from many miles away by the exotic scent of cloves and spices: 'But over and above the smell of cloves there was the smell of shark, one of the imports brought by the annual dhow trade which they'd caught on their way to Zanzibar and which were then deposited in great vats while they were salted and then re-exported largely to the African mainland.' The main gateway to the mainland was the port of Dar es Salaam, which was, for Darrell Bates, the realization of a dream: 'It was a beautiful harbour, landlocked completely with a very narrow entrance lined with palm trees and white buildings, and it was how one had imagined it to be. And it was a great moment, really, because almost ten years of my life had been devoted to this as an objective.'

Every landfall had its own never to be forgotten flavour. On the West Coast the Reverend Robert MacDonald had continued on down past the Slave Coast to the Bight of Benin, where his ship arrived off Calabar at nightfall: 'It was a kind of fortnightly run of the Elder Dempster liner; a gun was fired when the anchor dropped in the Calabar river and it happened that it was night just as we anchored and I remember being tremendously impressed by the first sounds of Africa. The crickets came out with their long whistling noises, and with the fireflies illuminating the whole area it was almost like a show of fireworks – and I wondered if I'd ever get accustomed to this kind of thing.'

But there could have been no more romantic or exciting introduction to Africa than that experienced by Bill Page – as well as by all those who came

Elder Dempster Lines

Passenger List

M.V. "ADDA"

The West African *mammy*-chair as seen from the deck of an Elder Dempster steamer in the 1930s.

47

to Accra by sea between the wars – as he was brought ashore by the Kru boatmen of the Gold Coast:

The steamers anchored a couple of miles offshore and there they rode gently rocking to and fro as the breakers came rolling in. And there we waited until the canoes – which they call surf-boats – came out. These were dug-out canoes made from one solid tree, with four men with paddles sitting along each side and one chanter at the back with a long oar to guide it and steady it. When they got alongside they would wait down below and on deck the *mammy*-chair would be got out. There were two seats facing each other in it and you could step in and then sit there. And this was winched up off the deck and then swung overboard and you were then suspended over the surf-boat below. Then they lowered the *mammy*-chair to within about four feet of the boat and as the surf-boat was resting in the trough of a wave they would let out the rope and you'd go down bang into the bottom of the surf-boat and step out. Then the Africans bent to their work and dug into the waves and got us travelling along well and of course the chanter at the back did his singing and they all joined in.

The surf-boat would go down into the trough between the huge rollers and you'd be completely out of sight of land, and nothing but waves around you. Then gradually you would mount again on to a crest and there you would see the shore again and slide down the other side. It was extremely hard work for these chaps and I was told that they didn't last long on this job, but they were of magnificent physique, with brown, shining and rippling muscles. As we got closer to the shore they would hold the vessel back until we were right on the crest of a breaking wave and then all together they would bend to it and drive us right up the shore. Then you had to nip out pretty quickly as the wave receded and the next one came in and, of course, the women were carried ashore by the boys. And so you went up the beach – and as you landed the heat hit you, like being hit in the face.

# four

# TAKING UP THE ROPES

*You would know you were in Africa if you woke up suddenly and found yourself there by the look of the sky, the clouds in particular, always brilliantly lit from the top with a dark line underneath. The sky and general colours are all of a very high key, very brilliant, so that the contrasts are very great and at the same time there is no softening. There are no soft greens, no grey, and shadows are equally dark, sometimes chocolate and sometimes a dark blue-grey.*

If Africa had a characteristic appearance and a characteristic heat it also had a characteristic smell. It was the 'quite unacceptable' odour of rancid palm oil that first impressed itself on Nigel Cooke when he arrived in Nigeria – that and the 'extreme vivacity of the African, which gave an atmosphere of great cheerfulness that sustained many Europeans apart from myself through many years of service'.

There were others whose first impressions were equally mixed. Seeing Freetown for the first time, Kenneth Smith was 'very dismayed at the little that seemed to have been achieved by a hundred years or more of continual British administration there. The town seemed to me to be a run-down shanty town and I went back on board ship considerably dismayed at the prospect of serving in what seemed to me to be the impoverished, run-down world of Africa.' Arriving in the Northern Rhodesian capital of Lusaka after a four-day rail journey up from the Cape, Robin Short took the 'rudimentary' local conditions for granted. Not until some years later was he able to make any sort of valid comparison: 'My parents, who had been in India, came out on a visit and were appalled by the disgracefully primitive conditions in which government servants were expected to live. They found the contrast between India and Africa very great, but, not knowing any better, we simply soldiered on.'

Almost by tradition, first-tour men spent a couple of days or more in government headquarters, while their seniors dispersed without delay to their various provinces and up-country stations, often catching the special evening boat-train that met their ship as it docked – in Lagos it left at 9 p.m. Nigel Cooke gained an early insight into what life as an Assistant District Officer would be like as his ship arrived at Lagos and the postings went up on the ship: 'I remember particularly an ADO who was coming back for his fourth tour, looking with amazement and disappointment to find that he was going back to the same station yet again – and this was a station on the Mambila plateau, the most remote in the whole of Northern Nigeria and very lonely indeed.'

After landing and proceeding through Customs there were certain conventions to be observed without delay. The most vital of these was still the dose of five grains of quinine a day. According to Martin Lindsay it was taken every evening with a pink gin and soda-water:

Even when you were out to dinner with somebody else the servant who brought the pink gin on a tray always brought a bottle of quinine with it so that nobody should forget to take his five grains a day. In spite of that most of us got malaria once or twice, although probably very slightly. The people who got it really badly were the second class – in the official sense of the word – white men, such as the foreman plate-layers and the engine-drivers who were miles away up-country living a very lonely life and who were often heavy drinkers. Their anti-malaria discipline was not good, and they used to get malaria very much worse than we did, which very often turned into blackwater fever.

Almost equally important – especially for those in government service – was the observation of protocol. Nigel Cooke had been warned and so he knew the form: 'When we arrived in Lagos we were taken to sign the Governor's book, the Chief Justice's book, the Chief Secretary's book. And furthermore, when one got to one's station not only did you have to sign the Resident's book but you had to leave cards in the appropriate places. I'd been told that a Resident should have a card and, furthermore, that any married couple should have two cards, but it was not obligatory to drop cards on married men who had not got their wives with them, or alternatively, bachelors without wives. And indeed, I left cards accordingly.' Edwin Everett was not so well informed:

It was the custom to leave cards very soon after your arrival. In fact we found this out when we were hauled up to headquarters and asked why we hadn't done it. The explanation that we didn't know anybody, we didn't know where they lived and in fact we hadn't managed to finish unpacking yet didn't get us anywhere. We were merely told that an officer would call that afternoon and drive us around so that we could leave cards, so we had to dash off into town and buy some blanks and fill them in and that evening a car arrived with an African police orderly who drove us around and kept stopping at various doors. And we just walked up the garden path and rang or knocked, and when the steward boy answered we said, 'Master in?' 'No' – we issued him with one card. 'Master get Missus?' 'Yes' – we gave him another card. Next day we were up on the mat again. 'Why did you leave only one card at Mr So and So's house?' 'But the steward boy said madam no here.' 'You silly fools, she was at the club.'

# Hugh Fortescue Moresby White. Born 15th September, 1891.

*District Officer, £880 p.a. and £72 seniority allowance.*

| | | |
|---|---|---|
| 28 April | 1915 | Appointed Assistant District Officer. |
| 14 May | 1915 | Arrived in Nigeria and assumed duty at Ijebu-Ode. |
| 23 June | 1915 | Transferred to Onitsha. |
| 24 Sept. | 1916 | On leave. |
| 15 Feb. | 1917 | Returned from leave and resumed duty at Ijebu-Ode. |
| 25 April | 1918 | Acting District Officer, Ijebu-Ode. |
| 24 May | 1919 | On leave. |
| 1 Jan. | 1920 | Returned from leave and resumed duty at Abeokuta. |
| 2 July | 1920 | Transferred to Ijebu-Ode. |
| 5 July | 1920 | Acting District Officer, Ijebu-Ode. |
| 14 Oct. | 1920 | |
| 1 Jan. | 1921 | Acting District Officer, Ijebu-Ode. |
| 28 Feb. | 1921 | |
| 11 June | 1921 | On leave. |
| 15 Jan. | 1922 | Returned from leave and resumed duty at Ijebu-Ode. |
| 25 Feb. | 1922 | Acting Resident, Ijebu Province. |
| 17 Mar. | 1922 | |
| 20 June | 1922 | do.      do.      do. |
| 30 July | 1922 | |
| 8 Nov. | 1922 | do.      do.      do. |
| 31 Dec. | 1922 | |
| 1 April | 1923 | Officer-in-charge, Ijebu Division. |
| 25 May | 1923 | On leave. |
| 13 Dec. | 1923 | Returned from leave and resumed duty at Owerri. |
| 19 Dec. | 1924 | On leave. |
| 24 June | 1925 | Returned from leave and resumed duty in Oyo Province. |
| 2 July | 1926 | On leave. |
| 6 Jan. | 1927 | Returned from leave and resumed duty in Oyo Province. |
| 8 April | 1927 | Acting Senior Assistant Secretary, Nigerian Secretariat. |
| 10 May | 1927 | |
| 3 June | 1927 | do.      do.      do. |
| 10 Feb. | 1928 | On leave. |
| 29 July | 1928 | Returned from leave and resumed duty in Calabar Province. |
| 21 Dec. | 1928 | Assistant Secretary, S.P. Secretariat. |

Educated at Malvern College, St. John's College, Oxford.

From the Nigerian Staff List 1929; a valuable reference book for
hostesses that showed not only details of age, appointment and salary of
every civil officer but also his exact seniority within each province at the
secretariat.

This custom of dropping and the returning of cards that followed it was not entirely without purpose, since it resulted in a considerable number of invitations to drinks and dinner. The practice was already on the decline when war broke out in 1939 and it was stopped by governmental directive for the duration of the war – never to be revived. But up to that time the extent of protocol continued to surprise many newcomers, including David Allen when he came to the Gold Coast in 1938: 'Everybody was really horribly and terribly aware of seniority in the civil service, so naturally at dinner parties you were very much seated in accordance with your status. There was this very firm feeling of status and seniority which went on for a very long time indeed though it got less and less as time went on.' The means by which this seniority was proclaimed was through the medium of the Staff or Civil Service List, known irreverently as the 'stud book'. This listed every official in the territory in order of seniority, together with such details as his salary, age, qualifications and his present posting: 'All formal entertaining was largely conducted with the Civil List in mind; the hostess was very conscious of where in the List the various guests appeared and took punctilious care to make sure that seniority was perfectly matched in the placing of her guests.'

The Civil List was also useful in other ways: 'One knew exactly where one stood with regard to all one's colleagues and how senior they were and how likely it was that they would get promoted and what one's own chances of promotion were and so on.' Going hand in hand with this status-consciousness was a certain formality of address. Very soon after his arrival in Lagos – 'my seniority at that stage was only about six hours old' – Nigel Cooke was addressed by the wife of a more senior official who expressed surprise 'that we cadets were so brash as to address an ADO of seven years standing by his Christian name. When I got to Bornu I don't think my Resident ever addressed me by anything other than my surname and, indeed, no one in that province addressed him by any other title than "Sir", and this included the senior DO. However, all the younger members of the Service and indeed quite a large proportion of those who'd come through the First World War were calling each other by their Christian names.' This observation of protocol was by no means confined to the European community:

When I went to my first council meeting the Resident told me exactly how many steps to take forward to greet the Shehu of Bornu when he entered the room. No steps were taken forward for the members of the council, and indeed they were not even sat in chairs, they sat on the ground. During the years that followed getting the chiefs to agree to their council sitting on chairs was one of the things which we were constantly pressing for, and of course, achieved in the end.

Before the war, and for several years after the war, it was not customary for administrative officers to shake hands with any Native Authority official other than a chief. This was not because we objected to doing so, but because it was assumed that the chief would object to your doing so. I remember the acute embarrassment of the Waziri of Bornu, who after all was the most senior person in the whole of Bornu Emirate after the Shehu, when I, in my greenness, shook his hand.'

But if protocol was a little heavy-handed and the atmosphere 'strenuous' at times, it was offset by a tradition of hospitality towards junior officers. David Allen's first few days in Accra were very typical:

Every day we had a detailed programme laid out for us which involved going out and meeting senior civil servants and hearing what they'd got to say to us. And then various social events were laid on for us. I remember one afternoon we went out and had a game of golf. In the evenings we were invited out to dinner by senior civil servants and I remember very well one dinner party we went to – I think it was with the Deputy Colonial Secretary – there was a lovely round mahogany table and no tablecloth on it, with everybody sitting round. What I remember is that the table was absolutely covered with ants; they just ran all over the place and nobody paid the slightest attention to this, and I thought, 'My God, for the rest of my time in the Gold Coast have I got to have ants running around on the dinner table?'

Over and above their hierarchical structure the administrators had other minor social divisions. There was the good-humoured contempt expressed by those in Northern Nigeria – the 'holy Northerners' – and Northern Kenya for those in the South; the suspicion of the men in the field, the district, for the men in the centre, the secretariat; the natural irritation of the experienced old hand for the inexperienced youngster, who would be told many times over that 'you've got to be two years in this country before you are any use to anyone.' Yet the administrators were themselves a group that was set not only above but also apart from the rest. There was, particularly in the early days 'a great division, unfortunately, between government officials and commercials and also between A class officials and B class officials'. The division between A and B class officials was the same as that found between officers and men in the services. On the one side were the administrators and, as time went on, more and more officers from the various support services. On the other side, with their own B class or second class clubs – and leading very different lives – there were the white 'NCOs', the Public Works Department foremen, railway engineers, civil contractors and other Europeans, usually out on short-time contracts.

The division between officials and non-officials was less marked but it was there all the same. 'Our lives didn't coincide,' states Donald Dunnet. Trading was trading and we had no connection with administration. We had no authority or powers. We were simply there, and we were rather looked down upon by some of the government people. We had terrific cuts in salary when the slump came on, and I remember one government officer saying, "Well, of course, you are traders."' Within the trading community itself there were other fine lines of social division and, as always, the first-tour man was at the bottom: 'Lagos society was very difficult for an assistant. First of all, trading assistants were not allowed to join the club, and there was a social division between assistants and what were called agents in those days – what we would call managers today. Having survived the rigours and all the ailments of West Africa and immeasurable quantities of alcohol, they had achieved this exalted state and they had no time for a first-timer. A first-timer was a term of contempt and derision – and a first-timer was left very much to his own devices.'

Attitudes towards Africans varied greatly between these different groups of Europeans – as indeed they varied greatly from colony to colony. Almost the first piece of advice that Bill Page received when he came to Lagos in the mid-twenties was to 'keep them in their place – and their place was obviously below! In those days the division between the races was very marked, but it wasn't unpleasant for the most part, and for the most part both sides accepted it.' As a convinced socialist, Bill Page was naturally critical of British Colonial rule:

I didn't think that our rule there was oppressive but I thought it was wrong and that it established the wrong relationships between people. But I also found that the government people I met were first class and far more friendly and prepared to mix with the Africans than the commercial community there. At Government House garden parties you'd see the higher people, particularly those who were commissioners from up-country, mixing very easily with the Africans and so would the missionaries, whereas the commercial people, and perhaps the lower civil servants, would be standing around, whites in one place and the Africans in another and not mixing at all.

Major differences in attitude towards Africans between one territory and another were due partly to the very different forms of social development within these territories, partly to the length and the nature of contact with Europe. In Nyasaland, for instance, which had come under exceptionally strong missionary influence since the days of Livingstone, the concept of partnership was implicit even if it was not greatly advanced. Administrators who served in this 'very small, very poor, not very important country' accepted that they were in something of a colonial backwater, yet shared a strong sense of family feeling, where 'everybody did tend to know everybody.' By contrast, the neighbouring territory of Tanganyika was the land of the 'tough German colonialists' where the inherited assumption was that 'an African or a wog was an inferior being, almost incapable of being taught, a first class liar and someone to whom one tried to be kind and at the same time train.'

When Robert and Mercedes Mackay came out to Tanganyika in 1934 they found 'layer upon layer' of snobbery:

For instance, we met some very charming railway people on the way and we said, 'We'll be meeting you, of course. We'll be meeting you at the club, I expect.' And they said, 'Oh no, you won't. We're not allowed to join your club. We have to have our own club.' The social layers and the social snobbery was almost unbelievable and unfortunately it particularly hit at people like doctors, forest officers and geologists – my husband was one. People like that who had gone to universities and had tremendous years of training and who knew practically everything about their subject, were ordered about by and practically had to kow-tow to a little boy with his mother's milk hardly off his teeth who drove around with a flag in front of his car because he represented the King! Now that was very galling.

First-tour men were almost by definition bachelors. If they were staying either in the capitals or in the larger stations they usually moved into civilian messes, where three or four young men could sleep under the same roof and share certain amenities. Such a mess was provided by the bank for which Bill Page worked in Lagos:

It was very pleasant if you had companions that were congenial – then it was absolutely first class, but if you didn't get on, you were in such close quarters that it was rather miserable. The heavy drinkers usually got into a mess on their own and therefore lived their own particular way of life without disturbing anybody else very much, but when you got a mixed mess then the non-drinkers would have their dinner at about half-past seven and go off to bed and at about eleven o'clock the drinkers would come in very happy and noisy, call the boys to bring out their dinner and disturb us generally which was rather an irritation. Each mess provided its own food. We shared a cook, but one member of the mess would be *chop* master, looking after the *chop* for a month. He kept careful accounts of all that was bought, instructed the cook to buy the food and paid him for it and made the menus. I found the food very dull, with a tremendous amount of minced beef. The cattle were bred up in the areas free from tsetse fly, which were hundreds of miles away, and were driven down by road and so were fairly tough when they got down to the coast and then of course you had to eat the meat fairly soon after it was slaughtered. So it tended to be rather tough and hence the minced beef and rissoles day after day, and if you had a *chop* master who had no imagination you would get banana fritters three or four times a week as well.

The institution of the mess was also to be found operating along rather more conventional lines among the various military units scattered through the colonial territories; the West Africa Frontier Force on the West Coast – with small detachments in Gambia and Sierra Leone, a larger formation in the Gold Coast and in Nigeria the Nigeria Regiment with four battalions and a battery – and in East Africa the King's African Rifles, with six battalions spread through Kenya, Uganda, Tanganyika and Nyasaland. The officers in these units were drawn from every regiment and corps in the British Army and included cavalry officers and gunners as well as those from the infantry. Whatever their origins all served as infantry officers and wore the same standard khaki drill uniform of an officer in the tropics: 'The only occasions when our regimental identity was evident was at night when we all dined in the regimental mess kits of our own corps, so that sitting at the mess table at dinner in Nairobi, the headquarters of the Kenya battalion, you had an astonishing scene of blue, green and scarlet mess kits of every corps.' In the regimental mess at Nairobi Brian Montgomery found that the conversation was 'almost entirely about experiences on safari, particularly the big game shooting. There was a very fine pair of elephant tusks, maybe fifty or sixty pounds in each tusk, in the mess and there were the heads of buck of various kinds also on the walls. And the prestige of a man who had shot a lion and an elephant, rhino and buffalo was very great. But the officer who'd never shot anything did not have much prestige and therefore, like other newly joined officers, I longed for the day when I would be sent on safari, with the independence and command of a detachment.'

When Brian Montgomery woke up on his first morning in his mess bungalow in Nairobi he heard for the first time the reveille, the 'Turkish rise' of the King's African Rifles. 'This bugle call was not the standard reveille of the British Army, but the Turkish reveille, a very tuneful call which none of us who served there will ever forget and which originated from the father of the KAR, Lord Lugard.' In addition to Lugard's original Sudanese and Somalis, the King's African Rifles drew its *askaris* from many other East African tribes – but not from the Kikuyu, who were considered to be lacking in the necessary martial spirit. What astonished Brian Montgomery when he first saw his *askaris* on parade was that they wore no foot gear: 'The uniform was a khaki drill tunic, khaki shorts, a *tarbosh* with a black tassel derived from the Sudanese origins of the KAR, blue puttees and no foot gear at all; the *askari* never wore boots. Their feet were iron-hard and the ground literally shook when they were given such orders as stand at ease – and the noise was tremendous.'

Another officer who had a period of service with the King's African Rifles was Anthony Lytton, who found the 'fleshpots' of Nairobi to be 'insidious and most liable to corrupt'. Playing squash and polo took up much of his time and 'several times a year there was a polo week when the settlers

# J. G. PLUMB & SON

## VICTORIA HOUSE, 117 VICTORIA STREET, WESTMINSTER, S.W1

A somewhat idealized image of the station club as represented in an
advertisement from one of the many firms of colonial outfitters offering
services in the 1930s.

descended in their cars from their remote ranches and farms from far and wide and gathered together and one danced from 10 p.m. to 6 a.m. One thought not at all, or very little, of the people up-country in remote posts, either alone or in twos and threes.' The Kenya settlers, of course, provided an element of society that was entirely absent from most colonies. Anthony Lytton found them to be distinguished by 'their enterprise, their energy and their resourcefulness in dealing with nature in its rawest and most difficult state. They were people of tremendous character – and their club gave an indication of what they were like by its rules and its customs. Muthaiga Country Club at one stage would not admit an official because the officials were always the brake on what the settlers thought it right to do and therefore for a very long time, right up to my period, there was a discord between the settler element and the officials.'

If Muthaiga was the most notorious club in Africa – 'full of rumour, intrigue and amorous occasions' – the English Club in Zanzibar was probably the oldest, set in an old Arab merchant's house with great brass-studded doors and catering for a 'very closed' English community. Although even the most junior members of the administration were accepted automatically, club membership was only open to the most senior members of the commercial and trading firms. The same distinction was made in such places as Lagos, where the Polo Club was open to managers and agents but not to their assistants – who had to be content with their own B class clubs, where they could go for a game of tennis or to play cards and where 'you just sat and drank and that made it a bit more tolerable – because there wasn't much else to do.'

Perhaps it was just as well that most young men, whether they were officials or 'unofficials' were soon packed off up-country. Darrell Bates had two days in Dar es Salaam before he was sent off to the small coastal station of Bagamoyo to which he had been posted:

I went out in an old lorry, surrounded by all the packages which I'd brought out from England, the tin bath and the camp chairs and the boxes and the shotgun and a few stores, and it was a long and very exciting journey through the bush. We didn't see very much – very few people, practically no animals – and it was the emptiness which struck me first of all, the emptiness and, to some extent, the poverty. And then suddenly, we were there; the driver said, 'There is the place.' There was a fringe of bush along the road, there were a few patches of cultivation, fields of maize, and there were a few scattered huts made of coconut leaves plaited and sewn with twine. And we turned a corner and there suddenly between the coconut trees I saw a Union Jack flying, rather tattered and forlorn on top of a very unpretentious white building. It was forlorn and lonely but it had a certain smack of authority and order. There was a flight of steps which led up from the road and on top of it a tall, thin angular figure stood with crumpled white trousers and a white shirt, and his face was long and lean and rather grey. 'Well, here you are,' he said. I didn't know what to say and I stood there probably looking rather foolish. 'Well,' he said, 'I'm off for my evening walk,' and off he went. I noticed that he had a fly switch made from the mane of a lion in his thin, bony hands and he twitched it to brush the flies off his face – and though I didn't know it at the time, it was to become a badge of office.

For officers whose postings directed them deeper into the interior, the journey could often take days and even, in some areas, weeks. As late as 1950 it took Anthony Kirk-Greene ten days to reach his district, culminating in the crossing of a river that had neither bridge nor ferry:

I arrived at the edge of the river and could see about·two hundred yards the other side, sitting on a Roorkee chair, a gentleman with a large hat on, a pair of shorts and a shirt – no uniform in Nigeria, of course, and no tie in the bush. And he was shaking hands with a young Assistant District Officer who was the man I was relieving. And we then – each from our respective sides – started to wade in. I had a puppy on my shoulder which I'd picked up in Yola from a veterinary officer, and when we got half-way and it was well up to my shoulders this other man reached me and said his name was Roger Dubullay and I said, 'That's a great coincidence because I'm Anthony Kirke-Greene and my grandmother said I might meet you somewhere in Africa. She knew your father very well indeed in India.' So then we passed on, he to his side and I to my side, and there was the Senior District Officer, who greeted me and said, 'Well, don't bother to dry out. Just get into the car,' and off we went for the last stage of this journey.

Bill Page had the unfortunate – and not altogether uncharacteristic – experience of relieving a man who had 'rather gone to seed. The three weeks while we were waiting for his boat to come and take him away were some of the most miserable I've had to experience, because it was very close quarters and you couldn't get away from him. He had a glass in his hand from nine o'clock in the morning and by the time the evening came it was more or less running out of his eyes and his mouth, and he would throw down the end of his drink on the floor or up the wall, wherever took his fancy.'

Most first-timers were luckier in their introductions to their first stations – even if the accommodation was somewhat stark. Few can have lived quite as uncomfortably as Bill Stubbs when he first began his police duties in Southern Rhodesia:

My hut was an ordinary native hut, wattle and daub with a thatched roof, about twelve feet in diameter and no door or window. I had no furniture, I had my tin office box which I used as a table and sat on a native stool to eat my meals. My bed consisted of two logs laid on the floor with a stack of grass between them over which I had my groundsheet and then over that one of my most useful purchases before I left England – a rolled-up valise affair of green canvas which is one of the things that the white ants don't eat, and one's blankets and pillow fitted inside it. I was quite content with this.

Philip Allison's first house was rather closer to the standard Public Works Department bungalow:

My first station was at Onitsha on the Niger, where I lived in a very attractive situation in a house with a splendid view down the river. My predecessor who had built this house had spent nearly all the money in erecting a solid concrete platform and hadn't got any money left to do anything except put up an erection of bamboo poles and palm-leaf mats to keep the rain out. It was a very attractive place, but terribly bad for mosquitoes and you used to sit up there at nights and hear the drumming coming over the water from Asaba and hear the frogs croaking down in the Niger swamps. And then the mosquitoes would drive you under the mosquito net. So I used to sit up in bed with the bush lamp outside trying to read *War and Peace* – or perhaps I'd go down to the club and drink beer instead.

It was said that wherever there were two Englishmen there was a club – and certainly, by the twenties, the old Scotch clubs where local Europeans gathered at a mutually convenient spot for drinks in the evening were being replaced by club-houses; sometimes station clubs that were little more than a meeting place with a bar and a snooker or billiards table, sometimes gymkhana clubs where officials and non-officials alike could gather in the late afternoon to play scratch polo or a game of tennis or squash – or even a round of golf on a rough course that had browns instead of greens. It was always considered vital for one's health to keep fit and active, however unsuitable the season might be for violent exercise, and sport in one form or another provided the means, coming naturally to young men who had been brought up to regard sporting activity as an integral part of their social life. What was just as important from a health point of view was that the club provided the opportunity to drink in company – because 'drink was unquestionably a major factor in life in the tropics; it was a very pleasant thing after the heat and burden of the day to rest and to have a long whisky and this was a very common form of relaxation. Drinks parties were almost invariably sitting-down drinks parties, but there was not the same feeling of having one glass after another in quick succession as you do at drinks parties in this country.'

The verandah of the station club also provided a natural setting for the exchange of shop and station news. At Lira in Northern Uganda, where Dick Stone was posted in 1938, it was where 'all the local officials – the DC and the ADCs, the District Medical Officer, the OC Police, the Agricultural Officer, the vet, the Community Development Officer and so on – gathered on Saturday mornings. We'd drink large quantities of beer and gin, and discuss absolutely informally the problems of the district – to see if we could work out a district solution to the current problems of the day. Perhaps these gatherings at the Lira Club were the forerunners to the more formal – and very successful – District Teams which were started a few years later by the Governor, Sir Andrew Cohen.'

But for the newcomer probably the club's greatest value was that it filled the 'rather difficult hour in the tropics between six thirty and seven thirty', a melancholy hour which could be passed in congenial company before he returned through the darkness to his own bungalow to have a bath and a late supper before retiring to bed. 'A house was something which one didn't ever occupy in the latter part of the day if one could avoid it,' recalls Nigel Cooke, 'because it was in the nature of a storage heater. In my early years I never slept inside the house, I always slept not only outside but wherever possible away from it, so much so that on one occasion when my steward brought my morning tea, I heard him tut-tutting with amazement because he could see the pad marks of a leopard that had gone round my bed more than once during the night.'

For a young man living on his own, servants played an extremely important role. They came to him by various means. Some were selected more or less at random from servants' parades held at headquarters, some were inherited from previous incumbents, some were brought in by other servants, some simply turned up on the verandah with their 'books', the testimonials or 'chits' from previous employers that always featured prominently in expatriate folklore. Here would be found such old colonial chestnuts as 'I'm sure this boy will do you as well as he has done me,' and 'This cook leaves me on account of illness – mine, not his.' Mocked though they were by employers, these 'books' were held in high regard by their servants, as Bob MacDonald found when he went down with a severe bout of malaria: 'I was very down and moaning a bit too much and I said to my steward boy, "Harrison, I go die." Harrison said, "Give me book first." In other words, give me my testimonial before you go.'

In the bachelor household the steward or house-boy was always the key figure, since the running of the household was left very largely in his hands. To assist him he had his assistant or 'small boy' – 'a youth who had to do all the menial jobs, like de-ticking the dog and cleaning the lamps and when you went from one house to another after dark he'd go in front of you waving his paraffin lamp to drive off the snakes and scorpions from the pathway.' There was always a cook and possibly his assistant or *mtoto*, and for those in horse country – as in Northern Nigeria – there would also be a groom and perhaps a water-boy. Very close and long-lasting relationships often developed between master and servant. Hugh Moresby-White's steward, Nduku – 'a most faithful servant' – came to him as a 'small boy' in 1916 and remained with him until he retired in 1944. Donald Dunnet's steward, Alexander, began in the same way: 'Living in grass huts as I did there was an awful lot of dust about and I used to get asthma and it was pretty painful. Well, he used to sleep at the end of my bed and make me hot tea during the night and look after me and really, apart from my wife, there's nobody who has done more for me in my life than this boy.'

Like most bachelors, Chris Farmer was content to leave the details of the catering up to his cook: 'It was up to him to produce my breakfast and my lunch and my evening meal as best he could and, after all, he knew better than I did what was available in the market. What I used to do was give him *chop* money, market money, enough for a week at a time and the meals would turn up. Sometimes he would use his imagination, sometimes he wouldn't. Occasionally I would get to the stage where if I saw another egg custard or another so-called pancake I would feel like screaming.'

Beyond a few unpretentious pieces of regulation furniture provided by the PWD, the bush bungalow offered few comforts. Lighting was mostly by Tilley or pressure lamp and paraffin refrigerators did not become widely available until well into the 1930s. 'You cannot imagine how primitive many aspects of life were,' asserts Clifford Ruston. Latrines – almost always cleaned out by prisoners from the local jail – often consisted of no more than 'a small mud hut with an open door, two upright pieces of wood with a horizontal piece and a small earthenware bowl and a pile of sand. And it was by no means unusual in the early morning to find a villager on his way to the well greeting one and wishing one a happy day's work!' In the bush supplies were always hard to come by. 'You might go into an up-country store and find nothing but cabin biscuits and bully beef and sardines,' recalls Edwin Everett, 'so you had to live off the country with its rather stringy chickens, the odd goat and anything more was considered a bonus. There was always rice, of course, and if you were really in the bush there would be a lot of bush fowl, partridge-like creatures infesting the African farms, and if you were lucky there would be anything from antelope to fish. But in some stations you just had to exist on tins and, therefore, if you were going to visit somebody either as a friend or on inspection, you'd take something with you. Even if it was only half a pound of butter, it would be gratefully received.' For those stationed near the coast or a railway line, newly imported supplies, known as steamer *chop* in West Africa, provided a welcome break in an otherwise monotonous diet.

In West Africa – where all food was referred to as *chop*, with canapés before dinner being referred to as small *chop* or (for some unaccountable reason) as *gadgets* – local foodstuffs and recipes made up only a small part of the European diet. The closest that most whites came to following native

ie new District Officer (David Allen) meets the local chiefs – the Nsutaheni and the
{iduasiheni – and staff at the Native Authority headquarters, Ashanti, Gold Coast 1940.

Social life thrived only on the larger stations; Zaria Races, N. Nigeria 1926, where infrequent amateur race meetings drew together officials and 'non-officials' from many miles around.

A new form of popular entertainment; the Resident together with Yoruba chiefs at the open-air Rex Cinema, Ibadan 1939.

In the bush district officials rarely lived in comfortable surroundings; the District Commissioner's house at Mandera, Kenya Northern Frontier District 1936.

The District Officer (Richard Turnbull) in his office, Mandera 1936.

The District Officer and the tribal *baraza*; in fact, two District Officers resolving a boundary dispute between two tribes – the pastoral Barabaig and their neighbours, the largely agricultural Wanyaturu, Tanganyika *c.* 1954.

custom was in the eating of the two great West African dishes of groundnut stew and palm-oil *chop*. Much of Philip Allison's first tour was spent in country where 'palm oil was king' – along the creeks of the Niger river:

The whole life of the creeks was palm oil and the food was palm oil and there was this glorified native dish called palm-oil *chop* which used to be served in European households on Sunday lunch-time, which was chicken stewed in palm oil, which had a golden-red colour – a bit like engine oil but more golden – and then served with peppers and rice and all sorts of side-dishes which the cooks called *gadgets*, consisting of fried onions, raw onions, chopped-up coconut, fried bananas, plain bananas, stink fish – which were fried shrimps – and all this was consumed with a lot of beer and gin to follow and lunch-time was liable to go on to four or five in the evening.

Other than at weekends, heavy eating – and drinking – was strictly confined to the evenings: 'You weren't allowed to drink until the sun went down and then you had your sundowners,' recalls Gerald Reece, who went out to his first district at Kakamega in Western Kenya in 1925. 'It was almost ridiculous the way they waited until the sun disappeared completely before they would touch a drink. I remember when I called one day on an old settler and he asked me to have a drink and apologized very politely – "If you don't mind, we'll have to wait, because the sun isn't yet down" – and kept popping out to make sure that the sun wasn't down. And after doing that three or four times he came back and said, "We're all right now, the sun has gone down and we can have a whisky."'

Civilian outfit as worn by officials and 'non-officials'. Walters and Co., 1925.

# five

# KEEPERS OF THE KING'S PEACE

*I suppose the District Commissioner under the old system of colonial administration exercised more authority than anybody exercises in any job I can think of. We really were – as the Africans always called us – 'father and mother of the people', we really were.*

Every province of every colonial territory was divided into districts, each administered by its own District Commissioner supported by a number of assistants and providing a system of dual government that underpinned to a greater or lesser degree various forms of Native Authority, ranging from the Northern Nigerian emirates where the power vested in the local rulers was paramount, to 'pagan' regions where local chiefs acted in subordinate roles and acknowledged the absolute authority of the DC. But whether his authority rested purely on his powers of persuasion or on a government mandate to rule, the District Commissioner was still the key figure in his district – a figure from whom every new cadet could learn.

In the event this was not always the case. Cadets very often found themselves thrown in at the deep end, where they learnt their jobs as they went along and as much by trial and error as anything else. But much depended on the personality of the DC himself. 'There were plenty of District Commissioners who would no doubt have been excellent guides in those early days, but I didn't have one of them,' remembers Charles Meek:

I had a chap called Cecil Steeble, an eccentric figure who in his early days had, I believe, been a chucker-out for Mrs Merrick, who was a notable figure in the night-club world of London in the early twenties. He was certainly built that way; a great, strong, robust, broad chap. I got on with him very well indeed but instruction came there none. In Tanganyika we were great proponents of the system of indirect rule which had been introduced by Cameron, and I had that explained to me in very short order. We had *liwalis* as headmen in charge of the areas within the district and I remember Cecil Steeble on, I suppose, my first day in the office sitting me down and pulling a sheet of paper towards himself and saying, 'This is the way it works, Meek, you have a *liwali* here and a *liwali* there and a *liwali* in the other place' – and he drew a series of small circles around the perimeter of the paper. Then he said, 'Here in the middle you've got me,' and he drew a large circle in the middle of the paper and said, 'You see, that's the way it works.' And so it did.

Pat Mullins's first mentor in Nyasaland was rather more helpful – but he, too, had his eccentricities:

My first District Commissioner was Harry MacGiffin and he was a real education in himself. He was a lively Northern Irishman, then in his late thirties, and an unconventional character, a man with a great sense of humour and a very good idea of what was important in district administration and what wasn't, and among the things that were not important in district administration in Harry's eyes was anything at all to do with paperwork. When he got paper from any source he chucked it in the 'Out' tray. Harry would specialize in not answering letters and regional headquarters in Tamale would bombard him with requests for replies and Harry was quite unmoved. I can remember him ringing up his neighbouring DC at Wa and talking on this very bad telephone line and saying, 'Gerard, I've had a seventh reminder from Tamale. I don't think you've ever had a seventh reminder, 'ave you?' On the other hand, outside the office he knew everything that was going on in the district and he could travel for miles and suddenly stop a man and ask him why he was carrying a stick, because he'd never seen him carrying a stick before and had he got an evil thought in his head? And this intimate knowledge of the African people in the area was incredible and I quite rapidly realized that I'd got to try and acquire a similar understanding of everything that went on in the locality.

In Ashanti, the central territory of the Gold Coast, George Sinclair and a fellow cadet considered themselves fortunate to be sharing an office with a District Commissioner who always set aside an hour at the start of a working day in which to receive petitions and complaints:

To us some of these complaints seemed trivial and some important, while others seemed to show that the complainant was a bit bonkers. But when the hour for complaints was over he turned to us and said, 'I know you two lads have been watching me very carefully. You may well have thought that I was wasting a whole hour going into these small matters when there was so much more important and urgent work to be done. But, I tell you, when the day comes when you no longer make time to listen to individual complaints, I hope you'll have the guts to go back to your bungalow, have a pint of cold beer, then write to your Chief Commissioner saying you feel you must resign as you are no longer fit to remain a member of the Colonial Service.'

Not only did we watch him at work, but occasionally, when he went out for meetings in various parts of the district, we went with him. But not for long, because he began to hand us the simpler tasks. We were sent off to inspect villages, to look at the water supplies and health arrangements. We were made responsible for the upkeep of a network of district roads; we had to look after the bridges and order cement and timber for their repair, and we had to pay the road-gangs and see that they were working properly and had the tools they needed. We were also sent out into villages to look into disputes that had been brought into the district office for our DC, and he would say, 'You had better go out and spend a few days in this area and listen to what people have to say and then come back and tell me what you think we should do about it.'

In addition to his European colleagues the cadet could also learn from the subordinate staff in the district or divisional headquarters. In East Africa these offices were known as *boma* and were almost invariably staffed by Goans from India:

There were Goan court clerks, there were Goan cashiers, and Goan district clerks. They were the most wonderful people; kind, generous and helpful and so superbly honest that one could scarcely believe that they came from the East. It has often been said that the Goans had a great graft and their graft was honesty; it was a matter upon which you simply could not fault them. Every young District Officer learnt one side of his trade from the Goans. He learnt how the government accounting system worked, how cash should be handled and how the records should be kept and he learnt about the office filing system.

As well as clerks there were also the African district messengers, 'the backbone of the administration', who acted not only as messengers but also as orderlies and bodyguards, 'a very fine body of hand-picked men, all from that district and varying tribes, but all completely loyal. They were a smart body under a head messenger and second messenger, neatly uniformed, unarmed and utterly reliable. Many a young District Officer learnt more from his district messenger than he ever did from the Colonial Service Course at Oxford.'

But it was no use having help on hand if one was unable to communicate, and here the Colonial Service Course began to assume real practical value – as James Robertson found in the Sudan: 'In my first district office there was only one English-speaking clerk and one could hardly take him away from his essential duties to interpret what the local people were saying to you and the result was that one staggered along trying to remember what one had learnt in London and trying to understand what the people were saying and I found this very difficult to begin with. But after I'd been there for a few weeks I was trekking round the villages with nobody speaking English at all and I soon learnt enough to get on – because it was the only way one could live.' Another way to learn the language was to employ somebody to teach you, in Moslem areas a *mallam* or learned man. This was how Clifford Ruston learnt Hausa: 'The usual process was to read from Frank Edgar's *Litafi na Tatsuniyoyi na Hausa*, which was a collection of folk-stories going deep into Hausa history, and he would then correct my pronunciation and elucidate any unfamiliar words. And one would consult Dr Walter Miller's *Hausa Grammar*. This and Robinson's *Grammar* were the only text-books on the language.'

An additional spur to the learning of local languages was the requirement that all newly appointed officers should pass a government lower standard language examination within a certain period – since success brought with it a cash increment and failure could result in dismissal from the service. The same regulation applied to officers of the King's African Rifles who were examined in Ki-Swahili – the lingua franca of East Africa – six months after they joined and risked being sent home as unfit for service if they failed to satisfy their examiners. This strong emphasis on language requirements was of obvious practical value, but it could never overcome a widespread, and obviously unsatisfactory, reliance on interpreters. Such dependence on a third party was almost inevitable, partly because of the nature of the service, where transfers from one district to another took place every few years. After studying Hausa and Twi in the Gold Coast, Patrick Mullins was transferred to Nyasaland:

I went to the Northern Province where the local language was Chitumbuka, so I got a sufficient standard to pass my lower standard government examination in Chitumbuka after about a year out there, and within two hours of doing so I was transferred to the Southern Province where no Chitumbuka was spoken at all and I was told that I had to take a second government language. So eventually I learnt Chinyanja and passed the language examination in that and shortly after doing that I went to Fort Johnston District where the Bishop of Nyasaland, an old-style missionary and a charming man, was insistent that I learn the local language which was Chiyao, and at that point I rebelled.

The need to have enough fluency in the local native tongue to be able to by-pass the official court interpreter was particularly acute when it came to taking on the role of district magistrate, the most obvious of the powers assumed by the cadet administrator. Authority to act came in the form of a judicial warrant handed over in a ceremony 'as solemn as a civil marriage service'. Hugh Moresby-White received his warrant from the Chief Justice of Nigeria: 'I remember he said to me, "Now one piece of advice I would like to give you. When you give your judgments never give your reasons. Your judgments will probably be right, but your reasons will probably be wrong."' Armed with this piece of advice and with a second class magistrate's powers to impose fines up to £10 and fifteen days imprisonment he duly went to court, which – as was very often the case – happened also to be his office: 'The accused in a criminal case would be brought in by a native policeman. I would be told what the offence was and the witnesses would be brought in one by one and I would listen to what they said and then pronounce a verdict.'

As his experience grew, so – provided he passed the appropriate law exams – did the magistrate's powers, although not all District Officers were required to act as magistrates, especially in those areas where an efficient native court system, such as that operated by the Moslem *alkalis* of Northern Nigeria, was already operating. But when they did hear court cases magistrates were bound to follow the standard codes of criminal procedure, which – even if 'you had virtually to be judge and prosecutor and defence as well' – went some way towards ensuring that the accused got a fair trial. 'There was no prosecution in my time,' recalls James Robertson.

There were no lawyers and the magistrate just had to try the best he could to get the truth and find the man guilty or not guilty. But there were none of the niceties of legal procedure which one would have expected in a court, and the language was of course the language of the people. The accused occasionally interrupted and was brought to order by the sentry and then when you'd heard all the evidence and asked questions you asked the accused if he had any questions to ask the witness and usually he said the witness was a liar. Then you heard what the accused had to say, you asked if the accused had any witnesses and if he had then you summoned his witnesses and at the end you wrote out what you thought the whole thing was about and the reasons for your finding. You found him guilty or not guilty and then the accused was allowed to produce evidence of character, which you took, and then you had to consider what sentence you were going to give. It was mandatory that if you found the chap guilty of murder then you sentenced him to death.

There were some who regarded the British legal system as both out of place and unsuited to the African temperament. On the East Coast, magistrates were plagued by an excessive fondness for *fitina*, the making of false accusations, which was said to be 'almost as widespread and universal as football pools in England'. There was, too, an irritatingly disrespectful attitude towards the majesty of the law, as illustrated by the well-known – and probably apocryphal – story of the Nigerian who went to a European friend and in the course of conversation revealed that he had a court case coming up before a British judge: 'He told his European friend that he was going to send the judge a gift of six cattle to incline his heart in the right direction. The European said, "For goodness' sake, don't do that. The judges are incorruptible. If you send the cattle you'll lose the case. Go to court, tell your story truthfully and you'll get the right verdict." Six months later the two met again and the European said, "Well, Adu, how did you get on?" And the other man said, "I sent the cattle, but I sent them in the name of my adversary."'

Nepotism, bribery and corruption could be found in one form or another at most levels of society. The official attitude was unbending. If government officers were offered a gift which they were bound to accept in order not to give offence, then they were required to return a gift of equal value: 'When you arrived at a station on tour it was the custom for a gift, a bowl of eggs or perhaps some meat, to be presented to you,' explains Edwin Everett. 'Now quite often this gift was the delegated duty of some minor official and he wasn't paid for it, so it was customary to pay the local market value, not directly to the donor but to give it to him as a gift. And if you were touring rapidly such gifts could mount up. I mean, at the end of a week, what do you do with five bowls of eggs?' Faced with this situation, officers took the precaution of taking with them supplies of tobacco or objects suitable for presentation as gifts. But sometimes there were situations when gifts were not returned. While issuing motor-vehicle licences Edwin Everett once noticed a £5 note at his elbow. 'It hadn't been there before so I said, "What's this? Take it away." And the trader in the office said, "Oh, that's not mine." So I said, "Well, it's not mine, take it away." – "No, sir, no, sir, it's not mine. It must be yours." So I produced a box of matches and burnt it and for some reason I never found money lying about the table after that.'

Perhaps the most serious problem for law officers was the sheer volume of paperwork involved, which made it almost impossible to comply with the requirements of court procedure. Faced with such a situation, and a mounting backlog of court cases waiting to be heard, some officers tended to take a rather more flexible approach when it came to handling the less serious cases, as Kenneth Smith explains:

Now take a very typical offence – a fight which might very well involve ten to fifteen witnesses. One knew that at the end of the matter it was going to be either an acquittal or a fine of the order of five to ten shillings. But to have copied down the evidence of the witnesses would have virtually meant that your list was brought to a stop. So I discovered for myself a routine whereby I listened in silence to the entire case and if I found the accused guilty I firmly entered on the appropriate form a plea of guilty. If, on the contrary, the accused was acquitted, I simply wrote on the form 'Charge withdrawn by leave of court', which meant, in fact, that there was no written record of these tediously prolonged debates.

Closely associated with the work in court were certain unpleasant duties associated with the execution of justice. District magistrates were required to witness punishments ordered by the court, perhaps in the form of six to twelve strokes of a cane, but very occasionally the hanging of a condemned man, which had to be witnessed in the company of a medical officer 'to see that all was tidy'. It was a judicial chore that most District Officers dreaded and went to great lengths to avoid if they possibly could. Very frequently Assistant District Officers were appointed superintendents of the local jail and in this capacity they would be required to see the prisoners turned out to work in gangs every morning and sent off to do various jobs about the station – cutting grass, digging ditches and, of course, emptying out the

.hunderboxes from the bungalows. Sometimes this work-force could be put to other use. Dick Stone used his prisoners at Lira to build a squash court: 'This, I think, was the first squash court to be built in an up-country station in Uganda and I remember that I built this squash court, including a little gallery, with the invaluable aid of a Sikh mason imprisoned for some heinous offence, for the princely sum of £26.'

Being a district magistrate was only a part of the work of the District Officer. Coming to Tanganyika as a 'brand new cadet', Frank Loyd was surprised by the immense variety of the work that had to be done each day:

There were petty court cases, there were matters affecting the African courts, there were things connected with the prison. But there was also road-building, tree-planting, the collection of tax, the exemption of tax from some of the older people or the sick; there were things like trading licences, matters connected with hygiene and extensions of the health service which the medical officer couldn't possibly cope with himself. All this together with endless miscellaneous things connected with schools, churches, and various individual problems that people themselves would bring forward because they rightly regarded the DO as the person to whom to bring their complaints and their problems.

Among the miscellaneous tasks that Frank Loyd found himself performing within his first few months were blowing up rocks in order to build a road through a rocky escarpment, laying on emergency relief following a flood – and dealing with a plague of locusts:

Locusts are a peculiar and rather frightening phenomenon of Africa, and when one thinks of them one still hears that awful noise that they make as millions of jaws chump away at the maize or whatever they are consuming at the time. When you are driving a car through locusts it is even more terrifying because you've got the windscreen wipers on and the locusts are so thick that the wipers won't really work; the whole windscreen becomes a sort of squishy mass and you can't really see anything through it. The stories about the trains getting stopped are perfectly true. Of course, we principally had to try to cope with them in the desert where the locusts themselves bred; the trick was to try and prevent them from ever getting away from the desert and becoming the destructive hordes that they did when they went further south.

Another essential part of a District Officer's job was dealing with petitioners. For Bill Stubbs the question of 'being available and willing to lend an ear' was the most important part of his duties: 'It was a nuisance sometimes when people turned up with a long story when one had other things to do, but, although sometimes one could do nothing to help, the fact that one was there and able to listen was a comfort to the person – and taught one a great deal about the African mind and how it worked and what was going on around one.' In regions where intrigue and corruption were endemic the need to be seen to be impartial was all-important. James Robertson's first District Commissioner at Rufa'a, Sam Budget, did this by having his petitioners in all at once:

They all sat in a mass on the office floor and he'd pick them out one by one. His idea was that in this way they would see what was being done and what was being said and there would be no accusations that the DC had favoured this man or that man – and also it meant that the *murasala*, the messenger at the door, wouldn't get any perk for letting so and so in before so and so. It had its advantages in that way, but it meant a frightful clutter of people, most of them spitting on the floor and coughing.

The new District Officer soon learnt that he was never really off-duty. 'We were the most accessible administrators you can imagine,' declares

Khaki Cawnpore
Pith Helmets
    16/6, 21/-, 25/6 *26/6*
Waterproof Covers
for ditto    5/6

Khaki Wolseley
Helmets
    18/6, 21/-, 25/6 *26/6*

DOUBLE TERAI HATS
Gentlemen's, Grey or Fawn
    27/6, 42/-

Ladies' Shapes procured at
short notice    from 42/-

White Minto Helmets
    19/6, 25/-, 28/6 *21/-*

Bombay Bowlers
    17/6, 21/-

From Walters *Tropical Outfit* Catalogue, 1925. The heavy Wolseley
Helmet was for official occasions, the Bombay Bowler for more casual
wear out of uniform and the Cawnpore Pith Helmet for use in the bush
and on sporting occasions.

Charles Meek. 'We were always open at any time for even the most humble villager to come in and see us and talk to us and put his troubles before us. Not only in the office; one's home was an almost equally open forum and many a time in the evening when I had been wanting to sit down and have a quiet drink or was playing a game of bridge with friends, I was interrupted by somebody who felt he wasn't getting a square deal or somebody who had a nasty emergency on his hands – asking for help and getting it.'

Not only did the law have to be upheld, public order had also to be maintained. Two potential sources of trouble in many otherwise peaceful and law-abiding districts were disputes between villages or neighbouring clans over land and quarrels over the succession to chieftainships. In Ashanti George Sinclair observed that, 'You remained a chief only while you carried the consent of the people, otherwise they would find good cause for "de-stooling you", as it was known, and finding a successor – and of course this led to deep quarrels between those who were in favour of a chief in power and those who wanted to replace him.' Occasionally these quarrels led to serious outbreaks of violence:

I can remember in my first few months being sent out with one other administrative officer, with one tour's experience greater than mine, to quite a serious riot. Two sides of one big division in Ashanti, called Igissu, quarrelled over the de-stoolment or retention of a chief, with the queen-mother being on one side with her faction and the chief and his supporters on the other and eventually with the help of the police and very little violence we got the two sides separated. We took three lorry-loads of cudgels, cutlasses and flintlock guns from the contestants. I remember keeping the two sides apart by sitting in the middle of the village street and having our lunch of two pineapples and one pint of beer – until one side yelled some very far-reaching insults at the other side and we found that the two groups were mixed up completely and we were in the middle. It took about an hour of talking, with the use of the few police we had, to get them separated again but that 'riot' went on roughly for three days.

Sometimes the disturbance of the peace was directed against the authorities, but it was seldom of a violent nature. There was the famous story of the Lieutenant Governor of the Southern Province of Nigeria in the 1920s, who was in the secretariat offices one day when a large crowd assembled outside: 'He went out and raised his hand and silence followed and he said, "What do you want?" They said, "Please, sir, we are a riot." He said, "I'm too busy for you to riot today, you must come back tomorrow." They said, "Very well, sir," and they went away quietly. The next morning they turned up and the Lieutenant-Governor sat down in a chair in the secretariat compound surrounded by a few officials and they told him what they objected to and he spoke to them and they went away quietly.'

But very occasionally there was rioting on a far more serious scale – as occurred in 1936 in Zanzibar in a dispute over the grading of copra. William Addis was with the Sultan of Zanzibar when news of the disturbance reached him:

I was in the palace when a man came rushing up very excitedly saying in Swahili to the Sultan, 'They are killing Europeans.' So I jumped up and said to the Sultan, 'I think I'd better go and see what's happening.' I ran back out and jumped into my car, which was a Morris Minor tourer with an open top, and as I was leaving my Provincial Commissioner arrived and said, 'Will you take me down, too?' So we both went down, neither of us armed, not even a walking stick in our hands, and as we turned the corner by the Customs we saw a large crowd of Arabs with their long double-bladed swords, all shouting. I spotted the Assistant District Commissioner and the Commissioner of Police being attacked so I drove into the crowd and told these two to jump into my car. Then one of the Arabs came up to me with a long curved knife and looked as if he was going to plunge it into my heart. He stared at me and plunged it into my tyres instead; he must have recognized me, that's the only explanation I have. So I had to back out with flat tyres with all the crowd rushing after us. The Commissioner of Police was badly wounded in the head and the District Commissioner had lost all his fingers. He was a keen cricketer and he said, 'Oh, well, I'll never be able to bowl again.' In fact, he had thirty-six wounds on him and he died that night from loss of blood and shock.

Leaving his wounded passengers at the hospital, Addis collected some armed police and returned to the Customs sheds. After opening fire and dispersing the mob he found the body of another colleague, 'a very pleasant Indian police inspector, with his stomach absolutely ripped open by those horrible curved knives they had and I remember so well how I went home covered with blood – because I'd carried this man – and said to my wife, "It's all right. I'm still alive." She said, "What do you mean?" "Didn't you hear the rioting?" "No." And she was only about a mile away.'

As a symbol of government and the keeper of the King's peace, the District Officer was a natural object of respect and flattery, addressed as *bwana makuba* (great master) or *zaki* (lion), or in such terms as 'you are our father and our mother – please help me in this . . .' As well as the flattery there was the awareness that he exercised a quite remarkable degree of authority – which he took for granted: 'One assumed a superiority and capacities which make one surprised now that we didn't have a bit more humility. But it induced a sense of responsibility which tended to bring the best out of one rather than the worst.' Any feeling of superiority was also tempered by the knowledge that the effectiveness of indirect rule depended on the co-operation and consent of others – and by the realization that power itself was something of an illusion, as Patrick Mullins acknowledges:

...ne simple people in the villages looked upon you too much as a 'fixer'. 'The ...overnment is our father and mother,' they used to say, but the father and mother ...ouldn't do very much for them. And so one felt a bit of a humbug, in a way. Sometimes one had local successes and one traced a missing relative in South Africa or one found that it was possible to send medicine to a particular village for distribution by the Native Authority, tiny little local successes like this. But most of the time they were asking you to do things for them and it was terribly difficult either to say no or say yes with a conviction that you were able to do much to assist. The whole country of Nyasaland was running on a few million pounds a year. And when you got down to the district level this was split up into penny packets. If one got a hut established as a native dispensary this was quite a major success. If one got a small wooden bridge erected over a river so that the population didn't have to go around a long distance to cross that river you'd achieved a considerable success. There was also a sharp contrast between one's own living standards and those of the people you were living with and so any feelings of pride were pretty shallow and short-lived.

And yet, for all that, it was still, as Charles Meek observes:

. . . the most exciting job you could do if you liked to wield authority as many of us do – not in a bullying way, not in a rough way, but always close to the people, always week to week, day to day with pressing decisions to make, not terribly difficult decisions because I think the simpler the society the more clear-cut the decisions are, but always with the weight of responsibility on you, from , in my case, the age of twenty. It didn't matter how old you were. I suppose I gained a bit by being lucky enough to start going bald at a very early age, and that was good and helpful. But the authority was always there. It was something you couldn't divest yourself of; all the weight of so many decisions, so many worries of other people, everything from their domestic worries – stolen goats, the row with the wife – to the question of who inherited the chieftainship, sorting out the border raids between the Barabaig and the Wanyaturu, stopping the Masai lifting cattle from the Sukuma. All this was the web and woof of our daily life.

However rich the experience, there were always drawbacks, particularly for inexperienced young men on their first or second tours in the outlying bush-stations: 'The worst part of it was isolation and loneliness. It affected some people more than others. Some people used to spend their free time hunting, others reading, others painting their houses. Others occasionally, but not often, took to drink. But then if they took to drink they were obviously no good at their job – and if they took to African women that also would have an adverse effect on their position and their duty. But some people obviously had reserves and it didn't seem to affect them.' Probably the least affected of the different expatriate groups in Africa were the missionaries. Their isolation was often as severe and their tours certainly

75

lasted far longer than those of their contemporaries in other walks of life but their commitment to a cause was undoubtedly greater. 'I never really felt lonely in any circumstance,' asserts Bob MacDonald, 'it was all too exciting. After all, I was right in the midst of first-century Christianity with all the problems that faced the early Christians. The people were by no means saints but their faith was tremendous and inspiring, and one just couldn't go wrong or feel lonely or neglected in a situation like that.'

There were, of course, others besides missionaries for whom loneliness and isolation held no terrors. Bill Stubbs also found that it was impossible to be lonely, particularly 'if one had an observant eye and enjoyed what one saw. But it was a great help if one could take a dog and I have always had a dog, generally small ones. They were very good company although of course in tsetse fly country you couldn't take a dog. I also almost lost one dog which was taken by a leopard but fortunately escaped owing to a thick collar which protected its throat – although it was badly mauled.' Stuck for six months in a remote Rhodesian post, 'in complete solitude' except for his servant Willie and the local Africans, Bill Stubbs went down with his first bout of malaria:

When I was unable to shoot game because of my fever, Willie killed off the last remaining fowls and for a short time we had no meat and we had to resort, on his advice, to his lining up a line of maize, and I would shoot from my bed into the hoard of doves that came down for it and these were made into soup. Luckily for me a fellow-policeman who was on patrol in the area dropped in to see me and he had quinine and dosed me heavily with it and I was carried out from that place in a scotch-cart, which is a two-wheeled cart pulled by oxen, a journey of about a hundred and fifty miles. By the time I got to the police post I was quite fit again, but it was an unpleasant experience.

Loneliness sometimes proved to be fatal. There was the District Officer in Northern Rhodesia, remembered by Robin Short, who cut his throat 'because he couldn't stand it any longer – luckily he recovered. Then there was an earlier DC in a particularly hot and unpleasant station who shot himself – and then there was a legendary DO who had been posted many years before at one of the more remote stations of the territory by himself who had gone mad and who was still in a lunatic asylum in Cape Town. But I emphasize that these were the exceptions.' Nevertheless, Robin Short himself on his first tour in Northern Rhodesia became unaccustomed to speaking his own language – except sometimes to himself: 'I remember on my first local leave arriving at a big European store in Chingola where I wanted some chocolate very badly – but I was unaccustomed to speaking in English. There was a great pile of chocolate behind this girl at her counter, and I approached her slowly and carefully and I chose my words with care. I aid to her, "Do-you-have-any-chocolate?" and the unfortunate girl was extremely worried and said, "Oh, oh yes, yes, yes! Take as much as you like!"' Placed in a similarly isolated position up the Nile, where the steamers came only once a month, James Robertson was regularly supplied with a month's copies of *The Times* newspaper: 'I never made up my mind what was the right thing to do about this. Did I start methodically from the beginning and wade through day by day until the next lot came? I think I usually cheated and looked at the last one or two first and then waded casually through the rest.'

There was only one sure way for the first-tour man to overcome loneliness, and that was to keep busy. In time, as Nigel Cooke's first Resident in Bornu Province taught him, the newcomer developed a natural resistance: 'You are lonely for the first three months. For the second three months you don't care and for the third three months if you hear there's a European in the neighbourhood you take off in the opposite direction.' As a prediction it was not so very far removed from Nigel Cooke's own experience:

For some time within the first three months that I was in Maiduguri I was heartily wishing that I'd never come. This might have been due to my being very young, to my suffering very greatly from the assaults of the mosquitoes and from the fact that I didn't feel terribly in rapport with the other members of the station, who were all that bit older than myself. I think it was probably at Christmas 1938 that I began to feel that I liked the place. Every administrative officer in the whole province came into headquarters and every European in the station was invited to dinner by the Resident, and one did feel that one belonged to something worthwhile. That year the Alou river came down and cut off the station from the native town, creating a broad expanse of water, and I was rowing about in it in a canoe with another ADO when he said, 'You know, Africa is an old bitch; it gets you in the end.'

Two images of the District Officer in the bush. From the Walters Catalogue, 1936.

# six

# GOING TO BUSH

*Most of us had seen a film called* Sanders of the River, *based on Edgar Wallace's book, before we went out and suddenly here was this thing, it was real; one was walking behind a long line of porters and the sun got up in the morning glinting on the spears of the porters – and it was just like the films.*

From the administrator's point of view the essence of rule was that it should be based on trust. Any suggestion of ruling by force was out of the question: the means to do so were not there. In the district in Nyasaland where Noel Harvey began his service in the early 1950s there were, in addition to the District Commissioner and his two assistants, one European policeman, one African sub-inspector, two sergeants and a dozen police – and an African population of a hundred thousand. His situation was entirely typical. In the absence of military support 'what power, what influence, what effectiveness you had was entirely through trust and trust came through knowledge, because Africans will not trust somebody they don't know. So it was very important that they knew you and you knew them.'

This knowledge was acquired by touring through the district, a process that was known as a safari in East Africa, as *ulendo* in Central Africa and as 'going to bush' or 'going on trek' in West Africa. Whatever it was called, travelling about the district had a mystique about it that was to be found in every territory and 'the mystique was completely justified, because although everything might be fine around the *boma* or station, it was only by going from village to village, looking round the houses, looking at the people, talking to them, looking at their crops, taking their tax census, all the routine jobs, it was only by doing that that one could find out how they were thinking and feeling.'

Touring was always held in the highest regard by senior officers, who saw it as the most important single aspect of ordinary administration – 'returns were called for; how many days under canvas one had done in each quarter – and if one had not fulfilled a fair number there were questions asked.' This was an attitude that the younger men soon came to appreciate and to share. 'I was told by my bosses that one ought to spend half one's time at least in touring,' recalls James Robertson, 'and so I tried to do that; half the time in headquarters and half the time going round one's district.' It didn't matter so much what you did on tour, Tony Kirk-Greene was told by his District

Commissioner, so long as 'you were seen, you were accessible and – ,
remember his words – that it was a visit and not a visitation.'

There were few unmarried officers who did not find touring 'a very
satisfying thing to do'. There was indeed the 'undoubted element of escap-
ism' as well as the fact that travel and bush allowances added considerably to
one's income. But there was also a powerful sense of romance about it all –
something that immediately conveyed itself to Tony Kirk-Greene as he
began his first tour:

Stepping out at the head of my line, with one policeman in front of me and a
government messenger behind me and the Emir's representatives behind him, all in
single line with a string of carriers. Early dawn had not yet broken at half past five,
I'd had a cup of coffee and I was thinking what a good advertisement it would be for
Nescafé; twenty-six miles a day on a cup of coffee. The carriers were piping and
neither then nor now would I be ashamed of the real romance, the *Sanders of the
River* touch. And I was always conscious of this, even in later years, riding out in the
early morning with the heat of the day to come. There was something very exciting
indeed about it.

Others besides officials found opportunities and reasons for touring.
Military officers in the King's African Rifles and West Africa Frontier
Force went out on recruiting tours to the tribal areas from which they drew
their recruits, traders went from one prospective supplier or customer to
another – and, of course, the missionaries went proselytizing. But for Bob
MacDonald it was not the image of Sanders that came to mind: 'It was the
old idea of a great long line like David Livingstone's, a whole line of head
porters with boxes on their heads. The villagers in each of the villages we
passed through supplied the carriers for this and when the first lot reached
the second village they'd dump everything in the market place and go right
back without a word. We would rest a while, the chiefs would tell small boys
to go and bring us coconuts from the trees and we would drink the coconut
water and meantime there would be a great row while they would be
marshalling the new carriers to take us on.' But not all his touring was done
in this classical manner: 'I've started off in a truck with a motor-bike and a
push bike in the back, going as far as I could with the truck, leaving it and
my driver there and going on on the motor-bike with a boy following me on
the push bike. When the motor-bike was no longer possible the push bike
could still go a bit, and might get me to the side of the river where a canoe
would be ready to take me on the rest of the way. That was the kind of
progress we made on quite a number of our visits, both on church work and
on school work.'

In West Africa, where the routine of 'going to bush' was well established,
it was customary to travel from one rest-house to another, rarely camping

under canvas – except where the rest-houses, often no more than simple circular huts with thatched roofs, were found to be bat- or bug-infested. In Northern Nigeria the travelling was mostly done on horseback, as Chris Farmer describes:

What would usually happen is that one would go out on a lorry with one's servants and the Emir's representative and a government messenger to the first take-off point of your tour, and you'd stay there in the rest-house for a night or two and then on the appointed day a gang of carriers would arrive whom you would pay, probably sixpence a day, or a shilling or something of that sort. They would turn up at about five o'clock in the morning and take away everything except the camp bed you were still sleeping on. Everything had been packed by your steward the night before, so they would put it on their heads and go off to the next rest-house. At about six I would get up, get dressed in my riding breeches, mount the horse and go off with my messenger and the Emir's representative to the next port of call. My 'small boy', as we called the second steward, would then pack up the camp bed and my razor and so forth and put them on the head of the last carrier. By the time I arrived at the other end the district head or the village head would be waiting to greet one and escort one into the rest-house. Shortly after your arrival you would find, as if by magic, that breakfast had appeared and somehow hot water had been boiled so that you could get into your tin bath and have a bath. Then after breakfast you would get on with the day's work.

Further south, in true bush country, Philip Allison's work as a Forest Officer took him, sometimes for weeks or even months on end, into the heart of the dense tropical rain forests:

Wonderful country, with attractive rocky rivers running through it and from time to time rocky hills sticking up out of the forests, *insulbergs*, with rounded bare rocks sticking above the two hundred foot tops of the trees. It was a wonderful thing to climb out of the damp forests on to the top of one of these sun-warmed granite domes and look down on the tops of the trees you'd been sweating along underneath for so long. There was a different smell and the senses all seemed to open up and you'd look down on the tops of the trees and you'd see one of those big hornbills – one damn near as big as a goose – suddenly plunging up out of the tops of the trees like a diving bird, a cormorant rising from the sea, flying along and then plunging back, lost to sight under the canopy again.

Sometimes there were encounters with other creatures of the forest. Robert MacDonald remembers how he and a missionary doctor once went out 'on a glorious early morning, the sun shining behind us and the long line of carriers with their loads on their heads going through a sunken path down the hill from a village. The doctor and I were at the end of the line when a leopard sprang from one side of the sunken road right into the air and was spreadeagled across the heads of the carriers – and in the sun he looked as if he were made of gold. There was very little excitement aside from a gasp of astonishment. They never even let down a load, they just kept on going.' In some regions there were lesser creatures to be avoided, such as the tsetse fly in the bush country through which Bill Stubbs toured, whose bite could sometimes prove fatal:

There was an instruction that if you went into tsetse country you had to cover your arms and legs, otherwise you couldn't obtain compensation if you died of it, but it was impossible because I've even been bitten through the canvas of a deck-chair. What you did was to have somebody with a fly switch brushing them off you as they settled, and you hoped for the best. They don't bite you when you're exposed to the sun, but they'll go to any point of you that is shaded, just up your sleeve or up the back of your shorts or, particularly, the shaded area at the back of one's neck.

For Bill Stubbs and for many others who went on *ulendo* or safari in Central and East Africa there was the added attraction of plentiful game: 'I was keen on big game hunting although I shot mainly for the pot rather than for the actual pleasure of shooting, but of course there was always more meat than one needed for oneself and in some cases for one's carriers, too, so you gave the headman a present of meat in which a good many people shared.'

An added pleasure for those who travelled in Central Africa was the reception given to the travelling District Officer as he neared his destination: 'The first thing you'd hear was the sound of clapping – and all the maidens of the village would come out, stripped to the waist and all they had on were a tiny little G-string in front and skirt behind, and all singing in beautiful harmony.' Where the women weren't singing they would be ululating, as Robin Short found in Northern Rhodesia:

Kaunda villages were quite small so you would have, say, ten or twelve women with their children coming out to see you, clapping their hands and ululating very loudly. But in the other districts you would have possibly two hundred women, quite a crowd, and they made a very loud noise indeed, and although it was great fun, after ten or twelve villages it did begin to wear one down just a little, particularly as the weather got hotter and hotter in the middle of the day. When one actually arrived at a village one was given a chair by the headman, who squatted on the ground or knelt, and clapped the traditional greeting, followed by his people. There was nothing servile in this. They were greeting in their particular fashion as they had always done and one replied by gently patting the place over one's heart with one's hand in acknowledgement and polite words of greeting were exchanged.

An equally stirring reception faced the District Officer as he approached a Hausa village in Northern Nigeria:

It would be quite normal for the district head to come out with a posse of horsemen, ride up at a gallop to greet you, accompany you to your rest-house and then come in and sit with you and pass the time of day. You would refer to all the normal subjects like the state of the rains, or the state of the crops, or the health of the people and you would exchange such greetings in Hausa as *Sannu da ruwa*, which meant welcome with the rain. And he would probably say, *Ranka ya dade*, which means may your life be long, and he would almost certainly be in his best robes. After he had completed his formalities the district head would probably go back to the district headquarters and you would arrange to visit the courts or you might well visit the tax office.

In the Sudan officers would also be escorted in by the local sheikh and some of his followers, sometimes mounted on camels. They were always offered very sweet tea, and sometimes coffee as well. There were occasions, as James Robertson remembers, when the reception was truly biblical:

Sometimes when you came to a village the sheikh would bring out a sheep and have its throat cut in front of you. Then the drill was that you had to step over this beast as it lay on the ground, to bring luck and to show that you were happy with your reception at the village. At one place they even slaughtered camels and there were these great brutes sighing out their lives. Some of my colleagues used to eat a dish called *marara* which the sheikh would bring you when you arrived at his village. This consisted of raw liver and lights and always seemed to me a most disgusting thing. I would never eat it and when they complained about this I would say that I had a religious scruple about eating anything that was raw in the way of meat, and that seemed to go down well.

Much of the time of touring officers in the Sudan was taken up with the assessment and collection of taxes; herd tax, based on the number of animals owned by an individual, and produce tax based on the Islamic tithe system known as *ushur*. For the latter, rough assessments of the area under cultivation and the expected yield had to be made by pacing one's camel or one's horse. 'In this way one could very often make some rough estimate of the area. But the assessment of the yield was more difficult. I used to cut down a certain amount of the crop and have it beaten out and then multiply it so that you got some kind of rough estimate. I would then take the list and judge the whole of it by this one field.' The assessment of herd tax also presented considerable problems – particularly when the herds belonged to nomadic pastoralists. But where there were villages the assessment was relatively straightforward:

... because the goats and sheep and cattle and camels and so forth and donkeys all came in in the evenings and were tethered in the village at night. I used to go out at about four o'clock in the morning with half a dozen police and surround the village and as the animals came out in the morning I collected them all together and then got the list from the sheikh of the village and crossed off 'Mahommed – three goats, two donkeys' – and so forth. At the end one still had a number of unclaimed animals and then one said to the sergeant or corporal, 'Now drag these off to the market and we'll sell them' – which meant that the owners came dashing out. Then you had to decide what to do. Did you fine all these people for not listing their livestock, or did you just put them in the list? I usually just put them in the list.

One of the principal duties of touring officers in Northern Rhodesia was the collection of taxes, a task that few officers enjoyed. 'I simply hated it,' declares William Addis, 'because it meant that all the young men had to walk five or six hundred miles up to the nearest copper town to get enough money to send home for the elders to pay their tax. And I knew that anyone who went up there with the slightest sign of leprosy would be turned back and would have to walk all the way back again, so anyone who had the slightest sign of it I'd sign off the tax register and say they were exempt.' Such direct handling of local affairs was far less typical of the African colonial territories as a whole than was the more delicate work of checking, scrutinizing and, if necessary, revising the work and decisions of the local Native Authority: 'Most of the hard work was done by the Africans themselves, who had a tribal structure of government with chiefs and headmen and courts and the whole paraphernalia of government, and the major part of one's job was to see that that functioned, as far as one could, fairly, efficiently and honestly. So the major part of one's job was really supervising them in the running of the show themselves.'

In Northern Nigeria this meant being accompanied on tour by the Emir's representative, who stood at the District Officer's elbow as he talked to the local Native Authority official. If a village headman complained, for example, that he had asked for a culvert to be built over a certain stream and nothing had been done about it, joint action could be taken:

One could turn to the Emir's representative and say, 'You'll bring that one to the Emir's notice, won't you?' and he would say, 'Certainly, may your life be long.' At the same time you knew jolly well that if, at the end of one's tour one didn't also mention it to the provincial engineer and get him to give a prod to the Native Authority head of the Works Department, that culvert would never be built. So we would go through the motions of making it appear that it was the Native Authority that was getting it done. Nevertheless, something which had not been done for a long time would, with luck, actually get done.

The main bulwark of this system was the traditional African one of the local councils and the chiefs, many of whom were, according to Dick Stone, 'the salt of the earth, and marvellous administrators. Whenever we were on a tour of inspection of a chief's area we had the chief with us to hear our words of criticism or praise. Many of them were astonishingly good, with a deep knowledge of all that went on in their area, and they laid the foundations of a first class administration within the district.' Since the effectiveness of the District Officer depended very largely on his power to influence and control the native administration, a good working relationship with the chiefs was essential. In the Kasempa District, where Robin Short began his administrative career, the senior chief was 'in his quiet way' a complete autocrat:

Chief Kasempa's judicial powers of course were defined by the Government, but his unofficial powers I suspect were very much greater because his people stood in awe of him. Generally because he was paid a government subsidy he worked with the Government to develop the people as much and as well as he could, but he wasn't a stooge or a stool-pigeon or a paid government employee. He stood very much in an independent position and this was particularly apparent when there were discussions leading up to the Federation of Rhodesia, when Chief Kasempa along with the other chiefs in the territory didn't hesitate to voice the very strongest opposition to the Secretary of Native Affairs and Provisional Commissioner and anyone else who came within hearing distance.

Another important local personality with whom the District Officer did well to come to terms was the witch-doctor or medicine man – 'any administrator worth his salt knew how to work not against the witch-doctors but with them.' When Charles Meek became the District Commissioner of Mbulu he found one such witch-doctor, Nade Bea, to be

. . . a much more important chap than any of the four chiefs that we had, important though they were. If one was wanting to get some big improvement in coffee cultivation, for example, the great thing to do was to get Nade Bea on your side. He was a remarkable old man; he was very, very old by the time that I'm talking about, white-bearded and I'm not exaggerating when I say that when he was born no European had been seen in the area and he'd never seen a wheel turn – yet he lived to be a wise adviser to a whole succession of administrative officers like myself and we rewarded him with some sights which must have been pretty astounding to him, flying him by aeroplane down to Dar es Salaam, having him shown over a big ocean-going liner and so on. He was a great ally to have going for one.

Witchcraft and the 'swirling tide of superstition which infests the African mind' were factors that administrators had always to take into account in their dealings with local people. There were still many areas of African life where the 'ju-ju mentality' prevailed and governed every aspect of daily life: 'If a man drowned in a river it was said that a spirit held him under the water. If a tree fell on a man and killed him it was said that a spirit pushed

## Camp Beds and Bedding

"X" Pattern, Improved Compactum Folding Bed, Malleable Iron
Fittings, best Green Rotproof Canvas

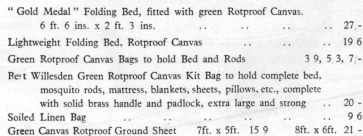

NEW HOOK JOINT

BED CLOSED

    6 ft. x 6 ins. x 2 ft. 6 ins.    ..    ..    .. 63/- 57/6

    7 ft. x 0 ins. x 3 ft. 0 ins.    ..    ..    .. 84/- 77/6

Wooden Mosquito Rods with solid brass sockets at joints for Bed 13 9

Folding Camp Bed, hinged joints, Birch frame, best Green
Rotproof Canvas.

    6 ft. 6 ins. x 2 ft. x 6 ins.    ..    ..    .. 39/-

    7 ft. 0 ins. x 3 ft. 0 ins.    ..    ..    .. 54/-

Wooden Mosquito Rods for above Beds    .. 12 9 and 14/3

"Gold Medal" Folding Bed, fitted with green Rotproof Canvas.

    6 ft. 6 ins. x 2 ft. 3 ins.    ..    ..    ..    .. 27/-

Lightweight Folding Bed, Rotproof Canvas    ..    .. 19 6

Green Rotproof Canvas Bags to hold Bed and Rods    3 9, 5 3, 7/-

Best Willesden Green Rotproof Canvas Kit Bag to hold complete bed,
    mosquito rods, mattress, blankets, sheets, pillows, etc., complete
    with solid brass handle and padlock, extra large and strong    .. 20 -

Soiled Linen Bag    ..    ..    ..    ..    ..    .. 9 6

Green Canvas Rotproof Ground Sheet    7ft. x 5ft. 15 9    8ft. x 6ft. 21 -

## Valises, Kit Bags, etc.

Wolseley Valise Regulation Pattern Brown or Green Rotproof Canvas
                        6ft. 6in. x 2ft. 6in. 51/-, 57/-, 67/6
                        7 x 3 ditto    .. 69/- and 79/6

Wolseley Valise in Waterproof Khaki Twill    ..    .. 39/6

Green Rotproof Canvas Indian Holdall    ..    .. 37/6

War Office Regulation Kit Bags,
    in Brown or Green Rotproof Canvas    ..    .. 60 -

Camping equipment for use when 'going to bush' or on safari. From
Walters *Tropical Outfits* Catalogue, 1925.

# Travelling Baths and Washstands

SHEET METAL BATH with beaded edge giving exceptional strength, fitted with lock in lid, solid leather straps, inside wicker lining.   Size 34 ins.   ..   ..   ..   .. 63/-

„ 38 ins.   ..   ..   ..   .. 72/6

Bath without beaded edge, and with outside padlock.  Size 34 ins.   ..   ..   .. 53/6

„ 38 ins.   ..   ..   .. 60/-

All our Baths have Wicker Linings, enabling contents to be lifted out without disturbance.

" X " Pattern combined bath and washstand with folding frame, Green Canvas bath and basin, complete in bag  ..   ..   ..   ..   ..   ..   ..   ..   .. 33/-

E. A. Pattern as above, but cheaper quality Canvas   ..   ..   ..   ..   .. 29/6

 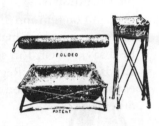

" X " Pattern Long Shape Green Canvas Folding Bath   ..   ..   ..   .. 25/9
Folding Canvas Bath only, in bag   ..   ..   ..   .. 12/- and 15/9
" X " Pattern Folding Washstand and Tray   ..   ..   ..   ..   .. 13/9
14 in. Enamel Basin and G.R.C. Cover with Strap   ..   ..   ..   ..   .. 10/-
16 in. Enamel Basin and G.R.C. Cover with Strap   ..   ..   ..   ..   .. 12/6
Green Canvas Collapsible Buckets, rope handle   ..   ..   ..   .. 2/9 and 3/9
" X " Latrine Seat, Folding   (Bag extra, 2/6)   ..   ..   ..   ..   .. 7/6

the tree. Everything was governed by these beliefs. You found it every-where. They had their *ju-jus* outside their houses, perhaps a pot on top of a hut to keep the evil spirits away. It might be a flute made from a human bone, it might be a wooden carving of a leopard, it might be the skull of an animal.' Such beliefs were understandable in earlier times, when men knew nothing. 'They only knew that when they went into the dark, dark forest they died of yellow fever and blackwater. What was it? They didn't know. It was the terror that seized them by night. It was evil spirits. Their men went out to sea, that cruel sea with those terrible waves coming in – and they were seized by the bar *ju-ju* and were drowned.' What was less appreciated was that these fears and taboos should linger on and be just as prevalent in the station and the *boma* as deep in the bush. A messenger would be unable to begin a journey after finding a broken twig lying on the path. Seeing a bicycle pump lying around, a clerk would become convinced that a spell had been put on him and disappear. 'They'd suddenly get it into their heads that there was a *ju-ju*. A man would not talk for three days and on the fourth day he'd say, "Well, I'm sorry but my *ju-ju* wouldn't let me talk."' In Martin Lindsay's Nigeria Regiment, where they were very keen on sports, it was considered to be good for morale for the two battalions to race against each other:

I remember we had a chap, a sergeant, who was leading by a hundred yards at the end of a three mile race when he suddenly stopped running and sat down. He said, 'My *ju-ju* won't let me finish.' And the Commandant said, 'We simply cannot have these *ju-jus* or else when we go to battle they'll all say "my *ju-ju* won't let me go."' So he was flogged and got twelve strokes with the *balala*, a rawhide whip.

But there were times when the official did well to acknowledge the force of local beliefs. On safari in his early days in Tanganyika, Darrell Bates was once confronted by a group of women who asked for his help:

For years there had been the custom that just before the rains they took chickens or pots of beer to a rain-maker in order to pray for rain, but people from the mission and people who'd been to schools said this was old-fashioned stuff and so this year they didn't do it and they got no rain and they were going to starve if they didn't get any rain. They went to the rain-maker but he said, 'You scorned me and I won't help you.' So they turned to me and said, 'We've come to you, will you help us?' It turned out that the rain-maker lived a longish way away, so I had to set off early in the morning and I walked nearly all day in the hills until at last in the evening I came to the place where he lived, which was a little hut on the edge of the forest. I found him there and I said I'd come to ask his help because the women of the valley had asked me to help them. At first he said, 'Why should I help them? They've rejected me.' But I said, 'Well, the children will go hungry and old people will suffer so I ask you not to help them, perhaps, but to help me.' And in the end he said, 'Well, I will pray for rain.' And I spent a whole day up there, a fascinating day talking to him. I found that like a doctor in England he had a certain amount of patter and a certain technique to impress the patients but that the elements of his craft were very simple: a basic knowledge of insects and birds and a belief in prayer. I hadn't brought anything with me when I went to see him but I noticed he was wearing a very old blanket so when I got back I sent him a new blanket, and three or four days later I was sitting in my house reading at night when I suddenly heard the rain start.

Touring officers were almost invariably well received wherever they went – even if 'it was never easy to gauge the reaction of the village African to what one was doing.' In Nyasaland Pat Mullins found the most common attitude to be one of passive acceptance:

It was a tradition of the country that they were hospitable to visitors and this went for the white *bwana* as much as it did for anyone else. Much of what the DC was always on about cannot have been particularly welcome to them, particularly the enforcement of agricultural rules or the collection of taxes, and I think behind it all most of the village Africans rather wanted to be left alone and not bothered on these subjects. But there was no active resentment; I think this was mostly town-bred. The villagers were polite and attentive and one always felt a little that they weren't too sorry when you went away again.

The usual way for the District Officer to meet the villagers was at a gathering, known in East Africa as a *baraza*, 'which took the form of a local meeting – both to explain government orders and policy and to hear complaints,' explains Dick Stone. 'So you'd have all the chiefs sitting with you at the high table, so to speak, while the people would be squatting on the ground below you – perhaps three or four hundred people and even sometimes, I remember, as many as nine hundred. And this was really the greatest entertainment to them; they loved their *baraza*. They saw the DO or DC on safari and they brought out their complaints and very frequently, because these people have a great sense of humour, they'd try to pull your leg and they'd say something outrageous and this was their fun in life. If they succeeded in making the DC turn a little pink in the face or stutter with rage then this was their day and they all roared with laughter. But of course the DC was also able to pull their legs a bit, and so we carried on these proceedings with the greatest of friendship and enjoyment.'

After the meetings and at the end of the day's work there would be 'the other half of the day's romance and pleasure', as Tony Kirk-Greene saw it:

This would come from going for a walk at between six and sunset, probably through a village and probably followed by a horde of children. You'd stop and talk to people and somebody might want to show you something; perhaps it was where there had been some guinea-fowl he'd spotted the day before, perhaps a snake that would live in a certain place, or a crocodile, or just showing you his farm. I always used to try and time my tour so that I was out the last ten days of the month, so that you got the moon rising and would be able to have your supper sitting outside, with no light on but with ample illumination from the moon.

When he toured Bill Stubbs often used to take a tribal story-teller along with him: 'In the evenings after all the work was done he would entertain the carriers, and usually the hero of the stories was *Wa Kalulu*, Mr Hare, very amusing but generally pretty ribald variations on the Brer Rabbit theme. Chandler Harris, of course, got all that stuff from Africa.' Sometimes the days would end more dramatically: 'Quite often in the evening of the second day the local people would put on a dance in one's honour, attended by several hundred young men and girls dancing away to their drums. And they often asked us to come in and join them, which we did – somewhat inexpertly but very much to their amusement.'

This was an experience shared by many officers on tour. George Sinclair recalls how:

When the drummers were inspired the call of their rhythm was irresistible and the whole village – men, women and children – were drawn into a swirling mass of dancers. We used also to listen through many nights to the Ashanti folk-stories, called *ananse* or 'spider' stories, interspersed with songs which often took the form of lampoons of some government measure or of a government servant. Occasionally, before one knew much of the language, one would find everyone roaring with laughter and then suddenly one realized it was a representation of one's own arrival in the village a day or two before.

Music and song, in one form or another, accompanied the touring officer through much of his travels. If he was touring on foot there would be songs and choruses passing up and down the line of carriers, and if he went by canoe there would be the work songs of the boatmen. Philip Allison recalls particularly 'a canoe song that a gang of canoe men used to sing taking us across the river from the forestry station to the station of the timber men. The leader sang, "You tiger, you!" and then the pullers all joined in, "You tiger, you!" – tiger was pidgin English for a leopard. Then there was another song where the chorus went, "Elder Dempster! Elder Dempster!"'

As the District Officer gained in knowledge and experience, moving from one district to another or even from one province to another, so he came to make comparisons: 'Every District Officer had his favourite tribe, that was natural. Different people got on with different tribes.' Fortunately, such tribal favouritism tended to keep pace with transfers, so that most District Officers professed to find the tribe with whom they were most closely associated to be the one whose virtues exceeded all others. For Robin Short it was the Lunda from Northern Rhodesia's extreme north-west corner who were the 'outstanding' tribe: 'They were intensely superstitious, intensely conservative, intensely secretive and spirit-ridden, but at the same time they had many attractive qualities and they produced men who by a combination of brains and character surprised one when one was in Africa at that particular time. They were courteous, well mannered, very ceremonious to their chiefs, polite and pleasant people – and they were willing to learn and willing to listen.'

For some it was the martial qualities of the tribe that were particularly attractive. This was a characteristic of the Nandis of which Dick Symes-Thompson was acutely aware:

They were a very fine warrior people who had fought successfully against the British when we first came to Kenya, and they had dominated the surrounding tribes with their force of arms. Although they were a law-abiding people – many of them had joined the police and the army – towards the end they began to get a bit disturbed and worried about the changes that were coming and I had one rather serious piece of trouble because they sounded their war horns, which meant that every Nandi of fighting age had to drop whatever he was doing and seize his spear and his weapons and rally to the horn. On this occasion the war horn sounded and ten thousand or more fighting men marched into the neighbouring district sounding their horns and shouting and causing a good deal of terror and alarm and it was my job to try and stop them and bring them back.

In West Africa the very much larger tribal association of the Ashantis had a similarly warlike reputation. For David Allen they also had 'special qualities that set them apart. They had certainly proved themselves in wartime as being the bravest and the toughest people whom we had to deal with in coming to the Gold Coast. I'm inclined to think too that they were in some ways the nicest people in the Gold Coast, a very friendly lot indeed and very easy to get on with, and although they were volatile and could change fairly quickly they always quickly came back again to this wonderful, easy, friendly, happy people.'

Sometimes it was a certain fellow-feeling that drew the District Commissioner towards a certain tribe, as Dick Stone explains: 'Over the years the British and the Acholi got on extraordinarily well together. I think they had rather the same sense of fun, the same sense of humour; they were fond of games, fond of hunting, and we seemed to see eye to eye very well indeed. Life was rewarding with them and most of us British expatriate officers felt that we had some sort of vocation for working with these people.'

In some instances it was the very intractability of the people that provided the satisfaction. Few tribes were more difficult by reputation than the

Kikuyu – with whom Frank Loyd worked for many years: 'Although as people they weren't so attractive or so easy-going and easy to get on with, nevertheless, in a different way it was much more rewarding to work with them because you did sometimes achieve results. It was much more wearing, much more difficult to do, took an immense amount of time and a great deal of patience. They were totally different in every respect to their pleasanter, quieter, more happy-go-lucky brothers in other parts of the country, but they did achieve many more results and the proof is that they are now running the country.'

Just about midway, geographically speaking, between the Acholi and the Kikuyu were the Kipsigis, who spoke what Richard Turnbull considered to be 'the most melodious, mellifluous language' he'd ever heard in Africa. 'They are a stock people – brilliant herders of cattle and devoted to them – and, of course, stock-thieving was their métier. It was their way of improving their herds and passing the time.' This stock-thieving reached such enormous proportions in the 1930s that on one occasion the Acting Governor of Kenya came up to hold a special *baraza*, where he told them that they were ruining the economy of the country and disgracing their names: 'The leader of the Kipsigis listened to what he said very carefully and then came forward and said they recognized the error of their ways; that owing to what he'd said this blinding light had flashed upon them and from that day forward they would steal no stock and become model citizens. The Governor was really extremely pleased. He said nothing but you could see him smiling to himself and reflecting upon what a word or two from the great would do. That night the Kipsigis came into the station and stole the entire government herd.'

This close identification with a particular people and a particular area only reached its peak after several tours as an Assistant District Commissioner, when the District Officer was finally given his own district. The officer who trekked extensively got to know his district and its inhabitants so intimately that he inevitably came to identify himself with it, until 'he regarded himself as a native of the district and would stand up for his district against anybody – including the governor.' A remarkable insight into the rapport that could exist between tribesmen and their local District Officer was once afforded to Violet Bourdillon when she and her husband were touring Uganda in the early 1930s. With the District Commissioner they visited a remote district headquarters where there was only one District Officer and no other Europeans:

In the evening they were going to do us a dance called the rag dance but they'd all got so frightfully drunk – celebrating our coming up there – that they couldn't do it. I remember the little DO, he was a wonderful man called Preston, who said, 'I'll go and get my men from jail.' So he trotted off and came back with all these jail-birds who solemnly divested themselves of every stitch of clothing in the moonlight – I can see them now – and started to dance. And he danced with them in the middle; I could see his little bald head bobbing up and down. I'd never seen a sight like it, never! And when it was over I said to the DC, 'That was a wonderful show.' And he said, 'Yes, they absolutely adore him. They call him "Our little one" and the only punishment in the jail is that they are not allowed to dance with him on Saturday nights.'

Even though such terms as 'my people' and 'my district' were officially frowned upon, they were an honest indication of how many District Officers and Commissioners felt – especially in the inter-war years when the burden of government lay more heavily on one man's shoulders. Bill Stubbs's first district was one of the more remote districts of Northern Rhodesia, and it was not well provided with supporting services:

It was about six thousand square miles in area and there was no police, no postmaster, no veterinary service, agriculture, education or anything. You were a one-man band and it was a great life. Although the responsibilities were heavy, the pleasure one got out of it was intense; having power – in the best sense – to see that one's people lived as reasonable a life as one could get for them. It was the feeling more or less of ownership that gave one pleasure, like inheriting a large country estate, but there was more than that; one worried about one's people and one would defend them, although it was a constant battle with the Treasury to get enough money and we had desperately short supplies for improvements, development and things like that. But the loyalty of the DC to his people was something which I don't really think one can describe. You felt almost fatherly towards them and you got a lasting affection for a particular district even though that district might not have been regarded as a particularly pleasant one. I was lucky in that I had three full years at my favourite station, but it was a matter of bitter regret to me that I wasn't allowed to go back for a further three years and see schemes that I had started grow into fruition. I had many senior jobs after that but nothing could compare with the life of a DC on an out-station and the rapport that one had with the people from that district. I used to dream in the local native language, in fact I occasionally do today – and the whole life was something I can't imagine being equalled or certainly not excelled in any other walk of life. It was something really unique.

ouring or 'going to bush' in West Africa; the Resident (Nigel Cooke) visits a remote corner
Adamawa Province, Nigeria 1959.

On safari in classical style; prospector on *ulendo* with head-porters fording the Kabompa river near the Congo border, N. Rhodesia 1935.

Touring by car, a modern convenience much frowned upon by old-fashioned Provincial Commissioners; the District Officer setting out on safari, Uganda 1925.

amping in the bush, N. Rhodesia 1935; officials usually slept under canvas in areas where st-houses or bush-huts were not provided.

Ablutions on safari; District Officer and collapsible wash-stand, Mbulu District, N. Tanganyika c. 1955.

The local Emir or district head meets the touring Resident (Nigel Cooke) on the outskirts of his district, N. Nigeria 1959. The open country and the absence of tsetse fly made it possible for officials in N. Nigeria to tour on horseback.

Confrontation on the Northern Frontier District; the 'Officer-in-Charge' (Gerald Reece) with two of his two District Officers meet a deputation of Turkana at Lodwar, near the shores of Lake Rudolf, 1947.

# seven

# MEN WITH SAND IN
# THEIR HAIR

*The frontier had its own mystique and officers who served there were tremendously attached to it. There were huge distances, camels, nomadic peoples, great heat and a feeling of spaciousness which was absent from the rather more crowded and populous districts in the rest of the country, and it did seem to draw out the character of the people who served there.*

While every district and every African province had its own remarkable qualities there was one particular group of territories that exercised a stronger hold over the British officers who served there than any other. Just as, in the days of the Raj, India's North-West Frontier maintained a strong hold over the lives and imaginations of its British frontiersmen, so the desert frontier regions of British Colonial Africa had their own unique and powerful character, drawing towards them a rather special kind of administrative and military officer. These desert lands were to be found on the fringes of Northern Nigeria and Northern Uganda, in British Somaliland and the Sudan, and along a wide belt of scrubland running across Northern Kenya.

It was this last area, Kenya's Northern Frontier District or the NFD, that had perhaps the fiercest reputation, although the term District was really rather a misnomer:

Kĕnya, as we used to call it – it's now called Kěnya – is divided roughly into two halves, the southern half of which consists of what we call the settled area where the white people had their farms and the agricultural natives had plantations, and the northern area which extends from Lake Rudolf to the Somali border and consists of about a hundred thousand square miles of acacia scrub, laval desert and patches of sand desert, roughly twice the size of England. The administrators in the southern half of Kenya thought we were mad to live there at all, but our work was entirely different from theirs and it called for certain qualities that produced what we thought was a fine type of young officer.

Another desert territory that also had more than a touch of glamour about it was the Sudan, with its vast scrub and dunelands and its provinces each the size of France. Life here and on the NFD was always tough and uncompromising – 'there was no softness about its nature' – and it developed these same qualities in the people who lived there and the men who went there.

95

For Gerald Reece, who first came to the NFD in 1925 and rose to become one of its almost legendary 'Officers-in-Charge', it was where 'real life' was to be found: 'Things were vivid and the people lived precarious lives and things seemed to mean much more than they do when one lives in a place which we regard as civilized. There was something genuine and real about it all, something clean and refreshing about the atmosphere, and those of us who'd had hard lives in the war found a certain peace in the solitude of the desert, where one is much closer to nature, getting away from modern civilization and all the pettiness of modern society.'

'Uncle' Reece's successor as Officer-in-Charge of the NFD was another outstanding frontiersman, Richard Turnbull, for whom the greatest attraction of working in these 'rugged and desolate surroundings' was that 'one was dealing with not only picked men in the service but with Africans who were enormously handsome and brave and alert and quite different from the likeable but not outstanding people further south.' This attitude was shared by many in the Sudan Political Service in the lands to the north and in particular by Hugh Boustead, one of the last of a distinguished line of Englishmen drawn to the great deserts of Africa and Arabia. For him the desert country was a place that 'got a great hold on you. Always there was a feeling that you were free, untramelled. You could go anywhere, there was nothing to stop you, and at the same time you were part of a moving family, to to speak, with the chaps who were with you.' For Hugh Boustead his 'moving family' was the Sudan Camel Corps, which he joined in 1924 – after adventurous careers in both the navy and the army – and which he eventually came to command.

Many of his early years with the Camel Corps were spent in remote corners of Kordofan Province, exercising a unique command:

The men were enlisted by the company commander, they were trained by him and they were discharged by him. You had probably 180 men and 230 animals to look after, and you had chaps who were ready to go anywhere within four hours notice. The camels would be carrying both grain for eight days and water for four days for the man on them, so that you could go off into the blue regardless of wells. And it gave you a freedom of the uplands of the deserts which was tremendous. When you left, all the good ladies of the company would come and sort of wail – ululate – to their men, and you'd go off on marches of approximately six hundred to a thousand miles. And the chaps got thoroughly interested, they didn't worry because they had their lunch late or they hadn't had their breakfast. It wasn't a case of where's my effing breakfast? They were most pleasant chaps to command because they were always so ready for anything. They moved like trains on foot; they were very fit, tough lads and immensely cheerful, always ready for a laugh and there was damned little vice with them. But we had to be very strict with them. If a chap going to sleep or through carelessness sat on the side of his saddle he'd give his camel a sore back and then he was not allowed to get on that camel again until it was healed. And he might have to run six hundred miles with the company. But there wasn't a court martial in the ten years I was there. It was unheard of. The worst thing you could do to a chap was discharge him — because it was just like a family.

Badges of the eight provinces of the Anglo-Egyptian Condominium of the Sudan. From the album of Sir Angus Gillan.

Sometimes these camel treks were made at night 'under a tremendous forest of stars. Then you'd come in the early morning and you'd go down to a well-field to water the camels and there you'd find lines and lines of camels all waiting under the palm trees with the herdsmen all round them there and you'd have to wait your turn. Then the chaps would go down to the well and start pulling up the water with all the accompanying noises of the camels gurgling and complaining.' It was very much 'a man's life' and not one suited to marriage: 'You got swept away while you were home, then when you came back you'd say, "Christ almighty, I must be mad! What's a girl going to do out here? She won't be able to enjoy this; she'd get damned bored and tired. Am I going to chuck this and go and live in some suburb at home or in some stuffy room in a barracks, with a very limited urban sort of life around you?" I couldn't have stuck it.'

The same dedication and camaraderie was to be found in the NFD, where there was 'a tremendous *esprit de corps*. We used to have silver cufflinks made from Ethiopian coins rather like threepenny bits with Menelik II on one side, and when a person really stayed a reasonable time in the NFD as a District Commissioner and had done well we gave him these cufflinks, which was rather like getting his colours.' Part of this *esprit* expressed itself in a feeling that the NFD was quite separate from the rest of Kenya. Its officers talked of 'going down to Kenya', and 'we would always say in extenuation if a man made a complete nonsense of something, "Of course, he's a Kenya man" – we didn't regard ourselves as part of Kenya.' The attitude in the South was rather different:

The North had a bad name in a certain sense; it was regarded by some people like joining the foreign legion and most officers couldn't or didn't want to stand more than eighteen months of it, after that they either got bored or their health gave way because of the heat, or they became nervous, so that was the average period during which an officer stayed in that territory. The result of course was that the Government in Nairobi used to have to send new officers fairly frequently, and very often there were not enough volunteers and so people used to be posted there and it was referred to sometimes as a sort of punishment station where you did your eighteen months and having got that over your name was erased from the list. Yes, we felt that in Nairobi they didn't understand.

The NFD's reputation as a punishment station was not entirely without foundation, particularly in the days of the one-man stations. It was to just such a station, just south of Lake Rudolf at Kolosia, that Gerald Reece was posted in 1927:

I took over from a man who was sleeping half in and half out of the door of his house. The houses in these places were just made of mud – you made them yourself out of local trees and an earth roof because there was no grass with which to thatch them – and this poor chap had a complete nervous breakdown and he found especially when it rained, which it very seldom did, but during the rainy season when the earth on the roof became heavier and the timber started to creak he was afraid of the house falling on him. On the other hand, he was afraid that if he slept outside – as a great many people did in Africa – his face would be eaten by hyenas. So he decided to put his bed half in and half out so that he could jump either way in an emergency. The man before him had died of blackwater fever and the man before him had similarly had a nervous breakdown and had had to be brought south by an Indian sub-assistant surgeon. The District Commissioner before him had committed suicide, so it was a gloomy place to live in, and of course in those one-man stations there was not a European within a three-day march and no motor transport or wireless or anything like that.

98

It was not an area to which wives were made officially welcome, although married quarters were eventually provided in two or three of the more accessible stations. Even after the Second World War conditions remained spartan in the extreme. In 1946 when Dick Symes-Thompson was first posted to Isiolo – the 'gateway' to the NFD and its Provincial Headquarters – he was given a house about half a mile out in the bush:

This was a thatched *banda*-type house with white ants that had affected the roof and when one ate one's meals the earth tended to drop down from the ceiling into one's soup, so it was rather uncomfortable. The bath was made of cement which somebody had fashioned with his hands to make a sort of bath and the lavatory outside was a pit, a long drop with a thatched roof over it, and I was rather frightened of this because a previous occupant had told me that I had to be careful going out there because he had gone in once and found a spitting cobra sitting on the seat which had then spat at him, so when I arrived I was actually very careful.

Standing in for Gerald Reece as Officer-in-Charge at that time was another great and eccentric frontier character, Hugh Grant, 'a great bayonet fighter and trick pistol shot and a splendid figure', who was to die later when a Masai warrior threw a spear at him – 'he threw his spear right through him and ran round and picked it up and ran away, leaving Hugh Grant dead on the ground.' Invited to Hugh Grant's house for supper on his first evening at Isiolo, Dick Symes-Thompson was advised to think of the two great rival groups on that part of the frontier – the Somalis and the Boran – as highlanders: 'He said that they were very similar; they had these clannish attitudes and clan frictions but when the common enemy arose they clung together. If I realized they were highlanders I wouldn't go far wrong.' When the time came for Dick Symes-Thompson to return to his house that night he was handed a 'very obscure' Diets lamp and warned to beware of the snakes on the path: 'It took me a very long time to get back to the house. Later on I would have strolled down without a light with no worry at all because I realized the dangers were more imaginary than real – although lions did often kill between my house and the rest of the *boma*.'

When Richard Turnbull first came to the frontier in 1936 his chief mentor was Vincent Glenday, a 'most wonderful fellow' who 'didn't allow you to get above yourself. He would constantly say to us, "Look here, my friend" – when he said "my friend" you knew he wasn't very pleased with you – "Look here my friend, in this place I want public servants not public dictators." He wouldn't allow you to say "my district" or "my people". You could say "the district" or "the people I administer" but you had to be very careful in your choice of words. All the same he took enormous pleasure in being the master.' This was particularly sound advice in view of the strongly independent-minded nature of the local inhabitants, who regarded themselves as 'not exactly independent – but they just know they are better than you are.' This became immediately apparent to Richard Turnbull when he held his first *baraza*: 'There were only ten people present instead of the hundred one would have down-country and after I'd spoken a charming old man got up and said, "Oh Turnbull" – none of this *"bwana"* nonsense – "you have made four points, I will deal with them in reverse order." And he answered me in the most polished debating manner I'd ever heard.'

The two principal tribal groups on the NFD were the Somalis in the east and the Galla to the west, neither of whom were the truly indigenous folk of the area:

The Somalis were the head of a great migration which had started in the fifteenth century from right up in the Horn of Africa, and had reached Kenya or the country which later became Kenya about 1900, and the Galla had been the previous masters of the area and had been forced to the west by the Somalis and were now rather pathetically huddled in a corner of their former kingdom. The Somalis were devout and very bigoted Moslems, and the Galla a most interesting people, pagans with a priest-king of the sort that one read of in *The Golden Bough*. The Somali was the better fighter and the dominant character in the area, but the Galla, having access to horses, could give a pretty good account of themselves. They also had a most revolting habit of castrating their enemies and handing the relics to their girl-friends, who would proudly wear them round their necks.

As elsewhere in Africa, different District Officers tended to like one tribe more than another – and usually the Somali came low on the list of preferences: 'He's accused of being treacherous, avaricious, unreliable and untruthful – a generally cruel and unpleasant person.' But this was not how either Gerald Reece or Richard Turnbull saw the Somalis. The latter considered them to be 'an extraordinarily attractive people':

They are always spoken of as being highly strung, and indeed they are, and they are spoken of as being unreliable and so they are, and they are spoken of as being constant in only one thing – their inconstancy. And all this is true. But of course they are loyal to themselves. The Somali knows what he wants and he's determined to get it and in the end he will get it. He will deploy any number of weapons and the biggest gun he has in his own armoury is that of flattery. He will come to you and say, 'I want my son to sit outside your office.' And you will say, 'Oh, why?' He will say, 'Because my son is going to learn to ride a horse and we know that you are a great horseman and if only your shadow will fall across our son twice a day we know he will learn something.' Now I'm not a horseman, in fact I once disgraced myself by falling off a mule on the Moyale Parade Ground. So why should the Somali say this to me? Well, he has a reason. The son will sit there for a month and in the end you'll find he's got a proscriptive right to the spot – and after six months he will produce a lease signed by Queen Victoria saying the place where he is sitting is Somali property.

The Somalis were also capable of employing more direct means to get their way: 'I got to know the more sophisticated Somalis on the frontier – that is to say the Ishaak – in an extraordinary way. They had an agitation of some sort which I was compelled to oppose and they collected a considerable sum of money and gave it to a chap to shoot me. He didn't do it – he went off to Aden with the money – but it set up rather a bond between us, and years later I would discuss this ridiculous episode with those who'd contributed and we would laugh heartily about it – and have a good gossip.' Naturally, it was the Somalis on whom the attentions of the administration were most directly focused:

Our main preoccupations in the NFD were to halt the great Somali drive to the south, then to prevent fighting between the Galla to the west and the encroaching Somalis to the east, for if a fracas started at one end of the line it would run like a powder trail to the other and the casualties could be serious. These conflicts could happen very easily and from the most trivial causes. A herd-boy might be insulted by another herd-boy. The herd-boy would send for his father, his father would send for his friends, and before long you might have a confrontation of half a dozen spearmen ready to fight for their particular prestige – and once the row had started it was difficult to stop it. An inter-tribal fracas amongst Somalis was fairly easily solved by calling a reconciliation ceremony where the injury suffered by either side was set off and the balance was paid in stock, either in camels or in sheep and goats or in cattle. But where you had the Galla and the Somalis each with a different tribal system and each with a different rota of penalties for everything from injured honour to the death of a man, it became much more difficult. But unless a proper peace meeting could be arranged and enforced there was a constant danger of the conflict spreading.

Maintaining law and order under these conditions was never easy. Nor did the specially adapted Indian Frontier Crimes Act always suit local conditions and local mores. Many officers felt, like Dick Symes-Thompson, that there was 'some conflict between the letter of the law and what one felt was justice – usually because the local custom of the tribe concerned regarded murder, perhaps, as something to be dealt with by means of compensation and the British law which insisted on bringing the offender to justice and hanging him seemed foreign to them. Nevertheless, it was very much part of our job to train people that the British law was a new law in the area which had to be obeyed and killing was wrong, and on the whole justice was done.'

Local attitudes towards British court proceedings were equally difficult to reconcile: 'The Somalis were expert at making you lose your temper. They had the most wonderful methods and unless you were very careful before long you were hopping up and down with rage. They would make you lose your temper by leaning back and laughing at you when you were speaking, meaning that what you were saying was so ridiculous, so beyond the credence of a reasonable man, that it was meant to be a joke. And if you could possibly never get cross you'd won an enormous victory.'

Hugh Boustead was faced with very similar problems when after ten years with the Camel Corps he transferred to become District Commissioner of the Western District of Darfur, almost at the very heart of the African Sahara: 'I introduced the talking stone, which was a stone that was kept in the court and the rule was that anybody who talked without that stone in his hand had to pay a five *piastre* fine. And that effectively stopped people because although they treated it as a great joke at first, when they found the five *piastres* were disappearing they treated it pretty seriously, and you stopped this great chatter going on which made the trying of cases almost impossible.' There was also the problem of getting hold of witnesses, which was solved by producing numbered metal tags: 'Anybody who received a bit of metal knew it was a sign that he was wanted in the court and if he didn't come in a few big court messengers would go out and bring him in and probably give him a couple on the bottom as they brought him in. So that was pretty effective.'

There was a strong feeling that imprisonment was not an appropriate form of punishment for a predominantly pastoral people. To Richard Turnbull 'there was something particularly horrible about locking a man up – and when you are dealing with people like the Boran and the Somalis who scarcely have been in a building all their lives, it's a terrible punishment to lock them up. I can remember old men coming into my office and sitting there sweating with fear in case the roof fell in upon them, because they'd never been in a building before.' It was an environment in which summary justice, in certain remote areas, made a great deal of sense – 'it wasn't a question of power. It wasn't a question of being a magistrate or anything else – you dealt with things on a human basis and you did what you thought was right. You couldn't consult anybody – they were too far off.' This applied particularly in the military detachments of the King's African Rifles that were stationed in the remote frontier outposts of the NFD, as Brian Montgomery explains:

Justice was rough – particularly in the context of military discipline. The KAR *askari* were perfectly disciplined but the military law to which they were subject was not the Army Act of the British Army but the colonial forces version of it. Very seldom was there any recourse to a court martial for a serious offence because it was so difficult to create one in the sparse garrisons that were so prevalent. The necessary machinery for reference to a higher court was simply not there and the accused might have to relax in jail for two months or more before anything would happen.

Therefore very severe powers were given to COs of detachments – but only for use in very exceptional cases. When a very serious case occurred, such as striking an NCO or rape, the CO would have to sentence the accused to summary physical punishment and he might award a sentence of, say, six lashes, in which case the accused would be paraded in front of the whole detachment, he would be stripped and laid down on the ground, where the sergeant would administer six lashes.

For these floggings a *kiboko* or rhinoceros-hide thong was used, with the detachment formed up on three sides of a square. But the occasion did not always go according to plan, as Anthony Lytton once witnessed on the frontier:

This particular malefactor was awarded twenty strokes with the *kiboko*. His trousers were taken down and the Sergeant-Major got ready to apply the blows – and the blows are always, by tradition, counted in Arabic. '*Wahid*' – down came the first blow. '*Thaneen*' down came the second. '*Thelata*' – as the third was coming down he picked up his bags and ran and the entire battalion broke ranks, yelling '*Kamáta, Kamáta* – Catch him, catch him.' The fellow outstripped the entire battalion but was collared round the legs by a corporal from the ration store who was a rugby footballer and caught him just as he was leaving the camp. And he was brought back and held down and the remaining eighteen were duly administered.

If justice was a little rough at times, so, too, was medical treatment if there was no trained medical practitioner on the spot. 'The first man I injected was rather sleepy with malaria,' recalls Anthony Lytton:

He was a Turkana. The dresser exposed his behind and prepared the spot with methylated spirits and so forth and gave me the syringe. After a great deal of palaver and preparation I plunged the needle into the hip of this victim, who at that moment instantly rose from the couch with the needle and syringe sticking out of his behind and hopped round the surgery until the needle fell out. He was pacified by the dresser and brought back and things were explained to him and he said to me that he had had a dream that he was being speared by his enemy. Another time, hearing of my exploits of sewing people up, a chief brought in his wife with her lips hanging in ribbons. 'How did that happen?' I asked. 'Oh, well,' she said, 'I had a fight with another lady. She bit me.' So I sewed her up and I think I only used one enormous stitch to pull the two bits of lip together and trimmed it up. I heard from the chief afterwards that he was very pleased with her appearance after my cosmetic surgery.

To assist him in the maintenance of law and order the frontier administrator had at his disposal a body of tribal police known as *dubas*:

Uncle Reece's policy was that the *dubas* should be selected from the most wealthy and distinguished families among the Somalis and the Boran so that we got the best young men in the country and they were proud and cheerful and very valuable allies if anything went wrong and in the frontier things *could* go wrong. They were very colourfully dressed in white *shukas* – which is a great white sheet – and a scarlet turban and they were really magnificent people. Their great strength was their local knowledge. When one went out on safari they were the ones who put up the tent, they were the ones who acted as interpreters, acted as messengers, acted as police, they protected the District Officer and they would be sent on various errands. For example, if there were an inter-tribal battle threatened among grazing tribes squabbling over a water-hole or over a bit of lush grazing, the *dubas* would be sent out to keep the peace.

In addition to the *dubas* there were also the *askari kanga*, government messengers who could on occasion show quite extraordinary courage and devotion to duty. While on service as a military administrator in the country south of Lake Rudolf, Anthony Lytton employed a Turkana messenger whose principal duty was to deliver the mail, including the weekly edition of *The Times* – through country which was infested with 'over-familiar' lions:

He travelled by night because he could travel more easily in bare feet and more swiftly, and he slept, lying up somewhere, during the day. He carried his two spears, as all Turkana do, and considered himself capable of dealing with any lion at any time, night or day, provided he had his spears. On one occasion he was late and explained that he had spent the night in a tree. He said, 'I don't get in a tree for a lion if I have my spears, but your newspapers are so heavy that I couldn't carry my spears and the bag, so I left my spears behind.' On a second occasion he arrived, as it were, too soon. He had travelled two nights and slept one day and he had done 124 miles. In this case he had driven a lion off its kill, put a haunch from the kill over his shoulder and left practically nothing for the lion. He was then followed during the night by the lion and arrived at breakneck speed with a damaged ankle.

Ultimately, the effectiveness of the administrator or the officer on attachment depended on his own skills and knowledge rather than on other people's. It took time to acquire such knowledge and, as always, the best way to gain it was through travelling on safari: 'The important thing was to go about simply, with animals and on foot so that you could see more of the people and talk to them and get to know them, not sticking to the roads but going to villages, however far away they were, and sitting down and talking to people. One used also to stop one's caravan whenever you met anybody, which of course is the way people in deserts do find out what's going on. It's not considered to be bad manners to stop a person and ask all about his business, it's the custom.'

Gerald Reece considered it part of his job to know everything that was going on in his district – and much of his information he gained from conversing with local people:

For example, one day I was going along with my camel caravan and I saw a small boy herding goats and I stopped and asked him where his father was. And he said that his father had gone to the station with two cattle that he was going to sell, and so I said, 'Well, you and your father must be getting very rich because the prices now on cattle are high.' And the boy said, 'No they are not, we only get 20s. when we sell an ox.' Well now that enabled me to find out that the headman to whom the Government had entrusted the buying of these cattle was cheating, because the Government was paying 60s. for each ox. In that way – without intruding on the privacy of people or spying in a way which makes them mistrust you – you got to find out a great deal about what was going on in their lives.

It was equally important to know about the land, and about water because, as Richard Turnbull explains:

We only had one running river in the whole hundred thousand square miles and two or possibly three seasonal rivers, which ran in the rains and in which you would find water by digging in the dry weather. In addition there were half a dozen well systems. Then there were possibly a hundred or more seasonal waters, pools which were there by nature, or pools which had been made merely by animals rolling. Even the giraffe rolling in the sand will make a depression which, when rain falls, will take water and will feed a village's sheep and goats possibly for two or three days, which is of great importance when you are moving stock and you want a staging point. We had to know where all these waters were and we had to know, of course, which of them had filled up in the rains, because the people would all be on the permanent waters during the very dry weather, with their homestead stock, but when the rain fell there'd be a general dispersal to the small pools and we had to make certain that this dispersal did, in fact, take place. As the season advanced, so the small waters would all dry up and the people would move back on to the larger pans. Ultimately, as the dry weather became more intense the homestead stock would move off back to the permanent waters, there – if our policy and their practice had been properly followed – to find the grazing dry but still existent.

Just as important as water was vegetation, which became Richard Turnbull's special interest to the point where 'I became a fearful bore to all my young men' and eventually had a species of acacia bush named after him – 'a very squalid little shrub which grows in a howling desert'. This specialized knowledge had enormous practical advantages, because it enabled him to follow the movements of the herdsmen:

For instance, the in-calf camels would have to get salt browse immediately after the rains in order to ensure that their lactation took place properly. And as one knew the salt browse areas one knew where they were likely to be. I'm proud to say that after four or five years working on it, I got to the stage where stock-owners found it very hard to diddle me over it. They would say to me, 'We must go to such and such a place and have grazing rights there,' and I would ask them why, and they would say

'Because the *bleforis fruticosa* is found there' – and I would know jolly well that it wasn't!

It was mastery of such intimate details that made life on the frontier such an 'extraordinarily rewarding job'. But at the same time it was a 'damned hard, lonely life and we did have difficulty in getting men to come back to it.' This was not surprising when one considered the position of an officer in such a place as Mandera, in the extreme north-east corner of the territory. This was where Brian Mongomery spent the most isolated six months of his life, speaking no other language but Ki-Swahili:

Towards the end of my six months I can see that I was over-conscious of small events which assumed too great a proportion in my daily thinking. For instance, we had to be very careful over the accounting and although I had an African clerk it was necessary to check very carefully that the amount of sugar or flour consumed by the platoon detachment in one week was not greater than the authorized ration. And if I found that my computation of the amount varied from that of the clerk by one ounce say, it tended to worry me greatly. And more so when the camel mail arrived with a note from the company detachment 250 miles away to say that there was a quarter-ounce discrepancy in my accounting for sugar. This seemed to matter a lot – which, of course, it didn't really – but I'm sure it was caused by isolation. Curiously, however, on safari that sense of isolation vanished and you couldn't have been happier, even by yourself.

As in the Sudan, these long safaris were made with camels – but baggage camels rather than riding camels – and they were 'always a delight' for officers on the frontier:

Starting off at four in the morning you went ahead of your safari, several miles ahead of the sixty-five camels, and you were alone with your orderly, who carried your rifle, and you had probably a native tracker who knew the desert. You carried your own sporting rifle – I had a .375 Manlicher – and of course you were out for the game shooting. You went ahead and then when it got to about eight o'clock or so it was time to go back and the tracker for some extraordinary reason was always able to find his way back to the camp, where you found the safari. We made camp, the camels were hobbled and turned into the bush to graze. It became very hot indeed about midday, nevertheless the cook produced a three-course lunch always which one was supposed to eat. I spent my time, because I was then a very zealous soldier, reading books for the Staff College examination. But I recall that very frequently I was asleep by the time lunch arrived. Then when the evening march was resumed at about four o'clock – and the sun always set at six o'clock in those latitudes – you went ahead again. But it was always absolute habit that when you came back to safari the *bwana*'s tent must be erected and his table and his bottle of whisky and his camp chair ready for him. Your bearer had your evening sundowner ready and you changed out of your bush shirt, put on clean clothes and relaxed in your chair with your evening drink until dinner was served by your bearer. The African cooks were extremely good; they had the facility of making virtually a whole meal out of one of those vultureen guinea-fowl which were so very good eating; they would make a soup out of it, followed by the most excellent cutlets and give you a savoury out of its liver, and they also were able to carve a complete bird in slices and put them together again so that you could take your slice without carving yourself. There was always a three-course meal and you then had your pipe or cigarette and your cold drink – because we used to carry the soda syphon in a *chagoul* or canvas bag which was carried on the camel and by evaporation always remained cool. Then, as the night went on you frequently heard the roar of a lion and there was always the cough of a hyena and the squeal of the jackal – all the sounds of the night in the African bush, aided of course, by the romance of the amazing starlit sky. You never slept in a tent but always in the open on your camp bed – and always with your revolver under the pillow in case of some alarm.

# eight

# THE DO'S WIFE AND THE GOVERNOR'S LADY

*She had been, I believe, a mannequin or something in Glasgow and she had married this young man and come out to this place with a house that was only fit for a cow to live in and no Europeans within seventy miles of them. And I said to her, 'My dear, you must have been terrified when you came here' – and she said, 'Coo, I was terrified.' 'I don't wonder,' I said. 'You must find it very strange.' And she looked at me and she said, 'I didn't mean that. I thought I shouldn't be adequate.' I said, 'Adequate? You are absolutely magnificent!'*

A somewhat idealized image of the colonial lady, complete with mosquito boots but with a vulnerable amount of exposed flesh above. From the Army and Navy Catalogue 1931/2.

There was a traditional condition known as feeling 'end of tourish', which was to be found in every territory quite irrespective of whether the tour lasted a year or three years. It was essentially a 'subjective condition – you thought the tour was coming to an end so you felt end of tourish', but it was still the case that towards the end of the tour most people felt run-down. This was caused not so much by sickness as by a combination of a hard climate, poor living conditions and, in particular, poor food. While such artificial stimulants as 'claret laced with soda-water to buck one up' might occasionally have been resorted to, the most effective remedy was an extended and generous leave: 'This was one of the glories of the service – for five months you were answerable to nobody. If you were wise you went by boat and the Government was paying for the roof over your head and the food down your throat and you were buying cheap drinks on board. It was all tremendous fun and you had enough left over to give yourself a good quiet holiday at home and no doubt three or four splendid weeks on the Continent as well.'

It was on such leaves, of course, that most men found – and in due course married – their wives. But not, in most cases, for quite a few years: 'Marriage for administrative officers was not really entirely a matter of personal choice. One of the terms of our engagement was that for a number of years you could not, in fact, marry without the permission of the Governor or the Resident.' The absence of married quarters was not the only reason for this ban, although certainly in the early years between the wars this was a major factor. Personal finances had something to do with it since most administrators – other than the Sudan politicals – regarded themselves as badly paid. But there were other very sound reasons for requiring a junior administrative cadre to be made up entirely of bachelors: 'The first thing you had to do when you went out there was learn about the country and the people and the language, and learning about the country meant going out on tour in the bush for weeks on end in often pretty unsavoury and unpleasant conditions and there was a danger that if a youngster went out there with his wife he would say to his Resident, "Oh, I can't go to that place, it's dreadful. My wife will get ill" – and so wives were discouraged.' This ban ended with the Second World War, when 'people were coming out of the forces and joining the Colonial Service who had been married for several years and they just wouldn't stand that sort of treatment, and so although in theory they were still expected to ask permission for their wives to join them, permission was never withheld.'

The natural sequence of events that most young officers seemed to follow was to become engaged after a second or third tour and to marry on the next leave, a routine that often coincided with a promotion from Assistant District Commissioner to District Commissioner, so that officers returned to Africa not only with a bride but also to their first full district. Not surprisingly, quite a number married within the tribe, finding their wives from among the sisters of fellow-officers or – rather more typically – from among those families where the tradition of colonial service was well established and understood. Betty Moresby-White, who married in 1936, qualified on both counts; both her grandfathers had been in the Indian Civil Service and her brother was then an administrator in Southern Nigeria – although he had never met her husband, who was stationed in the North. Mavis Stone had the same Colonial Service background, which included in her case a childhood in Uganda up to the age of four, followed by that cruel separation of parents and children that was so much a part of family life in long-established colonial territories like India, but which was then far less common in Africa. For such children there may have been a 'certain glamour' in having parents in Africa, but there was always a heavy price to pay: 'The children grew up with little contact and tended not to know their parents very well, and you grew up never really belonging anywhere. I was divided between Africa and England. When in England you got very homesick for Africa and when in Africa you felt homesick for England.'

Fiancées and newly married wives with this kind of colonial background had a pretty shrewd idea of the kind of life they were letting themselves in for, but there were many others who did not. 'My husband thought I ought to see the horrors of living in West Africa,' recalls Dorothy Ruston, who got married in 1925, 'so he took me to see *White Cargo*, a play then running in London. Fortunately, life in Northern Nigeria wasn't really anything like *White Cargo*.' Even Betty Moresby-White was ill prepared: 'I used to hear stories from my brother about things but I really didn't take it in very much. I never even thought to ask what standard my husband had got to and I was quite amazed when I got a letter from him from Nigeria with "The Residency" written on it. But it wouldn't have mattered where he'd gone; I'd have been happy to go too.'

No doubt most young wives went out with very similar attitudes – coupled, perhaps, in the early days with an awareness that 'one was part of a world-wide British Empire and in some way privileged to be part of it.' This was certainly how Nancy Robertson felt when she first came out to the Sudan in 1926:

We realized in a way that no modern girl can possibly do, that we were very privileged to be allowed to go there, because our fiancés or husbands were really the first generation after the military rule where women were completely forbidden except in Khartoum. And therefore we may have been a little bit scared but we realized that we had got to keep well and we had got to keep cheerful or else some superior government official would order us home. And therefore, I suppose we were conditioned to putting up with things that weren't very nice and enjoying things that were very nice very, very much more than more modern girls might feel called on to do – and, of course, with communications being so terrible, by the time the reply to your letter home to mother saying it was unbearable had arrived, four or five months had gone by and you were enjoying yourself.

Another quality that was still very much in evidence in the years immediately after the Great War was self-confidence – 'because in those days to be British was, in our minds anyway, to be absolutely top of the world'. Such self-confidence, together with the knowledge that 'you were much luckier than your contemporaries back home' made it easier for young innocents fresh from England to put up with the most extreme conditions. When Nancy Robertson first came to Geteina – a day and a night up-river from Khartoum – she found herself to be the only white woman in the area. This made her an immediate focus of interest, particularly among the local Sudanese women, 'very kind, very inquisitive people who knew nothing about the British. One of them said to me, "Why is it that the Turks" – and that is how they addressed us – "are always so rude, and why do they smell so bad?" And from then on I realized that to these people we smelt disgusting, because we were meat-eaters and we smelt like death. We might not like their rancid oil smell but our smell was as bad for them as theirs was for us. And that, I think, was a great help during the next twenty or thirty years.' All the same, 'it was terribly lonely, far lonelier than anyone could understand who has never been in that situation.'

The house that she first lived in was 'exactly like a hen-house surrounded by wire-netting to keep the mosquitoes and sand-flies out', which her husband had 'done his best to make as dreary as possible'. However, there were periwinkles in the garden and a few vegetables and 'just at the bottom of the garden there was the Nile – and even the name of the Nile in those days was romantic and exciting.' The same powerful aura of romance was found by Alys Reece when she first came to Marsabit, a volcanic outcrop in the heart of the Northern Frontier District of Kenya, in 1936:

I was remembering the awful stories I'd been told by the people on the boat about how bleak and bare the whole region was and how crazy everybody went there. The journey seemed to me to be absolutely endless, along a rather vague road that had been a camel-track and had been kept up enough for motor traffic, and the further we went the bleaker it got and I began to believe all the tales I'd heard on the boat. And then we came to the foot of the mountains and that was so incredibly beautiful that all my exhaustion vanished. We came to a place where elephant had just very recently crossed the road, there were steaming heaps of elephant droppings bang in the middle of the road and this was the Africa I'd come to enjoy. The roads on the mountains went through some very beautiful windy ways, with thick forest coming right down to the road and across it in places. The harvest was nearly ripe at the time, there was a wonderful moon and all the maize was shining in the moonlight. There were fires at each little hut as we got nearer the station, and we were passing through plantations, and it really looked too romantic and glamorous for words.

The local people were understandably curious about Gerald Reece's new bride: 'He was well known in that part of the world as a bachelor, he'd been there for years and everybody knew him. If we went out riding he'd stop and talk to anyone we met on the little hills and I can remember how embarrassing the conversation sometimes was. The usual greeting was "Is the maiden fat?" – which I didn't entirely like, but it really meant prosperous, I think – and how much had I cost, how many cows? And whatever Gerald answered it seemed to be questionable because they'd look me up and down and then they would ask me whether God had seen fit to send me an embryo yet.'

In the towns and larger stations new wives had easier and less dramatic introductions to colonial life. Communications improved rapidly during the inter-war years, with new ports and harbours being built along the coast and with better road and rail links to the interior – even, from 1930, an Imperial Airways service to both East and West Africa, with a flying boat that made the run from Poole Harbour to Lake Victoria in a series of short hops with frequent night stops. But deep in the bush and in the remote out-stations life changed very little. Certain corners and bush tracts remained permanently thirty years behind the times and never succeeded in catching up – so that the young woman who joined her husband in a bush-station in Northern Rhodesia in the 1950s could find herself in circumstances that, but for improved prophylactics and perhaps a fridge, was in no way radically different from the 'extremely primitive, very bush' life experienced by Dorothy Ruston in Nigeria twenty-five years earlier:

There was no refrigeration, no electricity, no means of keeping your food. Whatever you had was killed that morning and eaten either for lunch or for dinner. The excitement was really the boat train once a fortnight when you got your papers and your mail and you could, with luck, buy fresh butter – which, of course, didn't keep for very long. You might get some sausages and real English meat and sometimes you could even buy English potatoes. Otherwise you had to make do with yam. The cooks were extremely poor because there'd been very few women to teach them so one did one's best but of course it wasn't easy. The cook used to go with his cook's mate to the market and he would buy eggs and chickens and anything that he thought might be reasonable to eat, but the only place where you could actually shop would be what was called the canteen, which was run by the European companies, and they would have all the tinned things, tinned butter, tinned cream, tinned milk – everything had to be in tins whatever it was, jam or flour or anything.

Her husband's staff was made up almost entirely of Ibos who spoke pidgin English: 'You might have a little Northerner as a tennis boy who would carry your racquet up to tennis and retrieve the balls, but usually they were Southerners. The pay doesn't sound very much – the cook would have about £3 a month, the steward boy £2, then your second steward or your gardener boy would probably get £1 a month and the little boy that you took up to tennis, he would get 5s. – but of course, they were provided with housing and everything was extremely cheap then.'

In East Africa the role of the canteen was filled by Indian stores known as *dukas*:

There was no place, however remote, where one wouldn't find a couple of small Indian shops. Their owners were bully-ragged by the local Africans but somehow they survived and made a jolly good living. They bought the produce that the Africans brought in to them, and they sold the staples. They had in addition a most surprising range of tinned and bottled stuff. There were all those Eno's Fruit Salts in the old-fashioned wrapping with the children climbing the wall handing the grapes down to each other; there was Borwick's Baking Powder. There was Reckitts Blue – everything washed in Kenya in the early days always came out a bright blue. It was used in enormous quantities by every *dhobi* and every household had any number of Reckitts packets lying about. Ovaltine was another product which you'd find in almost every shop and when you were drinking camel's milk which had been held in a wooden container washed out with ashes it had a certain indefinable quality attached to it which didn't improve tea and didn't improve coffee, but Ovaltine went awfully well with it.

The young European housewife could always turn to more senior and experienced wives who 'took great delight in telling new wives out from England how to manage their houses and their servants', but there were always occasions when there was no one to turn to and where the housewife had to learn how to cope on her own. Here such stand-bys as *Chop and Small Chop; Practical Cookery for Nigeria* by Norah Laing and *The Kenya Settler's Cookery Book and Household Guide*, written by the ladies of St Andrew's Presbyterian Church, proved to be invaluable. The first was written by the wife of the Senior Resident of Zaria in the early 1920s and resolutely ignored all local produce ('groundnut oil is at the bottom of a great deal of indigestion'). It was superseded during the Second World War by the publication of *Living Off the Country*, which emphasized the value of such local produce as *paw-paw* leaves, for tenderizing the local *tukanda* (meat), or *yakua* leaves (roselle), to be used in place of vinegar or lemon juice when cooking greens or even as a cocktail. *The Kenya Settler's Cookery Book*, however, published in 1928, was very much in a class of its own. As well as giving all the standard recipes and a wide range of local recipes it also contained such wide-ranging household hints as how to make your own *mealie meal* soap, how to stiffen silks with gum arabic, and how to treat scaly legs in chickens or 'Nairobi eye', the bite of the Nairobi fly ('milk, calamine lotion or soda bicarbonate applied at once will give relief'). Also included was a list of items to take on safari and, most useful of all, 'it had a vocabulary which enabled you to speak to Kikuyu-speaking gardeners and two lots of Swahili, one for good Swahili speakers, called Ki-Swahili and one known as Ki-settler, the language of the settler. All this was a tremendous help, particularly when you were new to it all and weren't too sure how to begin handling your boys.'

Learning to run an African household was fraught with all sorts of difficulties, the first of which was having to overcome a reluctance in some households to take orders from a woman, a situation that usually ended with the senior steward or house-boy quitting the household – but not always. When Betty Morseby-White came out to Nigeria the head boy, Nuku, had already been with her husband for nearly twenty years: 'Poor Nuku afterwards told me that he was sure he was going to be sacked as soon as I arrived in the country because, he said, every Missus sacked the boys when they

# MISCELLANEOUS RECIPES AND HOUSE-HOLD HINTS.

### Alkama Sponge Cake.

4 eggs, 3 ozs. castor sugar, 4 ozs. alkama, $\frac{1}{4}$ teaspoon baking powder, $\frac{1}{2}$ teaspoon boiling water.

Beat the eggs and sugar together until very thick. Mix the baking powder with the alkama and fold lightly into the eggs and sugar. Add the *boiling* water slowly, turn into a tin 5 inches in diameter. Bake for about 25 minutes in a moderate oven. When the cake is cold ice it with Zaria sugar icing.

### Banana Chips.

### (A substitute for potato chips with fried fish)

Peel green bananas and slice lengthways or crossways as desired. Sprinkle with pepper and salt and fry up quickly in fat or lard. Pile on a dish and serve immediately.

### Bean Croquettes (Kwasi).

Soak native beans in cold water over night. In the morning remove from the water and grind finely in a food chopper or have a native woman grind them on her stone. Add enough water to make a stiff batter. Add *finely* chopped onion and salt to taste.

Drop by small spoonfuls into a saucepan which is about half full of hot fat, preferably groundnut oil. Care should be taken that the oil is not too highly seasoned with pepper or the bean cakes will be too 'hot' to eat. Remove from fat when they are brown. Serve hot with some sort of tart sauce, such as "Kukuki" jam.

Local recipes and local foodstuffs as found in *Living off the Country*, published in Nigeria in 1942. Yakuwa was an effective substitute for lemon juice.

first arrived. I told him that far from sacking him I was absolutely thankful for him, because he was so good.'

There were also language barriers to overcome and, where largely untrained servants were concerned, enormous areas of confusion that produced a rich crop of horror stories – the family silver cleaned with Vim, silk underclothes pounded on a stone, puddings decorated with toothpaste and plates dropped with the remark that 'its day had come'. Extraordinary disasters would occur during dinner parties and would be explained by the disarming apology that 'our heads went round'. 'I loved my black servants,' declares Violet Bourdillon, 'they were sweet and kind and lovely but they were dreadfully inefficient.' Even as a governor's lady she found it wise to check everything for herself, making sure that they hadn't 'turned the towels which the last gentleman cleaned his boots on inside out in order not to get new ones and so on'.

It was this inefficiency – from a Western point of view – that led to bullying and shouting, even if wives 'made a conscious effort not to behave like that.' There was what Beatrice Turnbull describes as

. . . an almost continual battle between African servants and their employers. It wasn't from lack of sympathy on either side. The real problem was each side had entirely different basic assumptions. East Africans – the people I'm talking about – had what I must call a tribal way of thinking, and it was extremely painful for them to be made to see or to have it pointed out to them that anything they had done produced any particular result. If there was an unlucky outcome of anything it was an affair of God, or of the Government, or of the weather, or me, or an unnamed malevolent spirit – and the only possibility of getting any change in this attitude was to become a nagger and try to get a man to see by going back carefully, step by step, that what he had actually done had caused the chimney to go on fire, or the laundry to flood. And if in the end you could induce him to agree, 'Yes, he had made the mistake' – from that moment on he was quite a different man.

Another source of irritation was the partiality for *ju-ju*, which usually found expression in an attempt by one servant to put a curse on another, although it could take the form of an 'affability potion', in which the opposite effect was desired. When she and her husband moved into Government House in Lagos in 1935 Violet Bourdillon inherited a cook named Mr William, who had been on the staff for twenty-five years: 'Well, we went on gaily for five years and then one day I went out into the compound and there was the most frightful screeching going on. It was a police raid and the next thing was I found that cook had been arrested; they'd gone into his house and found ten affability potions, each labelled: "To make my master look on me with the eye of favour". In fact, for five years we'd been given affabilities in our soup and tea.'

Despite this constant battle between the two cultures, a very genuine bond of trust and affection between mistress and servants did exist in many households. The European housewife got used to being addressed, for all her protests, as 'Ma' or 'Missus' – or as 'Memsahib' on the East African Coast – and she learnt to value her servants' honesty as far as money or valuables were concerned – while turning a blind eye to the customary perks in the way of tea and sugar and a little extra on the cook's shopping bill. She accepted responsibility for the upkeep and welfare of their families, in the African tradition, and she learnt not to visit the kitchen at the back or the

## English

129. An insect has eaten this.
130. Dig the garden.
131. Cut the grass.
132. Split the firewood.
133. Cultivate the soil.
134. I want to see your registration certificate and book.
135. Where have you been since you left your last master?

136. I do not give such high wages. If you work here, I will give you . . . shillings and food.
137. You are free every day from 2 o'clock till 4 o'clock, but at any other time you must be on duty on the premises.
138. No one is allowed to come here and sleep in your hut unless I give him written permission to stay.

139. I do not allow strange boys near the house.
140. Do not be sulky.
141. You are insolent! You must look pleasant (or pleased).
142. It is better not to be sulky.

## Ki-Swahili

129. Kimeliwa na dudu.
130. Lima bustani.
131. Kata nyasi.
132. Pasua kuni.
133. Palilia ardhi.
134. Nataka kutazama kipande chako na buku.
135. Umekuwa wapi tangu ulipotoka kazini ya Bwana wako wa mwisho?

136. Sitoi mshahara mwingi kama hivi. Ukifanya kazi hapa, nitakupa shillingi . . . na posho.
137. Una ruhusa kila siku kutoka saa nane hata saa kumi, lakini wakati mwingine wote lazima uwepo kazini huku.
138. Hapana awaye yote aliye na ruhusa ya kuja huku na kulala nyumbani mwako (S) (or mwenu, P); asipopata cheti kwangu mimi.

139. Siwapi maboi wageni ruhusa ya kuikaribia nyumba.
140. Usiwe kaidi, or, Usinune.
141. Mfidhuli we! Inakupasa uso wako uwe wa furaha.
142. Ni heri kutokuwa mkaidi.

## Ki-Settler

129. Dudu kwisha kula hii.
130. Chimba shamba.
131. Kata majani.
132. Pasua kuni.
133. Lima udongo.
134. Nataka kuona kipandi yako pamoja na buku yako.
135. Wewe kwenda wapi tangu siku ile wache kasi ya bwana?

136. Sitaki kutowa mshara kubwa nani hii kama wewe kuja hapa nita-toa shillingi . . . na chekula.
137. Kila siku, wapata ruhusa tangu saa nane mpaka saa kumi. Saa ingine, dasturi yako hapa nyumbani.
138. Sitaki watu wageni lala nyumbani yako hapa kama wataka ruhusa kwa wageni hapa, nitaandeka ba-rua, (or uliza mimi andeka barua.

139. Dasturi yangu, hapana wageni kuja karibu nyumba.
140. Usiwe mwenyi hati ya kunua.
141. Wewe jeuri! sharti wewe tezama chekalea.
142. Kutununa ni afadhali kuliko kununa.

Instructions for servants in Ki-Swahili and its corrupted form of Ki-Settler, from *The Kenya Settler's Cookery Book and Household Guide*, 1928.

staff quarters without plenty of warning. But two vital duties she always kept to herself; she supervised the washing of lettuce and other vegetables for salads in 'pot. permang.', as well as the boiling and filtering of water. A curious result of this constant boiling and filtering for Beatrice Turnbull was that when she returned to Britain she and her children were 'quite unable to drink a glass of water drawn from a tap. We could draw water from a tap into a jug and then pour it into a glass, but we could not drink water straight out of a tap.'

Even with a house full of servants it was not an easy life for a European woman and not all wives adapted themselves easily or even willingly to the colonial life. No doubt there were many housewives like Veronica Short who, when she first came to Northern Rhodesia, was fascinated by the life: 'I loved the Africans, they were all so friendly and it was a lovely climate, but after six months it began to pall and I'm afraid that for the rest of my ten and a half years out there I was just waiting for my husband to retire. And I think most wives were like I was; they'd taken on a job. We knew what we were doing when we married our husbands and although we might not have liked it we made the best of it.' Making the best of it meant living in 'rather horrid little houses' that were allocated to them which they were required to abandon at frequent intervals for other equally unhomely dwellings – 'because you were always moving on'. It often meant enduring months of appalling dry heat, when 'one had to be very careful or one ended up looking rather like a dried-up walnut', or months of extreme humidity when shoes and dresses turned green with mould and people at cocktail parties looked as if they'd been fished out of the sea, when 'if you dropped something while you were dressing you didn't attempt to pick it up – bending down would absolutely put an end to all your preparations.' It meant having cockroaches in the linen, silver-fishes eating their way through one's books, sitting in the evenings with legs either inside a pillow-case or in hot mosquito boots – and sometimes having to chase baboons or even elephants out of the garden. It also meant snakes. 'The thing that I was most frightened of at the beginning was the snakes,' declares Alys Reece:

The garden at Marsabit was very overgrown and there were any number of the kind of cobra that spit in your eye if you give them a chance – and although I was terrified of them I knew that if I flicked them on to the grass with a special hoe that I'd sharpened they didn't have much chance. They were always racing for cover but with the very sharp hoe I could cut them in half before they got to it – and I became really quite vicious over them. The other snakes that we had were puff-adders. I think they were as frightened of us as we were of them, but one would find them coiled round in the cool shade beside the loo seats, which was rather disturbing – and one would also find them coiled on the path that one was walking along. On one occasion Gerald trod bang on the head of one in the dusk and I was just about to step on it too when I saw its fangs moving, with its head sticking firmly in the mud.

Gerald teased me a bit about being scared stiff of snakes and it was a little ironic that shortly after that, when he was doing an early Saturday morning tour round the township, walking through long grass he got bitten by one. The snake-bite took effect very quickly; his temperature went to 105, he was delirious and his leg went black up to his waist. We had cut the place and done all the squeezing and all the old pot. permang. and that sort of thing, but there wasn't much I could do except try to keep the fever down by continually sponging him with lots of cold water and praying like mad – and by the Monday morning the worst was behind us. He had a very bad foot for some time and had to go around on safari in carpet-slippers, but apart from that he made a marvellous recovery.

In the larger stations such isolated horrors could be set against an active social life that centred very much on the club and the various sporting and social entertainments that went on there – the dances, fancy-dress parties, amateur theatricals, cricket weekends, gymkhanas and polo weeks as well as the private supper parties, with their endless rounds of *toasties* and small *chop*, and the weekend luncheons. While they provided a very necessary relaxation from official duties, such diversions also had their critics. Some wives found the other European women to be 'completely aloof from the people who really could have used their help. Their main topic of conversation was how frightful their servants were, how ghastly everybody was and why hadn't they been asked to the Governor's dinner the night before?' Also much criticized were the real casualties of colonial life, the wives who were 'really very unhappy in Africa and never fitted in. They hated to be parted from their children and they didn't want to be taken on safari so they had a lonely time because they were left on the station by themselves a lot. They were bothered by the lack of entertainment and facilities. They weren't interested in games or their gardens, so there was very little left to do.' For them life was perhaps 'a little dangerous, because some white women, unaccustomed to freedom from household chores and with nothing to do, assembled for elevenses in the clubs and became very easily involved in intrigues.' The fact that the men greatly outnumbered the women made Africa 'a terribly tempting place for a woman. There were lots of bachelors kicking their heels and they buzzed around married women like bees round a honey pot. Very few families hadn't got at least one man attached to the husband and wife, pathetically hanging on, hoping for crumbs that fell from the rich man's table. The husband might go off on safari and the temptation was stark. In Kenya it got to such a pitch that one used to say, "Are you married or do you live in Kenya?"'

By far the luckiest wives in Africa were those suited by health and temperament to a rough, outdoor life and who were able to become intimately involved in their husbands' jobs: 'This was the greatest satisfaction of being a colonial wife. You felt you were being constructive and productive and doing something that was well worthwhile and enjoyable.' This enjoyment was never more keenly felt than when they accompanied their husbands on tour. 'Camp life was to me the essence of Africa,' declares Mavis Stone. 'Both Dick and I felt much nearer to the heart of Africa and in much closer contact with the Africans, because somehow they were at their best then.' Touring through Northern Uganda they passed through

. . . magnificent scenery, long khaki-coloured plains with the flat-topped thorn trees and scrub bushes – and with a lot of game near the game reserves, particularly buffalo, waterbuck and elephant. You got the rather attractive little villages with woven fences, funny little granaries where they stored their food for the dry weather and chicken houses made up like little mud huts with thatched roofs and stuck up on stilts. And everywhere the children, the fat babies and the *totos*, the children that were half-grown, all legs and smiles. The men standing around on one leg leaning on spears. The women always graceful, always carrying loads on their heads – even a matchbox I've seen them carrying on their heads – never anything in their hands. And their babies on their backs, of course, with gourds over the heads of the babies and flies – flies everywhere.

One of the remarkable features of these tours was the way in which the cooks managed to produce high-quality meals cooked in *debbies*, four-gallon paraffin tins with the tops cut out and made into portable ovens. 'The cooks were marvellous,' recalls Alys Reece. 'They made bread in holes in the ground and they would carry the bread in the half-way stage in cloths on the camel and as soon as the fires were made in the evening out it would come and they would bake the bread at night in a hole in the ground, with cinders. We had one cook who used to make beautiful éclairs the same way on tour.'

It was nearly always the evenings in camp that held the greatest attraction – certainly for Mavis Stone:

We always had a camp fire which we used to sit round. It was usually lit at sunset which we would sit and watch and there was supposed to be a blue flash which you did just see as the sun disappeared and then it got dark very quickly. Then the mosquitoes came out, so you'd want to have had your bath in the back of the tent, an old-fashioned hip-bath where you had to swat at the mosquitoes while you were having your bath. But it was very refreshing and then you got into your trousers and mosquito boots and a long-sleeved shirt and you went and sat by the camp fire and had your drink. And the night sort of closed around you and you were very aware of the stars – and usually from the village that was not far away you would hear the noises of the people calling and chatting and quite often the drumming that went on. Wherever we went there was nearly always a dance laid on. In Acholi, particularly, they did the most beautiful dancing with little drums and leopard skins and those magnificent head-dresses that they wore made out of sisal, almost like long blond hair. They did this leaping and dancing and it was almost like a ballet.

There was one aspect of married life in Africa with which it was particularly difficult to come to terms. 'Until the Second World War there were no European children in Nigeria,' recalls Dorothy Ruston. 'You didn't anticipate taking your children out, so they had to be left at home. Every married couple had to face the problem of what would happen when they decided to have a family. It wasn't easy to decide that you must spend part of the time at home with the children and part of the time with your husband. Some people decided that perhaps it was better to have no children at all.' To say that there were no white children was perhaps putting it too strongly, for there were always children to be found in the settled areas and in the healthier climates and among the mission communities. And if most couples sought to have their children born and reared, as far as possible, back home in England, there were always the exceptions. Three of Alys Reece's children were born during her first few years at Marsabit:

Having a baby in those days was rather a pantomime, as one had to go all the way down to Nairobi, which meant two or three days travelling and a long stay in Nairobi. And when my first child was born it turned out to be a daughter which wasn't at all the right thing to do by local standards and poor Gerald had to put up with a lot of commiserations. All the old men called on him in a ceremonial fashion and wrung his hand and wished him better luck next time. One Somali servant that we had produced a fertility emblem that he insisted I hung over my bed. He was a bit worried about its being second-hand, but it was a dreadful thing and shrieked its message. It was a huge ostrich egg with a lot of conch shells rather representative of fertility, and this had to be hung over my bed and I used to wake and see it in the night and be terrified of it and I was very glad indeed when I could hand it back and say that, yes, it had worked and it was fine. But another daughter arrived and poor old Ibrahim thought it was partly the fault of his second-hand fertility emblem. However, the women of the place were very interested and all the young women called to see the baby and play with it and were very nice and comforting and then, some time later, our first son was born and when I came back to Marsabit I was staggered by the reception that I got. With the girls the men had just sent their wives or daughters to congratulate me, if you could call it that, but when I came back with a son it was quite a triumph, and all sorts of old men appeared with a terrific range of presents from a beautiful white ox to bunches of bananas and hens and all sorts of things like that to celebrate the birth of our son.

Bringing up small children in the tropics presented all sorts of difficulties. The most serious health risk was malaria, since the taking of quinine or methadine as a daily dose was not good for children. But even after the Second World War, when the introduction of paludrin removed the threat of malaria, there were still plenty of other dangers. Even when there were servants and, in East Africa, *ayahs* – 'a very wonderful race of women who really did love their charges and ruled them with an iron fist' – trained to look after and care for the children, the need to be on the alert was always there. Veronica Short's constant worry was the fear of rabies: 'On almost every posting we had there was a rabies scare, which meant that all the local dogs had to be tied up. But then there were always dogs that would escape from the villages and run through the *boma* and if your children were playing in the garden you were never quite sure whether they had touched the dog, because my children were fond of animals and very apt to pat any dog that came near, so this was one of the things that always haunted me while I was in Africa.' Then there were such minor hazards as – in Nyasaland – the *puttse* flies that laid their eggs on the washing as it dried in the sun. If the washing wasn't well ironed there was always the risk that the eggs would hatch and the grubs work their way into the skin. This was what happened to Noel Harvey's son Christopher when he was two years old: 'He got rather pale and complained of a sore head and we found there was a boil coming up, so we took him round to the doctor and the doctor treated it as a boil and said that we must wait until it came to a head. When it finally did we went in and the doctor said, "This is *not* a boil." He took his two thumbs and squeezed and out from the boil came a most revolting little maggot.'

The risk to life may not have been so acute as it had been in earlier years, but it was still a risk that on rare occasions had to be taken seriously – as Sue Bates found one night in Tabora:

I wasn't sleeping very well and I went in to look at the youngest child and I found that his cot was completely black with ants. Soldier ants had been working their way right through the house – and his cot had been in the way. They'd got under the netting and through the netting and his ears and his nose and his mouth were full of ants so he couldn't cry out. We had buckets of water so we put some in a basin and we held him more or less under and tried to pick all these things out and he started to cry and so that was all right. Then we got the other two children and we put the four legs of our iron double bed into tobacco tins full of paraffin and the five of us spent the rest of the night in the bed. And by the morning the ants had worked their way through the house and they'd eaten all the cockroaches and pretty well everything else there was to eat. It was a rather horrifying experience because if I hadn't gone in to see him he would have been killed.

But there were always compensations to be set against the privations and the risks. For the children these first years in Africa were ones of rare privilege, with love and affection lavished on them by all the household and constant attention focused upon them wherever they went. Alys Reece recalls how, when her three children were a little older, they were visited by

he District Officer's wife led an isolated and often lonely life. *Above*, Margaret Gillan, Jebel
arra mountains, Western Sudan 1935. *Below*, Betty Moresby-White at breakfast, Ibadan
39. Her staff at that time consisted of Famous the cook, Ndukri the cook's mate, the second
use-boy and two gardeners.

The Governor (Sir Alan Burns) in full ceremonial regalia; a uniform said to have been devised for the Crimean Campaign, Gold Coast *c.* 1945.

The Governor (Sir Richard Turnbull) in mufti; an exchange of gifts at an up-country *baraza*, N. Tanganyika 1958.

The Governor's Lady (Beatrice Turnbull) on safari; boating down the Rufiji river with the
local District Commissioner, Tanganyika 1959.

The reality of Mau Mau; a young
District Officer, Kikuyu Guard,
questions Mau Mau suspects,
Kenya 1953.

*Below*    The Chief Minister –
and future President – and his
senior staff; Julius Nyerere with
his Permanent Secretaries and
Provincial Commissioners
shortly before Tanzanian
Independence, Dar es Salaam
*c.* 1960–1.

. . . two stark naked warriors with their spears who came and sat down on the lawn just outside the house. The following day they came back and just took up the same position again. They didn't look at all hostile, so I wasn't frightened by them but I got a little bit curious and at last I sent a note down to the District Commissioner and asked him who they were. And they were Geluba from the far corner of the province who had been brought in as witnesses in a murder trial. They had heard rumours of a little girl with white hair who rode her own pony and they were waiting to see this happen. So Sarah, who had very blond hair at that age, obligingly and very seriously got on her pony and did a neat little gallop round and they shook hands all round and went away delighted.

This African childhood was very rarely prolonged: 'The children couldn't stay after a certain time because the tropics were bad for them and there was no proper schooling. They had to go off to England to boarding school.' Then came 'the awful choice which comes sooner or later between husband and children', a choice that was undoubtedly 'the saddest and most controversial part of the lot of the colonial official'. Some wives stuck by their husbands, others went with their children. Most tried to do a bit of both, staying on in England for several months after their husband's leave was up and coming back early a month or two before the next leave was due. For some parents, like the Mackays, it was 'a very, very painful choice to make and in the end we left the Colonial Service.'

Just as the First World War effectively brought one era to a close so the advent of the Second World War marked quite unmistakably the ending of another. On the day that war was declared in August 1939 Mercedes Mackay had been having 'a particularly riotous day' with the other Europeans on the station:

We were playing a cricket match in which all the men dressed as women and all the women as men. There were some absurd costumes and some very peculiar cricket was played, and I remember going on as a soldier dressed in my husband's solar topee and carrying his rifle. Various other idiotic things happened and we were all laughing so much that we could hardly speak when suddenly a car appeared and a man got out and said, 'Come quickly to the club, the Prime Minister is about to speak.' So we beetled off in our cars round to the club and we all stood round in our ridiculous costumes and they turned on the wireless and there was that fatal announcement. And I remember looking across at the Inspector of the Public Works Department, who had dressed himself up in a long, black flowing dress with a red wig as a madam of a brothel, and he was standing there with tears pouring down his face. It was one of the most tragi-comic situations that I can ever remember.

# nine

# WINDS OF CHANGE

*We have seen the awakening of national consciousness in peoples who have for centuries lived in dependence on some other power . . . In different places it takes different forms but it is happening everywhere. A wind of change is blowing through this continent, whether we like it or not.*

HAROLD MACMILLAN Address to the Joint
Assembly of the South African Parliament
3 February 1960

When Alan Burns first went out to Nigeria in 1912 there was 'no thought in anybody's mind that Independence was to come within our lifetime, and at that time we none of us believed that the Africans were fit for self-government. It was only after the Second World War that people began to realize that sooner or later – and probably sooner rather than later – there would have to be Independence. Even then they didn't think – not even the Africans themselves – that Independence was coming as quickly as it did.'

The war and its aftermath brought about many changes, both in circumstances and attitudes, not the least of which was the sudden revelation that pith helmets need not be worn. When Philip Allison first came to Nigeria,

. . . there was usually quite a lot of discussion if you were at a drinks party during the day on a Sunday morning at somebody's house; some people thought that if you wanted to go out to relieve yourself in the compound there was just time to go out and do this without putting your hat on, but many people religiously put their topees on before they went out to relieve themselves in the garden. But during the war when British soldiers came out and walked about bareheaded and nothing terrible happened to them, people realized at last that nobody ever really suffered from sunstroke. What they'd been suffering from was heat-stroke – due to wearing a heavy helmet for one thing, no doubt. But that was one of the things that the war exploded for us.

There were also sudden dramatic improvements in living conditions, such new drugs as paludrin and sulpha-guenodine became available, refrigerators became standard issue for all government servants – 'and for once they started by issuing these refrigerators to the lower paid before the senior officers were offered them' – and improved air services brought Africa and Great Britain that much closer, making it increasingly possible for wives to shuttle between husbands and children – even for the children themselves to come out and join their parents for a summer or winter holiday. The war also added a new word to the colonial vocabulary – 'development'. 'It has to be remembered that a country like Tanganyika was chronically short of money between the wars,' explains Charles Meek, 'so there was nothing whatever to spend on development. Each colony was supposed to subsist on its own and if you had very little, as Tanganyika did, in the way of primary produce in high demand, sisal, cotton, a bit of coffee, then the country was going to be hard up – and poverty-stricken it certainly was. It was only during the war with the passage of the first Colonial Development and Welfare Act that the coming of better times was signalled. They were slow in coming but slowly the momentum of development did build up and the pace got faster and faster.'

In the district this new aid expressed itself in development plans which not only 'enthused all of us white administrators but also caught the imagination of the Africans' so that comparatively small sums of money – in Charles Meek's district of Mbulu it was £90,000 spread over five years – provided the basis for ambitious self-help programmes in which the local young men were drafted in to provide free labour in the dry season.

With this development came the concept of the administrator as chairman or co-ordinator of a District Team rather than as the isolated head of a district or province. There were, too, a number of other shifts of emphasis in district work, heralded by a dramatic increase in paperwork. 'This seemed to grow and grow,' recalls Bill Stubbs, 'and towards the end of my service it was even necessary to recruit a brand new kind of officer who went in many cases even to out-stations to assist in the growing paperwork which took so much of the administrator's time and took him away from the other more important duties.' The District Officer found himself 'increasingly embroiled in political matters, not necessarily on a local level but on a regional or even a federal level'. The commonest expression of this politicization was in the introduction of democracy into the fabric of tribal life. In Tanganyika Darrell Bates found himself charged with replacing a 'rough and ready system of democracy, which largely consisted of knocking off the chief if they didn't like him' with a system of electing local representatives that accorded to some degree with English-style democracy:

We would invite the people to a gathering to nominate two advisers who would sit on a council to advise a chief. And shyly and slowly people would come forward and say, 'We nominate him' – and 'We nominate him' – until I had perhaps seven or eight different people. Then I told those who supported them to stand behind the candidate of their choice and then I took the person who had the least votes and said, 'Now, you are a non-starter – you go and stand behind your second choice,' and this went on until you had the two with the largest number of supporters. This was a form of democracy that was open and reasonably honest and so in this way democracy came to a small corner of Africa.

Elsewhere very similar experiments in local democracy were being carried out. 'From 1950–51 onwards life in Northern Nigeria was dominated by elections,' recalls Nigel Cooke. 'Initially there was a very indirect form of election, with hamlets electing people to go forward to a village area and a village area to a district and a district to an emirate and so on. It was all in stages and very, very indirect, but gradually with regional and federal elections the pattern changed to more and more direct elections. And of course the more direct the elections grew the more danger there was to law and order.'

In the meantime changes were taking place among the administrators themselves. Although the post-war generation came from very much the same background – the public schools and Oxbridge in most cases – the war had undoubtedly created a gulf between the two generations, a gulf accentuated by the freeze that had been put on recruitment for most of the duration of the war and by the fact that only the youngest members of the various colonial services had been allowed to join up. In Northern Rhodesia a line had simply been drawn through the Staff List and 'only those DOS under thirty were allowed to go to war.' Those who were forced to stay on – sometimes under threat of imprisonment if they attempted to join up – had served out enormously extended tours of duty, which had further accentuated their isolation. As a result these older administrators, many of whom prided themselves on their liberal outlook, were caught out by the new post-war mood of egalitarianism. When Tony Kirk-Greene came to Nigeria in 1950 most of the senior administrators were men who had gone out between 1920 and 1935:

The big gap was between them and those of us who came in after the war. People who came out after the war were more likely to question the hierarchy, question why things were going to be done. The whole structure seemed to be very different after World War Two. And I think the real breakthrough came with a younger group of us recruited after World War Two when we decided that we would spend much of our time getting to know the new élite. We were convinced that this was where the future lay. Instead, as our seniors had done, of paying all the attention to the elders, the chiefs and senior Native Authority officials, we went for the younger educated élite, people who had been to secondary schools, occasionally to university. And this made all the difference. I'm not blaming people for not doing this before the war. I think in that kind of society – both European society and the Colonial Service hierarchical society – this would have been impossible. This easy mixing, having young educated Nigerians to your house, playing Scrabble and, particularly, mixing them with some of the other Europeans who were also interested in getting to know the new Nigerian. I think this was the big change-over.

This difference of attitude was in no way confined either to West Africa or to the youngest generation of administrators. In Tanganyika Charles Meek also felt that:

There was a gap in the thinking between young and old. The older men, Provincial Commissioners, members in Dar es Salaam under the old membership system of government, found it very difficult – and quite understandably so – to appreciate the urgency that people of my age, in their late thirties, felt, and the consuming feeling that it was no longer possible to think as we used to think of handing over power in very deliberate slices. We used to believe that you could give them a little bit now and see what they made of it and in ten years time give them a little bit more. This wasn't going to work. Not in the tide of opinion that the nationalists had set up, operating against a background of world opinion, particularly American opinion and UN opinion, which was totally hostile to all our conceptions of colonialism.

There were other ways, too, in which the differences between the generations were making themselves felt. One of the principal features of district life that was disputed by the post-war generation was the importance attached to touring by their seniors. There was a feeling that perhaps some of them 'toured for touring's sake.' This was not helped by a prejudice in some quarters against touring by any means other than on foot: 'After the war ADOs were asking for advances to buy cars,' Nigel Cooke recalls. 'Now this was not commonly given and I remember one very pompous Resident saying, "No, Smith, I will give you an advance for a pair of boots, but not for a car."' To some extent the issue was resolved by the arrival of four-wheel drive and the Land Rover, which 'revolutionized administration in East Africa. Your people were always accessible, then. You might have an exciting time getting to them, but you did get there. And it really altered things for us.'

Another new arrival in the district, and a further by-product of the war years, was an altogether new model of colonial wife. Not only was she freed from many of the constraints that had inhibited her predecessors but she also had more positive ideas about her role and was often determined to do 'as much as a woman is allowed to do in an African male society', involving herself in local African councils of women or such organizations as the Girl Guides rather than simply offering token support to 'the charity of the Lady Governor of the time'. Even more significantly, the ending of the war also released a professional work-force of women trained in leadership for whom service in the colonies was a natural progression from their war work. One of these was Catherine Dinnick-Parr, who had served during the war in the WRNS and who was appointed in 1947 to work among the Tiv people of Northern Nigeria as an adult education officer. Although she was by no means the first woman educationalist to go to Northern Nigeria – Sylvia

Leith-Ross had been appointed as the first Lady Superintendent of Education as early as 1926 – her work in the bush was as much a pioneering venture as anything that her male colleagues had been through in the earlier days:

I left by car on the road which leads from Benue Province to Ogoja Province, which is in the Western Region of Nigeria. I was told to drive to milestone 40 and then turn right. There was a path there, even though I couldn't see it, and we drove some distance down this bush path and came to a local school. Then we were told to drive back to a certain tree and to plough through the grass, which was at least six feet high, which we did, and there was this one room with a little wooden verandah and a thatched roof. There were huts in the compound for the boys and there was also a round mud hut as a kitchen. We unloaded the car and I told my steward, Sam, that I would have to go and salute the chief, who was the head of the clan. I knew I couldn't make a mistake about his compound because it was at the end of this bush path, and also it was surrounded by tall trees which signalled it was a chief's compound. There were twelve old gentlemen sitting on the ground and in front of the middle one there was a deck-chair. I had very little Tiv then, but I could salute them all, 'M sugh u', which means, 'I greet you'. The man in the middle put his hand out for me to sit on the deck-chair, which I did, and it immediately collapsed. Eventually a dog came out and sniffed at me, then a woman came out and she put her foot by mine. I was wearing open sandals and she was obviously saying to them all, 'Well, at least her feet are the same as ours.' Then she felt me more or less all over and although I was covered she was obviously saying, 'Well, she's the same as us even though she's wearing clothes.'

Her first problem was to become accepted – by both blacks and whites. Although 'most of the Europeans I met were very kind and helpful, I think they thought I must be a little strange being on my own.' Meeting another European in the bush she asked him to join her for a drink, 'and while we were sitting drinking he kept turning round and I couldn't think what he was looking for. I asked him if he'd lost something. He said, "No, I'm just looking for your husband." So I said, "But I don't have a husband. I work here." "But", he said, "we don't have any woman working on her own in the province." And I said, "Well, at last you have met one."'

Catherine Dinnick-Parr's principal objective was to get the Tiv people interested in female education. But in order to work with the women she had first to be accepted by their menfolk:

I had to be very, very careful in case I did something which they wouldn't like and I found it very difficult at times to keep my thoughts to myself and my mouth closed. But if they thought that you were trying to wipe out all that they believed in, they would not have been willing for you to stay and work with them. The position of the women in the family has to be understood and one cannot just run in like a bull in a china shop when they are doing something which we consider is absolutely wrong according to our culture.

By walking round the village compounds every day and getting to know the people and their customs – 'whether you felt they were right or wrong that wasn't for you to judge' – Catherine Dinnick-Parr not only learnt a great deal – 'learning by watching what the women were doing, how they worked, what foodstuffs they put in their dishes, seeing their babies, talking to the women, listening to the old men telling their stories about former days' – but also built up trust. Then she was able to start classes, first in one village and then another – 'they would wait until my car arrived and then a drum would be sounded and they would come in' – concentrating particularly on hygiene, child care and cookery. 'Always in every class there is one woman who listens. She may not agree with everything you say, but she does put some of your things into practice. The next time you go to visit her hut you find that it has been swept out, she's tied a rope between two huts and she's putting the sleeping mats and the sleeping clothes out in the sun to kill any germs there may be. She's made a little platform of mud on which to prepare her food rather than doing it all on the ground and she's covered all the pots which have food in them.'

Just as Catherine Dinnick-Parr found some of the Tiv customs hard to understand, so no doubt the Tiv people found some of her own customs equally inexplicable:

In an evening in the bush I always wore a long evening dress to keep up my morale but also one had to wear mosquito boots; there were mosquitoes and sand-flies everywhere and the long dress was a great help. I remember when I was at Mbaakon the Development Officer would come along and have dinner with me – he in a dinner suit and I in an evening dress – and we would walk along the bush path talking and everyone gathered to see us. They were all so excited. I think they wondered why we got all dressed up and covered ourselves when it was so frightfully hot. In an evening I would often play my gramophone records. I had an old-fashioned gramophone that you had to wind up and I had hundreds of records and the ones that they liked best were one by Tom Lehrer called *Pigeons in the Park* and *Dreaming of a White Christmas*. These tunes they absolutely adored and they'd ask for them to be repeated time and time again. All the village would come. We'd sit round and we would have these records on and then always there was a drummer with his drum and he would start drumming and they would start dancing. And it was absolutely beautiful, particularly by moonlight and I can't tell you how friendly they were. And although I was often on my own I was safer there than I would ever have been anywhere in England today.

Some years later Catherine Dinnick-Parr was posted to Kaduna where, as Chief Education Officer, she found herself up against 'tremendous opposition to girls' education that went on year in and year out'. There was a great difference between the education in the Moslem far North and in the Southern region of Nigeria: 'In the Southern part there was the mission influence and many girls attended school. But the missions were not permitted to work in the Northern region, where there was still tremendous opposition to female education of any kind, due partly to religious beliefs and tribal customs, particularly early marriage, or to the loss of a young wage-earner and the loss of a young pair of hands to do the chores. It was very, very hard going to get the girls into school.' The change only came in the early 1960s when it became obvious that 'if the country was to go forward then the women must go forward with the men. The modern Northern Nigerians now quote an old Arabic saying, that "a country where the women are not educated is like a bird with only one wing."'

Another teacher who came out to Northern Nigeria was Joan Everett: 'I remember being rather staggered to see a girl walk to the window, firmly grasp her nose and blow violently out of the window, and I couldn't help thinking that this was a slight change from my girls at Sherborne.' Both for her and for Mary Allen, who came out by air to teach in Accra in 1950, 'being a single woman in a small station had enormous advantages because one was rather in demand.' Not unexpectedly, this led to an alarmingly high drop-out rate among their fellow women educationalists: 'This was a constant source of consternation to the people in headquarters because no sooner had they got somebody who they thought was going to stay with them for some time, than they were smartly snapped up and married.' Indeed, both Joan Everett and Mary Allen followed this pattern by getting married within a few years of their arrival in West Africa, the former to a police officer, the latter to a District Officer.

The immediate post-war period also saw the start of a decline in the independence of the district office, with a corresponding growth in the power of the provincial or central secretariat. It was to this hub of government – sometimes referred to as the 'scratch box' on the Gold Coast, and as the 'biscuit box' in Northern Rhodesia – that most administrators gravitated as they rose up the ladder of promotion: 'Most people resented going into headquarters; a few were honest and said that they actually enjoyed life at headquarters, and most of us once we got there found there were certain attractions in it, but we felt we were saying goodbye to the touring which we had enjoyed so much as Assistant District Officers.' However, objections to working in an office at headquarters were tempered by the knowledge that promotion came more readily to those who had had secretariat experience:

The District Officer who didn't want to serve anywhere but in a district and who had become an expert in district work had comparatively few opportunities of advancement. He could become a Senior District Commissioner and he could become a Provincial Commissioner in charge of a province where there were perhaps six or seven districts under his control, but he was not usually thought worthy beyond that of promotion to the higher reaches of government. Whereas the secretariat officer had his sights perhaps on becoming the Financial Secretary or the Chief Secretary of the territory and eventually, perhaps, on a governorship.

The fact that nearly all officers were required at some time or other to serve for a period in the secretariat did not prevent a very wide degree of suspicion, bordering on contempt, growing up between these two partners in government – 'the same sort of feeling as exists between a line officer and a staff officer in the army' – which expressed itself in mutual distrust:

The secretariat officer didn't think that these bush-whacking DCs really knew much about what was going on. He thought that they weren't all that well endowed on top, that their letters were not quite up to secretariat standard and that they didn't understand the drift of government policy. On the other hand, the DCs reckoned that if you got a secretariat man away from his car and off a metalled road he would lose his way, and that he didn't understand the language or the country. He was just a good chap on writing letters on subjects on which he wasn't really fully conversant and what he really needed was to come out to a district and get his knees brown.

To officials who, until their most senior years, lived simply and roughly and for whom 'money was always a preoccupation', the matter of promotion and the public recognition of their services meant a great deal. This recognition was most often expressed in the form of a 'c' after some twenty years of service – with perhaps a 'κ' to follow for the high-fliers. But it was not the fact of the award but its timing that was really significant, and this caused considerable heart-searching as every New Year's Honours List was published: 'You tended to scan it to see whether contemporaries of yours in other branches of the service or in other territories had beaten you to it, and where you had been beaten to it you tended to make allowances by saying, "Well, of course, he was lucky. It was a small territory and therefore he got his 'c' earlier than he would have done had he served on with us here in Tanganyika or wherever."'

The peak of the administrator's career was to be found among the governorships, which came in four grades of importance. Nigeria, Kenya, the Gold Coast and Tanganyika all merited a class one governorship; Sierra Leone, Uganda and Northern Rhodesia came into the second category; Nyasaland, the Gambia, British Somaliland and Zanzibar fell into class three. A fledgling governor might serve an apprenticeship on some small Pacific island before moving on up the ladder – provided that he had satisfied his masters in London that he was the right man for the job. Just as the selection of cadets had been greatly influenced by one man, Sir Ralph Furse, so the selection of governors in the post-war period was very much the responsibility of another key figure in the Colonial Office, Dennis Garson, on whose 'A' list were to be found the names of those regarded as fit material for governorships. Kenneth Smith remembers him as a 'naturally unobtrusive chap', who spent much of his time slipping largely unnoticed in and out of various colonial territories and who 'reached the height of his influence in the early fifties when it was his job to assemble these lists for the key governorships when it became necessary for political reasons to replace a governor who had clearly run out of steam in his capacity to cope with local problems.'

The most pressing of these local problems was everywhere the dramatic rise of African nationalism, a phenomenon that could also be said to have had its roots in the war, which had given soldiers from both East and West Africa a glimpse of 'what was happening in other territories round the world – in India, Ceylon, Madagascar and so on. They saw that they all had Independence – or were about to get it – and so they thought that it was time that Africans should also get Independence.' When this awakening of political consciousness was first observed in West Africa it was not viewed with undue alarm. The principle of Independence itself had never really been a major issue: 'All of us who served in the African colonies never had any doubt in our minds from the start that our job was to bring these countries forward to Independence.' But what became increasingly a matter for dispute was the question of the time-scale, because 'everyone was talking about eventual self-government – with the emphasis on the word "eventual".'

At the end of the war there was still 'very little belief that we would be called upon in the course of our careers to hand over to the people we were working with.' Even as late as 1950 – only eight years before Ghanaian Independence – recruits on the Colonial Service Course in London were being assured by a 'much-respected and not illiberal' governor of the Gold Coast, Sir Charles Arden-Clarke, that 'there would be jobs for us there during our lifetimes and the lifetimes of our sons.' This reluctance to face facts was certainly not due to personal motives, because there was undoubtedly a widespread awareness that, in principle, 'we were there to do ourselves out of a job.' But what actually happened, as Darrell Bates found, was that 'once one arrived in Africa and was actually involved in the day to day administration it seemed so remote, to be perfectly honest, that I didn't really give any thought to it. I didn't conceive that a situation would arise in which they would run their own affairs without our help in my lifetime – and how wrong I was.' David Allen, in the Gold Coast, admits to a very similar attitude towards Independence: 'The fact of the matter was that we'd all looked upon Independence – in so far as we had thought about it at all – rather like a young man thinks of old age; something that's going to happen sometime, but it's a very long way ahead and one doesn't pay much attention to it.'

It was the issue of Africans' running their own affairs – in a word, 'Africanization' – that provided the main stumbling block in every territory's progress towards self-government. It was argued that 'there were insufficient trained Africans both in the civil service and outside it to govern the country without it' – but at the same time programmes for the advancement of such a skilled work-force were not being effectively promoted. Nor was opposition to such Africanization programmes entirely one-sided. In Nigel Cooke's opinion the administrator's reluctance in Northern Nigeria to train up or advance Africans for district work could be attributed 'very largely to the deference with which they treated the chiefs' views. They did not want African administrative officers. I had an example of this when I was in Kano, when the chief complained about his African DO taking his wife in the front of his car. I had to explain to him that times had changed and that the African DO was perfectly entitled to carry his wife in the front of his car.'

This failure to build up an indigenous executive cadre was widely recognized as perhaps the greatest error of colonial rule – and, with hindsight, the 'slowness with which we brought people to manage their own affairs' was universally and deeply regretted. Yet this failure was, in James Robertson's opinion, brought about not so much by a lack of will as by 'a lack of imagination'. In 1942 he was one of a group of senior officers in the Sudan whose opinion was sought by the Civil Secretary about the possibility of promoting Sudanese officials to the higher administrative posts: 'Practically everybody said, "No, we couldn't run our province if we had to have these chaps" – because they were not educated enough. I don't think the thing was a rearguard action; it was a wish for good government. They reckoned that they wouldn't get as good a service and as good administration as they had from British officers. They couldn't see that if a country was going to be independent you must take risks and get ahead with these things.'

In fact, Sudan's Africanization programme was in advance of that of the other African colonial territories, and in 1956 it became the first of the British-ruled territories to gain its Independence. When James Robertson was appointed Governor of Nigeria in 1955 he found the contrast between the two territories very striking. In particular he was surprised 'at the delay which had apparently occurred in Nigerianizing the services', and one of his first acts was to call for plans to bring this into rapid effect. In some institutions Africanization was already well advanced, notably in the

Church, which had a long-established tradition of equal partnership. Yet even here a 'paternal attitude' among the older missionaries had been very evident to Bob MacDonald when he first came to Calabar in 1929, and what had changed this attitude was the fact that, through its mission secondary schools, Nigeria had started to produce young men who were proceeding to British universities and coming back as lawyers and doctors and teachers – 'and it was just stupid for us to patronize or be paternal to people who were just as well educated and as widely read as we were. That kind of change brought the older missionaries into line and led the way to a system of integration which gradually handed over the whole of the work and property and the control, from a mission council which was composed of white missionaries to the Senate of the Presbyterian Church of Nigeria. And it came very easily, very happily, very gently.'

Rather more surprisingly, integration in the world of West African commerce was also well advanced. There had always been a tradition of business co-operation between white and black traders that went right back to the days of the slave trade, but the first real breakthrough in integration came with the 1930s slump when many European companies cut down on their white staff, thereby creating vacancies in jobs that had previously been regarded as exclusively European. When Donald Dunnet had first gone out to Nigeria in 1920 it had been taken for granted that 'the white man was superior – and I'm afraid as a young and rather cocky young man I accepted that as a fact. That's the way we lived and that's the way we thought. In those days they said an African could never be a cashier or an African could never do this or that, but, in fact, some of the Africans did the jobs a lot better than any Europeans had ever done.'

Even if they were behind the Sudan in Africanization and integration, Nigeria and the West Coast territories were still a long way ahead of East and Central Africa. The contrast was immediately apparent to Mercedes Mackay when she and her husband transferred from Tanganyika to Nigeria in 1941:

We arrived in the docks in Lagos and the first thing that happened was that our luggage was all put into a blazing hot Customs shed and instantly up marched a very smart-looking black man all in uniform. He said, 'Open that one, please,' and started fumbling all through my underwear and generally sorting things out, and I was absolutely flabbergasted. I couldn't believe my eyes, they were popping, almost literally – that an African would dare to even dream of doing such a thing! A few days later we went to Government House for a cocktail party and there, to my equally amazed eyes, were Africans dressed in dinner jackets and black ties and moving around and being introduced as Mr So and So, Mrs So and So. And you shook hands with them, which was something quite unheard of – and I suddenly began to look at these people and heard them talking perfectly normally, and I realized that they were not only human but most charming human beings. And from that moment on my colour prejudice just faded away.

The first organized anti-Government demonstrations took place on the Gold Coast in February 1948 – 'when Nkwame Nkrumah organized a march on Government House one Saturday afternoon, a time when many people were playing cricket and others were out on the beaches bathing – a move that caught us completely by surprise'. But the one event that really shook British self-confidence more than anything else, and forced home the message that Britain's days in Africa were numbered, was not strictly to do with nationalism at all: 'Mau Mau was the most horrible experience that Kenya has suffered. All civil wars are said to be infinitely more savage than wars between nations and this was certainly true of the Mau Mau business. It was almost unbelievable that the Kikuyu could have inflicted such casualties, and with such brutality, on people of their own sort.' Beginning as sporadic outbursts of violence in the Kikuyu districts of Kenya in 1952, the Mau Mau rebellion took such a hold that eventually a state of emergency had to be declared. For Richard Turnbull, then Minister for Internal Security, quite as much as for the rest of the white population of Kenya, the Emergency had all the characteristics of a nightmare:

The atmosphere of Mau Mau was horrible. Worse than any other civil disorder that I'd ever heard of, or been associated with. Long after the Emergency we were still digging up bodies in Nairobi that had been buried and, as for the forest, goodness knows how many Kikuyu are still buried there. I always think of that passage in Philip Sidney's *Sistina*: 'The scenes I hear when I do hear sweet music, the dreadful cries of murdered men in forests'. There were all kinds of interpretations, most of them, I'm afraid, face-saving from our point of view. But land was at the bottom of it and the whole Mau Mau exercise was part civil war and part rebellion. It was civil war against those Kikuyu who were comfortable as they were, who may have been keen nationalists but were moderate nationalists and were prepared to follow constitutional methods, really the Kikuyu 'haves' against the Kikuyu 'have nots'. The rebellion side of it was a determination to create such havoc in the European farm areas that the Government would have to reach accommodation with them. There wasn't a very large number of European deaths, but those seventy farmers killed were killed in the most savage and terrifying way, and they were seventy of the best.

Two other administrators who were also intimately involved in combating the Mau Mau were Frank Loyd, District Commissioner in the Kikuyu districts of Fort Hall and Kiambu, and Dick Symes-Thompson, who found himself in the thick of it when he came to Kericho in 1953:

I must say the shock of arriving in a district where dead bodies were lying about and people were living in fear of their lives under threat of attack with *pangas* – which is a large type of knife – was very frightening and for the first two or three weeks I was more frightened than I have ever been in my life and I found it difficult to sleep. I was worried about what might happen to myself and my family and I was worried about the situation and how it was to be got under control and so on. It was enormously difficult to know who was the enemy and who was not and this particular situation was tremendously impressed on me when I went round the locations which were for the most part under the charge of young District Officers, Kikuyu Guard – they were called DO's KG – who had had a little military training in the Kenya Regiment after having been at school in England or out in Africa and they were put on their own in charge of an African location of, say, twenty thousand people and given a few tribal policemen and told to recruit loyalist Kikuyu Guard to carry out their defence and to start getting control of the locations. Well, each one built his own guard post, which consisted of a little mud fort and a bamboo house in which the officer lived with his few guards and police and a big ditch around it so that they could be safe from attack at night. And when I questioned these District Officers saying, 'What is your situation, are you safe from attack?' they would say, 'Well, I think I trust three of my men, the others I think are sympathizing with the enemy but I am not quite sure.' This was a terrifying situation for me.

The fight against Mau Mau was won by taking the most drastic measures: 'We decided to concentrate the whole of the population in the district into the villages and this was done. Of course, when it was first begun it was bitterly opposed but because we put all the Kikuyu into the villages this meant that it was easier to consolidate land and once we had started doing this land consolidation, and the people themselves had seen what it actually meant on the ground, it gained in popularity and in Kiambu District we had the curious situation where there were people clamouring to get on to the priority list.'

The war against Mau Mau and the long-term effects of Mau Mau were far-reaching. Above all, 'it led to a realization of what enormous power they – the Africans – had if they but cared to use it.'

# ten

---

# THE FLAGS COME DOWN

*One of the strange things about our presence was the reluctance with
which we appeared to go in and the speed with which we came out.*

For many officers in the field the late 1950s were years of 'tension and
impending tragedy. One could see the clashes coming and we simply didn't
know really what was going to be done about them. We thought vaguely that
the Home Government was moving far too slowly and that there was this
gulf fixed between the nationalist demands and the pace at which we were
allowed to move. Quite clearly there was going to be trouble and we were
going to be caught in the middle of it.' As far as they were concerned the
wind of change had begun to blow long before Macmillan's celebrated – and
belated – speech in 1960:

It was scarcely a prophetic utterance, it was something that we ourselves had
realized for many years and was received pretty cynically by officers in the field.
The Home Government had had one policy under Alan Lennox-Boyd as Colonial
Secretary, which was a policy of a fairly rigid paternalism with talk about eventual
self-government perhaps over the next generation. And then, at the end of 1959,
there was a change of Colonial Secretary and a change of policy, a belated recognition of what was going on when Ian MacLeod came in on a progressive liberal ticket
and we all marched off in the opposite direction, where it was quite clear that
independence for all the colonial territories in Africa was coming within the next
few years.

Until that change of direction there was a strong feeling among senior
administrators that successive Home Governments and British politicians
were not supporting them: 'It was pathetic how little they knew and how
little they cared.' However, with the advent of modern air services the
phenomenon of visiting politicians became increasingly familiar: 'People
came out who didn't know anything, more prepared to talk about what they
thought about it than to take the word of the man on the spot.' Violet
Bourdillon recalls how such visitors to Government House in Nigeria
during the war 'always knew everything. I used to say to my husband,
"What are you going to tell them?" He'd say, "What's the good? They

know it all.'" Occasionally the politician out from home ventured up-country. When Nigel Cooke was Senior Resident in the Jos Plateau Province a 'senior cabinet minister' once dropped in and asked to see some naked pagans:

So the next day we went down the road and when we were about thirty miles outside Jos we saw an old pagan aged about sixty-five wandering along traditionally dressed, which meant to say he had nothing on at all. The politician shouted, 'Stop! Stop!' because he wished to take a photograph. So I got out of the car and went up to the man, slipped him a shilling and said, 'Do you mind if this man takes a photograph? He's an extremely important person from the UK.' So the old gentleman stopped in his tracks and stood there stolidly, while the politician got out of his car and very laboriously took a photograph. But it was from the rear view, and it was then that I realized that these people were not as unsophisticated as I thought, because when I said to him, 'Would you turn around?' – so that this politician could take what would now be called a full-frontal – he said, 'That will be another shilling.' I felt that I had indeed fallen rather low, acting as a pimp for a visiting politician.

But it was not only the Home Government that was 'perpetually being surprised and brought up short by developments'. Almost every territory had to suffer the agony of rioting or of civil disturbance to a greater or lesser degree as it failed to come to terms with nationalist demands. In Nyasaland, so long regarded as the most pacific of territories, the crisis came in 1959 – and it began in Noel Harvey's Karonga District:

Karonga, when I'd first been there, was a very peaceful total backwater, an area of love and trust and affection, with very, very little happening. Your monthly security report was really a joke; you would struggle to think of half a page worth of things to say. Going back after a year and a half away, suddenly you found yourself being spat at, you found people afraid to talk to you, a completely different atmosphere, an atmosphere of dumbness and distrust. Now when I got back we went straight into the thick of this tension, and it built up to a point where, on a Sunday at the very beginning of March, the DC came into my house and said, 'Noel, they are holding an illegal meeting right outside my house as a gesture and they want to see what I'm going to do about it.' And I said, 'Oh.' And he said, 'We'll have to do something, won't we?' And I said, Yes, I'm sure we shall.' Then I looked at him and said, 'What do you think we ought to do, Gordon?' Here was a toy-town situation; we had an African police officer, one sergeant and three constables on the station, and the meeting was of about three hundred people. So the DC and the African sub-inspector and myself went and arrested the leaders of the meeting, who were all sitting round a table waiting for us to come. We none of us had arms; obviously it would have been ridiculous to carry a gun. The DC came in his car because he thought that he would then take the leaders of the meeting in his car and appear to drive them right outside the area of the settlement. In fact, what he was going to do was go round in a big loop and come back to the police station and charge them. Well, all we did in fact was to leave plenty of time for the 347 people left at the meeting to get to the police station and be waiting for us when we got there. They then pressed so tightly on the police station that we couldn't get out of one office and out on to the verandah and back into the next office to get the charge papers, and we had this ludicrous situation where we had to say to them, 'Look, we know you, you know us. You are going to hear more about this, but we can't actually formally charge you on paper now. Off you go.' Meanwhile they ripped the flag off the DC's car, smashed his windscreen, planted an axe in the bonnet and bust the windows in the police station. And that actually was the first riot of the emergency.

Those caught up in such emergencies were no doubt unaware that they were part of an over-all pattern of events that was being followed with depressing consistency right across the continent and elsewhere; 'a repetitive pattern of leaders of African opinion being arrested, imprisoned and brought back as future governors of their country'. Patrick Mullins witnessed this cycle of mistakes twice, first in the Gold Coast, then in Nyasaland:

It happened to one particular colonial officer I can think of, first of all as a senior official in the Gold Coast with Nkrumah, then as Governor of Cyprus with Makarios, and finally as Governor of Nyasaland with Banda. In each case they had to graduate from prison before they could pass an essential stage in their journey towards becoming rulers of their own countries. In Ghana they wore 'PG' on their caps – 'Prison Graduate' it stood for – and they realized better than we did that before they were going to get anywhere they'd got to go to prison and then be brought out again and reinstated. And the reason for this I think was because the governors and indeed the colonial administration generally – as well as the Home Government – couldn't accustom themselves to the pace of the change that was beginning to sweep Africa. They were always holding on until too late and making their concessions too late, and then having to make much larger concessions and adopt far shorter time-scales than we thought they were going to have to do.

After the Sudan, the next African territory to complete the cycle was the Gold Coast. Its peaceful transition from Gold Coast to Ghana provided a valuable model for the others to follow. One of those who participated in the hand-over of power was George Sinclair:

The two main catalytic agents apart from Nkrumah and the two nationalist movements themselves were Sir Charles Arden-Clarke, who came as the new governor shortly after the riots, and Reginald Salaway, with his background of experience in India. Charles Arden-Clarke was completely different from the governors that we had experienced. He came to us with a realization that new forces were on the move and they'd got to be made to work constructively rather than to be held back. The phrase he used was, 'I believe in making the inevitable the basis of my policy and I believe it is better to channel water to useful purposes rather than dam it up and let it overflow and destroy the country below it.' He caught the imagination of leaders who had been in prison and got them to work with him and we then embarked on what was a real honeymoon period, with the overseas administration and all the departments working together with the politicians, and African staff coming up towards senior posts as fast as we could bring them on and as fast as they could take themselves up there. And this was for many people, I think, both African and European, a golden period.

Dressed in elaborate uniforms designed, so it was said, for the Crimean campaign – 'the white uniform was quite cool but the blue uniform was devised by the Colonial Office to kill off governors' – the retiring governors of the late 1950s made easy scapegoats as symbols of discarded policies that had been tried and found wanting. There were, indeed, diehards among them, as well as tired men who had stayed on a year or two longer than they should have, but there were others who had in their time been considered dangerously liberal. It was their fate to be replaced by a last batch of governors – realists who bulldozed their territories through into Independence – of quite exceptional quality.

Nigeria's last colonial governor was Sir James Robertson, the very antithesis of the pompous colonial official of popular imagination and 'not a chap who got excited about protocol or pomp'. Although he accepted the necessity for ceremony, 'whenever the opportunity came I used to take my glad rags off and go about in my shorts and shirt – and I don't think that did me any harm. What one heard was that the Nigerians were very pleased that one sort of got down to their level and talked to them and didn't throw one's weight about too much.' As the Governor's Lady Nancy Robertson shared the same unassuming outlook. What had most struck her when she and her husband moved into Government House in Lagos in 1956 was the fact that she now had her nightdress ironed every day:

But I think it was probably lonelier for me than it had ever been even in the very early days because I had to be very careful about what I said. The only time I said what I thought, which was over Suez, I was indirectly ticked off. It was also very tiresome until I had a little car of my own because I couldn't go out to coffee without ordering a Rolls-Royce or its equivalent and the people who were going to be there had obviously put on stockings for the only time in six months. It didn't make for comfortable living, but from the other side I had the privilege of meeting people and entertaining people that I would never have approached in ordinary life.

Although there were arguments over timing as well as friction and disharmony between North and South over the question of federation, the actual transition of power in Nigeria took place without a hitch. 'It is the fashion to talk about the fight for liberation but in fact there was no fight in Nigeria. The whole thing went incredibly smoothly.'

In Tanganyika, however, the situation was rapidly deteriorating when Sir Richard Turnbull took over as governor in 1958. 'Governor Turnbull, when he came to us was very different,' recalls Charles Meek. 'I remember, from the speech he made at his swearing-in, my neighbour saying, "He's come to pack us up." Well, so he had. The whole trend which he was to follow through with such skill and persistence in the next three and a half years was to speed up this process of Independence which had looked so infinitely remote to us in my early days, and which was suddenly rushing upon us at a breakneck speed – but a speed which could not be slowed down at all without the risk of the most violent bloodshed and disruption.'

Richard Turnbull began his governorship with appalling disadvantages:

I came there as the hammer of the Mau Mau, the oppressor of nationalists, the associate of the wicked Kenya settler, and all these were pretty strong factors working against me. Luckily I'd been speaking Swahili for thirty years and I spoke it with some fluency and could cap any proverb in Swahili with another proverb in Swahili, and although my accent was a horrible Kenya one, that was my trump card – that and my friendship with Julius Nyerere were the two things that saw me through. Because when I arrived in Tanganyika and recognized how extremely strong the Tanganyika African National Union was I decided that what I must do was to get in touch with the leader of TANU and find out what kind of a fellow he was and let him see what kind of a chap I was and see if we could work together. Luckily I had a very gentle, generous leader of the opposition with whom I immediately came to terms, and we became close personal friends, and that was Julius Nyerere. What the position would have been if I'd had a blundering bully-boy to work with I don't honestly know.

Governor Turnbull now accepted that in Tanganyika, as in so many other territories, 'the old axis of the administration and the African authorities, the chiefs and chiefs in council, which previously held the country together, was disintegrating.' Instead, there was 'a very tricky path' to tread: 'I had to move fast enough with Julius Nyerere to meet the demands of the wilder element of TANU, because if I had kept Julius down to the speed that I wanted and that the Colonial Office wanted he would have been discredited. But if I went as fast as Julius's men wanted him to go then the Colonial Office would have been extremely alarmed and the administration in Tanganyika would have been horror-struck. So I had to tread this rather tricky path with the greatest care.'

It was now this question of pace that provided the major cause of heart-searching among government officials, the great majority of whom would agree with Anthony Lytton's opinion that the hand-over of power was 'too swift at the end, too slow at the start'. In Kenya Frank Loyd feared, as did so many of his colleagues in other territories, that 'there simply wasn't going to be time to achieve an orderly Independence. This came as a great shock and surprise, and we wanted time. We were too involved and too fond of the country and our friends in Kenya to want to have to rush to Independence. We didn't think we would be able to do this in such a short time and in the event I am more than delighted that we were proved so conclusively wrong.' Another common fear was that 'in some ways the machine was going to go backwards: government was going to be less efficient, possibly more corrupt after Independence.' Yet it was also realized that this was not really the main issue: 'The important point was that they had to learn to run their own show and the time had come where there was absolutely no option at all but that they must start running it themselves.' To Joan Everett in Nigeria the African point of view was expressed in very much the same terms: 'I remember an African friend saying to me that when the Romans were ruling Britain Boadicea didn't seem to think that they were the right people to be in control and, in the same way, even if Nigeria *wasn't* up to Independence standards in the eyes of the rest of the world, they wanted Independence and if there were going to be any mistakes they'd like to make them themselves.'

After the months of feverish activity and negotiation that had led up to it, the actual hand-over of power often came as something of an anti-climax. Ceremonies, church services and parades followed in quick succession, culminating in the lowering of the old flag at midnight and the raising of the new: 'The Prime Minister and I walked out together,' recalls James Robertson:

I had to wear my uniform, feathers and hat and medals and things and we stood on a little dais and the Union Jack was illumined by searchlights and the band played 'God Save the Queen'. The lights went out and the flag was lowered and then the new Nigerian flag was hoisted to the top of the flag pole. The lights went on and the bands played the new Nigerian anthem. And I noticed the Prime Minister was really affected by this, tears were running down his face when I turned and shook him by the hand and congratulated him. But to me it was a parade, it wasn't nearly so emotive as the bit in my own house. We hadn't any official ceremony for this but I and some of my staff gathered and stood by as the Union Jack came down and I must say that this was the most moving part of the whole show for me.

Different individuals celebrated or noted the coming of Independence in different ways. 'I spent the evening of Independence Day alone,' recalls Philip Allison. 'I could have gone to various parties but somehow I never got there in the end. I sat alone in the rest-house in Abaykuta listening to the new national anthem, "Nigeria we hail thee, our home and native land" being played on the radio. I was working in the museums in a job I enjoyed and I'd have gone on longer doing this, but I wasn't so preoccupied with it that I wasn't prepared to think of a new life in England. I was comparatively young so it wasn't all that of a wrench – I can't pretend it was.' In Adamawa Province in the North Cameroons Nigel Cooke lowered the flag outside the Residency: 'I don't think that I or the other administrative officers felt any particular emotion about the occasion – and the next day we went back to work as normal.'

Inevitably the coming of Independence brought casualties in its wake. There was, in particular, 'one constant feature of development' that disturbed many administrators – 'the necessity to abandon friends who believed we were there for keeps'. Kenneth Smith saw it happening in varying degrees in all the territories in which he served, 'from Zanzibar on to the Seychelles, to Aden and the Gambia. Always the foreign servant, such as myself, has retired home to his pension and a search for another job, but he is unhappily aware that he has left friends who trusted the continuence of the British presence very dangerously exposed to the incoming régimes.' Nowhere was this concern more evident than in Kenya with its recent experience of Mau Mau: 'Naturally we were very afraid that the chiefs and the Kikuyu District officials and others, who had remained throughout staunch supporters of the Government and had done very good work with us, would be victimized in an independent Kenya. This, in the event, proved to be totally wrong and in fact many of those men either remained in the jobs they were doing in the administration or were promoted into others, and to this day have remained as some of the pillars of the Government in Kenya itself.'

Nevertheless, there were territories where such fears were indeed realized, as in Malawi – formerly Nyasaland – where 'the Africans on the spot were categorized as stooges and traitors, having first of all been loyal to the previous régime. No provision was made for their future and many of them suffered at least professionally, if not in other ways, and we felt there had been a betrayal of them.' By contrast, European officials who chose to stay on were made very welcome: 'Those who wanted to come away were provided with pensions and with compensation for loss of their careers. Those who wanted to stay were received in a most friendly fashion by Dr Banda, who made room for European civil servants in his Government for some years after Independence and quite frankly told his Africans that they wouldn't get those jobs until they were of a standard where they could really occupy them.'

It was the same in most newly independent territories, where 'life went on much the same but the facial colour of the officers next to you changed.'

A great many officials did stay on for perhaps one or two tours after Independence before beginning to feel – as Nigel Cooke did – increasingly conscious that they were becoming redundant: 'I remember saying to the Superintendent of Police on one of the rare occasions when I was in my white uniform that I felt I was an anachronism and it was about time I left.' And so in their turn they too became constitutional casualties. 'We saw our chosen careers fading away when we were all at our most vigorous,' observes Charles Meek, 'deprived of the prospects of all the glittering prizes which young men aspire to when they enter a great service like my own. Some will have felt things harder than others; there are some, I am sure, who felt that it was all wrong that Independence should have been conceded as early as it was. I believe that it was a fact of life, that it had to be.'

And so the anachronisms – 'we are now an extinct species as colonial servants; the conservationists didn't reach us in time' – began their departures, taking their leave always with mixed feelings, with hopes and fears for the future, pride and regrets about the past, and sharing the conviction – for all the prevailing mood of hostility towards anything that smacked of colonialism – that their work had been to some good purpose. Mistakes had indeed been made and, in Sir Alan Burns' opinion:

The greatest mistake was to expect an average colony to support itself. But when one considers colonial rule one has got to remember what was there before it started. Cannibalism, slavery, human sacrifice and various other abominations all existed in Nigeria and the Gold Coast. So I'm quite certain that colonialism was a good thing from the point of view of the African native himself. It taught him respect for the law, it removed him from the constant fear of witchcraft and it taught him also that you could have a democratic government instead of the absolute rule of the chiefs.

Sir James Robertson also believes that to judge Britain's colonial record it is necessary to know about the past:

I think a great deal is now spoken by people who don't know very much about the background to our rule in Africa. When we took over many of these countries there was very little government, there was very little civilization, there was a great deal of inter-tribal warfare. Our policy in these countries was, as Virgil said, *imponere paces mores*, to impose the ways of peace, and that's what we did, and we developed them as best we could. One of the things that our critics seem to forget is that we had no money. The British Government gave us nothing for many, many years. In Sudan, which I know best, when Kitchener defeated the armies of the Mahdi at Omdurman in 1898 there were no railways, there were no telegraphs, there were no schools, there were no hospitals, there was no sort of modern government with ministries or anything of that kind. And when we left the Sudan there was a system of railways, there was a system of roads, there was a police force, there was an army, there were hospitals, there were schools, there was even a university. This was all done in the space of about fifty-eight years – and you could walk from one end of the Sudan to the other more safely than you could walk in the back streets of London, without any fear of danger. We had set up a civilization which had not existed before.

But the imposition of a *Pax Britannica* meant also the imposition of alien ways and customs that had little relevance to African life. A prime example in Sir Richard Turnbull's opinion was British parliamentary democracy: 'We always thought that the political system that happens to suit us in this northern part of Europe is suited to Africa and to the extraordinary tribal society that exists there. It is not. The single party state is what's wanted, although I must admit that we were badly shaken when we first came across the single party state. For us who grew up in the thirties and saw the dictatorships arising, the single party state and fascism are not so far apart and to us it was very distasteful.' In very much the same way there were differences of opinion as to the efficiency – or indeed the relevance – of the English legal code in the African context. Nowhere was the contrast more apparent than in Northern Nigeria, where Nigel Cooke found that 'the administration of law was seen in a very different light by Moslems and the British. We were always against native judges carrying on cases in their houses, and were all in favour of the pomp and ceremony of the law. And this was brought home to me when a new Chief Justice for Northern Nigeria came to Bida, which is the headquarters of an important emirate, and explained at length why he was building a new court-house which would add prestige to the region and increase trade and so on. And he received what I saw to be an absolutely stinging rebuff when a member of the council looked at him and said, "Can you explain what this has to do with justice?"'

Even more damaging to African sensibilities was the initial assumption of racial superiority which had long continued to be expressed in the form of benevolent paternalism: 'When the paternalistic era became a bit outmoded we perhaps weren't very clever in dropping it and adjusting ourselves to getting the right sort of relationship with the new, educated, politically minded African. We preferred dealing with the backward people who we thought were manly and honest and straightforward – we didn't perhaps like so much dealing with the clever politician.' A very similar 'early and abiding error' was made in concentrating 'too much on the happy and progressive development of rural agricultural communities and too little on what was happening under our noses in the big urban centres. Your urban population was never treated with the careful analysis of its hopes and fears that events subsequently proved they required.'

These were the errors of extreme conservatism, a negative side of British colonial rule that was nevertheless, in the opinion of most of those who served in the African colonial territories, outweighed by its merits. 'In our moments of depression we would wonder whether really we were doing any good,' declares Sir Gerald Reece:

I myself came to the conclusion that the British were doing more than perhaps most other nations would do in that we were serving a purpose. Undoubtedly we interfered with the Africans, sometimes by trying to introduce our own way of life which didn't suit them, but, on the whole, I believe that the British did set an example for them to follow if they wanted to do so. Our attitude to such things as honesty and tolerance, our belief that an absence of bribery and corruption amongst officials produced the best results, and above all the idea that if we have a responsibility and are put in charge of others, it is up to us to serve the people in any way that we can. That was a great lesson I think that the British have left behind in Africa.

And was it all, in the light of later events, a waste of time? Chris Farmer, looking back on his own experience in Nigeria, believes that it was not: 'Of course, it's easy enough looking back to be cynical and disillusioned. It's easy to say, "God, what a mess they've made of it." But then you look back over English history and you say to yourself, "Well, look, we and the Nigerians together" – and it *was* a partnership, you know – "in the course of a mere sixty years we brought Nigeria along a road which took us British unaided in this country how many hundreds of years?" And so, looking at it in its historical perspective, I don't think we did badly.'

And so the British departed, sometimes accompanied by regrets – 'because one regrets leaving the country where one's left a large chunk of one's heart, as one regrets leaving the life one lived and the job that one was doing' – sometimes with relief – 'ninety-nine per cent sheer joy at going home, one per cent great sadness'. Some left with tears: 'I will admit to crying as I saw the Land Rover drive out of the gate carrying my personal servants, with whom I had very happy relations for many years and of whom I was very, very fond – and I much feared that they were going to have a far less happy life in the future.' Others left with a sense of satisfaction, 'from the fact that in spite of all the dire warnings before I went to Africa that I would never survive, twenty-eight years in tropical Africa didn't seem so bad.' Some 'dreaded the flatness' that lay ahead after what was 'the most vivid part' of their lives, and some faced the future rather more pragmatically: 'I loved my thirty years in Africa but when finally I came back to England I came back to the country in which I was born and which I dearly loved. I no longer have some of the joys of living in Africa and I'd love to go back, but I have no desire to go and live there again.'

With every departing ex-colonial there went 'the memories which you live on in your old age'. Perhaps the 'recollection of camels rolling in the dust around a big fire at the end of a long walk'; 'hippos surfacing and sounding like very old men laughing at jokes'; 'the herdsmen whistling to their cattle as they munched their way through the long grass'; 'the coming of the rains after a dry spell – suddenly down it comes, like thunder, and we all rush out and just stand there and get drenched in it – and then up comes the beautiful smell of grateful earth'; the sound of the African dove – 'for all the world like the bouncing of a ping-pong ball, only very musical' – and the sounds of 'house-boys chattering on the back of the verandah and laughing their lovely, fat, uninhibited laughter'; the smell of wood-smoke in camp or from village fires and the universal African sounds of cocks crowing at dawn and the drums beating at night: 'It wasn't right on the doorstep, it was down in the town, and so it used to rise up to the Residency and you could hear this going on all the time until eventually, of course, you didn't hear it at all because it was like mosquitoes – you hear the pinging to begin with and then you don't hear them any more. And the drumming was comforting in a way, it was the feeling that everybody was content, and if there hadn't been any drumming it would have been a bit sinister somehow.'

Coming home in the mid-1960s was a depressing experience for many ex-colonials and their wives. They came back to an England where the public image of colonialism and the colonial servant was very different from their own: 'I think we were viewed at home as a lot of rather superior beings who'd come along via the Somerset Maugham route, living in luxury and drinking gins in large clubs and flying their flags in large cars as they passed through their districts.' Even more wounding was the 'complete lack of interest in what had happened in Africa in the last fifty years. It was all forgotten, as though it had never been, and all that replaced it was an aura of bright optimism about how much better it was going to be without us.' Veronica Short was asked by friends what her husband had done in Africa: 'When I told them that he had been a District Officer it meant nothing to them at all, they had no idea what he had done. This I found rather sad because I felt that he and all the other people in the Colonial Service had done an extremely good job with very little reward and all that seemed to have been ignored by England and the world at large.'

There was perhaps one final consolation. With Independence the last of the barriers between the races had come down, so that now – 'We find that we can be completely at ease and talk in the friendliest possible way and there isn't, as perhaps some people might expect, a legacy of hatred or dislike. One feels that one is back with real friends and they always say, and I'm sure they mean it, "Do come back we'd love to see you."'

WALTER THOMAS

# Elder Dempster Lines
## Passenger List

# NOTES ON CONTRIBUTORS

Sir William ADDIS, KBE, CMG, Brilliant Star of Zanzibar, 3rd Class; born 1901; joined Colonial Service 1924; served in Zanzibar and N. Rhodesia; Private Sec. to Sultan of Zanzibar 1939–45; Colonial Sec. Bermuda 1945–50; Governor of Seychelles 1953–8; Foreign Office.

David ALLEN, MBE; born 1916; joined Colonial Service 1938; ADC Kumasi, Gold Coast 1938–40; DC Mampong 1940–42, Obuasi 1943–4, Kumasi 1945–8; Secretariat 1949–50; DC Kumasi 1950–53; Asst. Regional Officer Trans-Volta Togoland 1953–5; Perm. Sec. Min. of Health 1955–8, Min. of Economic Affairs 1959; retired 1959.

Mary ALLEN (née Moon); born 1928 India, father in army; teacher for the Army School, Accra 1950–52; married David Allen 1953; lived in Gold Coast 1950–58, two children born in Gold Coast.

Philip ALLISON, ISO; born 1907; joined Nigerian Forest Dept. 1931; Forest Officer Anambra and Rivers States, S. Nigeria 1931–3; Ondo, Oyo, Ogun and Benin before and after Second World War; in 'Middle Belt' during war; working tours of other territories for Nigerian Govt.; retired from Forestry 1960 to collect traditional art for Nigerian Museums 1960–62; pub. incl. *Cross River Monoliths, African Stone Sculpture.*

Sir Darrell BATES, CMG, CVO; born 1913; joined Colonial Service 1935; ADC Bagamoyo 1936–7, Kiberege 1937–8, Mbulu 1939–40, Tanganyika; King's African Rifles 1940–43; seconded Colonial Office 1944–7; DC Same, 1948–9, Tabora 1949–50, Tanganyika; OAG Seychelles 1950–51; Deputy Chief Sec. Somaliland 1951–3; Colonial Sec. Gibraltar 1953–68; pub. incl. *A Fly-switch from the Sultan, The Mango and the Palm, A Gust of Plumes.*

Lady Susan BATES (née Sinclair); born 1923; brother Sir George Sinclair, Colonial Service; married Darrell Bates 1944; lived in Tanganyika, Seychelles and Gibraltar; two of three children born in Tanganyika.

Lady Violet BOURDILLON; born 1886; married Bernard Bourdillon, ICS, later Governor of Uganda and Nigeria, 1910; accompanied him to India,

Iraq, Ceylon, Uganda 1932–5 and Nigeria 1935–43; three sons born in India and Baghdad, of whom two joined Colonial Service and one joined Colonial Office.

Col. Sir Hugh BOUSTEAD, KBE, CMG, MC; born 1895; RN and SA Brig. 1913–19; Gordon Highlands, Turkey 1921–4; joined Sudan Camel Corps 1924, commanded SCC 1931; joined Sudan Political Service 1935, DC W.Dist., Darfur 1935–40; Col. Sudan Defence Force Brig., Eritrea 1941–5; rejoined SPS 1945; Brit. Agent E. Aden 1949–58; Dev. Sec. Muscat and Oman 1958–61; Brit. Pol. Agent Abu Dhabi 1961–5; pub. *The Wind of Morning*.

Sir Alan BURNS, GCMG; born 1887; grandfather Auditor-General, Leeward Islands, father Treasurer St Kitts-Nevis; Colonial Service Leeward Islands 1905–12; Asst. Sec. Nigeria 1912–24; Cameroons Exped. Force 1914–15, Egba rebellion 1918; Colonial Sec. Bahamas 1924–8; Deputy Chief Sec. Nigeria 1929–34; Governor Brit. Honduras 1934–9; Colonial Office 1940–41; Governor Gold Coast 1941–7; Acting Governor Nigeria 1942; pub. *Nigeria Handbook, History of Nigeria, Colonial Civil Servant*.

Nigel COOKE; born 1916; father mining engineer N. Nigeria 1910–51; joined Colonial Service 1937; ADO Maiduguri, N. Nigeria 1938; military service 1939–43; Prov. Admin. as ADO, DO, Senior DO and Acting Resident N. Nigeria 1943–57; Resident Benue Prov. 1957–9; Senior Resident Adamawa Prov. 1959–61, N. Cameroons Plebiscite; Senior Resident Jos Plateau Prov. 1961; Senior Resident Kano Prov. 1961–2; retired 1962.

Joyce 'Catherine' DINNICK-PARR, MBE; born 1912; WRNS 1943–7; Woman Education Officer, Special Duties, Tiv Division, N. Nigeria 1947–51; Organizer Home Economics Kaduna, touring N. Nigeria 1951–9; Chief Educ. Officer (Women) N. Nigeria 1959–63; retired 1963.

Donald DUNNET; born 1899; after demob. joined Miller Bros. (Liverpool); posted Lagos, African and Eastern Trad. Corp. (later merged into UAC) 1920; Port Harcourt and other stations E. Nigeria 1922; opened trading posts Enugu–Makurdi railway 1926–8; Native Foodstuffs Officer and Palm-oil Mill Manager 1930–31; Dist. Manager Onitsha 1932–4; Asst. Manager Port Harcourt Area 1934–41; Govt. Lend-Lease 1942–4; Merchandise Manager W. and N. Nigeria 1944–5; Director UAC Motors 1946–61.

Mrs Marjorie DUNNET (*née* Wiles); born 1900; married Donald Dunnet 1928; went to Nigeria 1930; lived in Port Harcourt, Ibagwa, Onitsha, Calabar, Usambura (Ruanda Urundi), Lagos; left Nigeria 1948.

Edwin EVERETT, OBE, QPM; born 1916; joined Colonial Police Service, Nigeria, 1938; Sub-Inspector Lagos, Badagri 1938–40; RWAFF 1940–43;

recalled Nigeria Police Lokoja 1943–4; Adviser, Native Authority Police Bornu and Bauchi Provs.; Asst. Commissioner of Police 1945–61; Commandant, Preventive Service, Member, Board of Customs and Excise 1961–5.

Mrs Joan EVERETT (*née* Way); born 1923; taught at Sherborne School for Girls 1945–9; joined Colonial Education Service 1949; Woman Education Officer Sokoto, N. Nigeria; married Edwin Everett 1950; two daughters brought up largely in Nigeria; taught at St Saviour's School, Lagos 1961–4; left Nigeria 1965.

Christopher FARMER; born 1921; joined Colonial Service 1942; ADO Kano, Hadejia, Katsina, 1942–5, Nigeria; Private Sec. to Chief Commissioner N. Prov., 1946; Secretariat, Lagos 1947–9; DO Hadejia, Kano 1950–51, Zaria 1952–7, Senior DO Kabba 1957–8; Acting Resident Kabba Prov. 1958; Senior Asst. Sec., Premier's Office and Deputy Perm. Sec. Local Govt. N. Region 1959–60; Acting Perm. Sec. 1961; Resident and Prov. Sec. Bauchi 1961–3.

Sir Angus GILLAN, KBE, CMG, Order of the Nile, 2nd Class; born 1885; joined Sudan Political Service 1909; Deputy-Inspector El Obeid 1910–12, Asst.-Inspector Nahud 1913–16, Asst. Political Officer, Sudan Western Frontier Force 1916; DC Nyala, Darfur 1917–18; Abuhin, Red Sea Prov. 1919–20; Deputy Governor Berber Prov. 1920–21; Deputy Governor Nuba Mtn. Prov. 1921–8; Governor Kordofan Prov. 1928–32; Asst. Civil Sec. 1932; Civil Sec. 1934; retired 1939.

Harry St. Leger GRENFELL, OBE, MC; born 1905; grandfather Earl Grey, director BSA Co. and Administrator S. Rhodesia 1896–8, mother accompanied C. J. Rhodes Matopo hills 1896; worked in Lupa goldfields, Tanganyika 1932–6; joined BSA Co. Rhodesia 1938; war service 1939–44; in charge BSA Co. office Lusaka, N. Rhodesia 1946–56; Executive Director BSA Co. (merged Charter Consolidated) 1956–70.

Noel HARVEY; born 1929; joined Colonial Service 1953; ADC Karonga 1954, Mzuzu 1956, Mzimba 1958, Nyasaland; DC Rumpi 1958, Karonga 1959, Mzuzu 1959–60; Admin. Officer Soche 1961, DC Blantyre (Urban) 1962–4; married 1956, three children born in Nyasaland; retired 1964.

Anthony KIRK-GREENE, MBE; born 1925; grandparents in India; war service Indian Army; joined Colonial Service 1949; ADO Adamawa 1950–54, Bida 1954–5, N. Nigeria; Private Sec. Min. of Works, Kaduna 1955–6; DO Bornu 1956–7; Inst. of Admin., Zaria 1957–9; Senior DO 1960; Chief Info. Officer N. Nigeria 1960–61; Reader in Public Admin., Ahmadi Bello Univ., Zaria 1961–7; pub. *Principles of Native Administration, On Governors and Governorship, Biog. Dict. of Colonial Governors.*

Mrs Sylvia LEITH-ROSS (*née* Ruxton), MBE; born 1883; father W. African Slave Patrol 1840s, brother Royal Niger Constab., later Lt. Governor S. Prov. Nigeria; in 1906 married Capt. Arther Leith-Ross, WAFF, N. Nigeria, died at Zungeru 1908; returned to Nigeria 1910, studied Fulani; first Lady Supt. of Education, Nigeria 1926–31, invalided home; research Nigeria 1934–8; worked for Lagos and Jos Museums 1956–69; pub. *Fulani Grammar, African Women, Nigerian Pottery*.

Sir Martin LINDSAY, Bt., CBE, DSO, King's Polar Medal; born 1905; father Gurkha Rifles; joined Royal Scots Fusiliers 1925; seconded 4th Bttn. Nigeria Rgt., Abadan, 1927–9; explored through Belgian Congo to E. Africa 1929 and later explored Polar regions; MP after war service.

Sir Frank LOYD, KCMG, OBE; born 1916; joined Colonial Service 1938; ADO Embu 1939, Garissa 1940; war service, Ethiopia 1940–42; DC Mandera 1942; Private Sec. Governor 1943–5; DC Moyale 1945, Kakamega 1946; married Katherine, daughter Kenya settler 1946; DC Kapenguria 1947, Nyeri 1948, Fort Hall 1949–53, Kiambu 1954; Prov. Commiss. Central Prov. 1956, Nyanza 1959; Acting Chief Commiss. 1960; Perm. Sec. and Sec. to Cabinet 1961–3; Commiss. Swaziland 1964–8.

Noel Anthony LYTTON (Lytton-Millbank), 4th Earl of Lytton; born 1900; grandfather Viceroy of India, uncle Governor of Bengal; joined Rifle Brigade 1921; seconded 4th Bttn. King's African Rifles, Kenya 1922–7; Nairobi 1922–4; Administrator Samburu and Turkhana Dist, NFD 1924–5; rejoined Rifle Brigade 1927; pub. incl. *The Desert and the Green*.

Rev. Robert MACDONALD, OBE, MA, DD; born 1903; became Church of Scotland Missionary 1929; stationed at Ikot Inyang, Itu, E. Nigeria 1929–52; Admin. Superintendent and Chaplain, Itu leper colony 1952–67; left Nigeria 1967.

Mrs Mercedes MACKAY; born 1905; married Robert Mackay, mining geologist 1933; with husband to Mines Dept., Tanganyika 1934; stationed in Dar es Salaam, Mwanza, Lupa goldfields, Mbaya; three children born in Tanganyika; local corresp. *East Africa Standard*; with husband to Geological Survey, Nigeria 1941; stationed Jos, Kaduna, Ibadan; worked in Ibadan local radio; left Nigeria 1950; pub. *Indomitable Servant*.

Charles MEEK, CMG; born 1920; grandfather Indian Army, father Resident Nigeria; joined Colonial Service 1941; ADO Lindi 1941–3, Shinyanga 1943–5, Maswa 1945–7, Arusha 1947–9, Tanganyika; DC Masai 1949–50; Mbulu 1950–56; Secretariat 1956–8; Minist. Sec. 1958; Perm. Sec. and Sec. to Cabinet 1959; Head of Civil Service 1961; retired 1962.

Nona MEEK; born 1921; WRNS 1941–6; married Charles Meek 1947; lived in Arusha, Masai, Mbulu, Dar es Salaam 1947–62; three children born in Arusha, Tanganyika.

Lt. Col. Brian MONTGOMERY, MBE; born 1903; grandfather ICS, father Bishop Tasmania, uncle Commiss. Kenya, brother Chief Native Commiss. Kenya; seconded to 3rd Bttn. KAR, Kenya 1927–32; stationed Nairobi and Wajir, Mandera, NFD; transferred to Indian Army; Diplomatic Service.

Betty MORESBY-WHITE (née Brandt); born 1918; both grandfathers ICS, brother Nigeria Admin. Service; married Hugh Moresby-White 1936; lived in Abeokuta and Oyo until 1944.

HUGH MORESBY-WHITE, CMG; born 1891; joined Colonial Service 1914; ADC Ijebu Ode, Onitsha, S. Nigeria 1915; ADC Ijebu Ode 1917–18; taxation riots, Abeokuta Prov. 1918; Ijebu Ode 1920–22; Owerri 1923, Oyo Prov. 1925–7; Secretariat Enugu and Lagos 1927–32; Resident Abeokuta Prov. 1933–40; Senior Resident Oyo Prov. 1941–4; retired 1944.

Patrick MULLINS; born 1922; joined Colonial Service 1950; ADC Damongo, Gambaga, Bole, Northern Territories Gold Coast 1951–2; Secretariat Zomba, Nyasaland 1952–5; ADC Mzimba 1955–6, Chikwawa 1958–9, Fort Johnston 1959–60; Secretariat, Clerk Legislative Assembly 1962–3; Princip. Sec. Pub. Serv. Commission 1963–4; retired 1964.

William PAGE; born 1904; junior clerk Lloyds Bank 1921; joined Bank of Brit. W. Africa 1926; clerk and cashier Accra, Gold Coast 1927–8; cashier Bathurst, Gambia 1928–30; joined Abbey National Building Soc. 1930; later teacher.

Lady Alys REECE (née Tracy), MBE; born 1912; married Gerald Reece 1936; lived at Marsabit and Isiolo in NFD, Kenya, and at Hargeisa, Somaliland; two daughters, one son born in Kenya, one son in Somaliland; pub. *To My Wife – 50 Camels*.

Sir Gerald REECE, KCMG, CBE; born 1897 New Zealand; war service, solicitor; joined Kenya Admin. Service 1925; ADC Kakamega, Kacheliba, Kolosia; DC Mandera, Moyale, Marsabit, NFD; HBM's Consul for S. Ethiopia 1934; Officer-in-Charge, NFD 1939; Senior Pol. Officer Borana Prov., Ethiopia 1941; Prov. Commiss., N. Prov. Kenya 1945; Governor and C.-in-C. Somaliland 1948–53; retired 1953.

Sir James ROBERTSON, Kt, GCMG, GCVO, KBE; born 1899; grandfather and father in India; joined Sudan Political Service 1922; ADC Rufa'a, Kamlin 1922–5, Geteina, Duein 1925–30; Duein, Rosieries 1930–33; DC Nahud 1933–6; Sub-Governor White Nile Prov. 1937–9; Deputy Governor and Acting Governor Gezira Prov. 1939–41; Asst. and Civil Sec. 1941–5; Chief Sec. 1945–53; Brit. Guiana Constit. Commission 1953–4; Governor-General and C.-in-C. Nigeria 1955–60.

Lady Nancy ROBERTSON (*née* Walker); born 1903; married James Robertson 1926; lived and travelled extensively in White Nile, Fung, W. Kordofan and Gezira Provs., Sudan 1926–53 and in Nigeria 1955–60.

Clifford RUSTON; born 1900; father Lagos Stores Ltd 1895–6; after demob. joined Lagos Stores Ltd, Lagos 1919 (later merged into UAC); posted Zaria 1921, Kano 1921; stationed in Zaria, Kano, Jos, Makurdi as District Manager 1923–39; war service RWAFF; Gen. Manager covering Benue, Plateau, Bornu and Adamawa Provs. 1940–51; transferred Head Office UAC, London 1951.

Dorothy RUSTON (*née* Rayner); born 1903; married Clifford Ruston 1925; accompanied him to Zaria, Kano, Makurdi and Jos; crossed Belgian Congo to S. Africa 1943; left Nigeria 1951.

Robin SHORT; born 1927; Rifle Brig., Palestine 1947–8; joined Colonial Service 1950; ADO N.W. Prov. and Copperbelt, N. Rhodesia 1950–57; DC Mwinlunta 1958–60, Lundazi 1961–3; Native Courts 1964–5; retired 1965; barrister and magistrate; pub. *African Sunset*.

Veronica SHORT (*née* Vail); born 1927; Sadler's Wells Ballet 1946–54, toured Europe, USA, S. Africa; married Robin Short, Chingola, N. Rhodesia 1954; four children born N. Rhodesia, two at Kitwe, two at Fort Jameson.

Sir George SINCLAIR, Kt, CMG, OBE, MP; born 1912; joined Colonial Service 1936; ADC Ashanti, Kumasi, Gold Coast 1937–9; Military Service 1940–43; DC Ashanti 1943; Colonial Office 1943–5; Secretariat 1945–50; Regional Officer Trans-Volta Togoland 1952–5; Deputy Governor Cyprus 1955–60.

Kenneth SMITH, CMG; born 1918; grandfather ICS, brother Colonial Service, Nigeria; joined Colonial Service 1939; Cadet Tanganyika 1940; war service RAF; Appts. Dept., Colonial Office 1945; DC Zanzibar 1946–8; Res. Magistrate Pemba, Zanzibar 1949; Colonial Sec. Seychelles 1949–52, Aden 1952–6, Gambia 1956–62.

Mavis STONE (*née* Dauncey Tongue); born Uganda 1924; father Prov. Commiss. Uganda; trained Boschetto Agric. College, S. Africa; WRNS 1943–6, war service Kenya and Ceylon; married Richard Stone 1948; lived in Acholi, Toro and Buganda 1948–62.

Richard STONE, CMG; born Kenya 1914; father Prov. Commiss. Kenya; joined Colonial Service 1937; ADC Toro and Lango 1937–9; war service with KAR in Abyssinia, Burma and India; DC Acholi and Toro 1947–54; Perm. Sec. various ministries 1954–9; Resident, Buganda 1960–62; retired 1962.

William STUBBS, CMG, OBE; born 1902; father ICS, brothers ICS and Sudan

Political Service; joined BSA Police, Rhodesia 1921–4; transferred N. Rhodesia Police 1924; transferred Administrative Service, N. Rhodesia 1926; DC various districts 1926–39; Labour Dept. 1940–44, Labour Commiss. 1944–9; Prov. Commiss. 1949–54; Sec. for Native Affairs 1954–7; Pub. Services Commission, Somaliland 1960.

Richard SYMES-THOMPSON; born Nairobi 1923; grandfather Commiss. Basutoland, father coffee-planter Kenya; war service 1942–5; joined Colonial Service 1946; ADC Isiolo, Garissa, Kitui, Meru, Tambach, Nakuru, Kenya 1946–9; Secretariat Nairobi 1950–53; married Gillian Brooke Anderson, father Colonial Service, Kenya 1952; DO Kericho 1953–4, Limuru 1955–6; DC Embu, Teita, Naivasha 1956–7; Nandi 1958–63, Kiambu 1963–4; retired 1964.

Lady Beatrice TURNBULL (née Wilson); born 1908; secretary to Lord Reith; married Richard Turnbull 1939; lived in Meru, Nairobi, Kapenguria, and toured extensively in NFD 1939–58; one son born in Kitale and family of three raised in Kenya; lived in Tanganyika 1958–62.

Sir Richard TURNBULL, GCMG; born 1909; joined Colonial Service 1930; ADC Kericho, Kitui, Kisumu 1931–5, Kenya; DC Isiolo, Mandera, Moyale, NFD 1936–40; DC Meru 1941; Secretariat 1942; DC Turkana 1943–4; Secretariat 1945–6; Prov. Commiss., N. Prov. 1948–53; Min. for Defence and Int. Security 1954–5; Chief Sec. 1955–8; Governor and C.-in-C. Tanganyika 1958–61; Governor-General Tanzania 1961–2; Chairman, Land Board, Kenya 1963–4; High Commiss., Aden 1965–7.

# A SHORT GLOSSARY OF
# ANGLO-AFRICAN WORDS, PHRASES
# AND SLANG

---

In addition to those words and phrases that occur in the text I have added others that have a particular relevance to the British colonial period. Most will be seen to be derived from one or other of three main sources: pidgin in British West Africa (WA), Swahili in British East Africa (EA) – which also looked to Anglo-India for some of its argot (e.g., *ayah* for nurse) – and (to a lesser extent) Afrikaans or sometimes 'kitchen-kaffir' in British Central Africa (CA). Apart from such official terms as 'district', very few words or phrases seem to have been able to transcend these three distinct regions. Thus the term used to describe the process of trekking or touring about the district has its own regional variations; safari in East Africa, *ulendo* in Central Africa, 'going to bush' or 'going on trek' in West Africa.

---

A

| | |
|---|---|
| A class | – administrative officials and others of officer rank, as distinct from B or second class officials |
| ADC | – Assistant District Commissioner, junior District Officer occasionally responsible for the administration of a subdivision within a district; also aide-de-camp to a governor |
| *alkali* | – Moslem judge or lay magistrate administering Mohammedan law in N. Nigeria (Hausa from Arab) |
| Ashanti chicken | – dish made up of one fowl, with bones removed, stuffed inside another (WA) |
| *askari* | – soldier in King's African Rifles (Turkish), thus '*askari kanga*' – government messenger (*kanga* – waist cloth) |
| *ayah* | – native nurse (EA; Anglo-Indian); known in Swahili as *yaha* |

# B

| | |
|---|---|
| *bafu* | – bath (EA; Swahili) |
| *banda* | – thatch shelter (EA and CA) |
| *baraza* | – official gathering or meeting (EA; Swahili), lit. verandah |
| *barracki*-Hausa | – simplified Hausa used by officers in Nigeria Regiment |
| *bature* | – white man (N. Nigeria; Hausa) |
| *beef* | – animal (WA; pidgin), thus 'angel he be God beef, he have wings for back and fly for top' |
| *boma* | – district or divisional headquarters (EA and CA; Swahili), literally an enclosure from early days when government posts were enclosed in a *boma* or thorn *zariba* (*v.* 'station') |
| Bombay bowler | – casual pith helmet or *sola* topee as opposed to formal cork sun-helmet (Anglo-Indian) |
| boneyard | – area of ocean lying between Canary Islands and Sierra Leone, also known as 'Elder Dempster boneyard' |
| book | – bundle of employers' references carried by servants |
| boy | – personal servant (pidgin) regardless of age or size, also known as 'steward' or 'house-boy', supported by his assistant or 'small boy' – or even 'small-small boy', thus 'lantern boy', 'turney-boy' – driver's mate and engine cranker |
| BSAP | – British South Africa Police (Rhodesia) |
| *bugg-bugg* | – insect (WA; pidgin) |
| *bundu* | – N. Rhodesian and EA term for bush |
| bunduki | – gun (EA; Anglo-Indian *bundook*) |
| bush | – forest and uncultivated land and provincial areas away from headquarters (WA; pidgin), thus 'going to bush' (*v.* 'touring'), 'a bit bush' – rather wild, 'bush house' – basic rest-house as distinct from catering rest-house, 'bush lamp', 'bush shirt', 'bush hat', 'bush allowance', 'bush happy' – state of mind engendered by prolonged absence from civilization or without leave, and 'bush-telegraph' – local communications system that preceded official communications from headquarters |
| *bwana* | – master, term for European (EA; Swahili), thus '*bwana* DC' and '*bwana makuba*' – big master |

## C

c
— Companionage, specifically Companion of the Order of St Michael and St George (CMG), the order most often conferred on senior colonial administrators, sometimes known as 'Call Me God' (v. 'K')

canteen
— up-country shop or store (WA; pidgin) usually run by European or Syrian trading companies, known in early days as 'barter-rooms' or 'factories'

chagoul
— canvas or leather water bag (EA; Anglo-Indian)

chop
— food (WA; pidgin) thus 'palm-oil chop' traditionally eaten at Sunday lunches, 'chop box' – reinforced provision box, 'small chop' – canapés (v. 'gadgets' and 'toasties'), 'steamer chop' – shipboard meals or food newly landed, 'chop master' – person responsible for ordering food in the mess, taken in rotation, 'Pass chop!' – a call for food to be served

CNC
— Chief Native Commissioner (Kenya), later MAA – Minister for African Affairs

the Coast
— usually taken to refer to West Africa generally (v. 'old coaster')

condominium
— joint rule as exercised in the Anglo-Egyptian Sudan

craw-craw
— skin irritation (WA; pidgin), said to be caused by excessive starch in laundry, also known as 'dhobi-itch' (EA; Anglo-Indian)

## D

dash
— gift (WA; Portug. pidgin) thus 'topside dash' – gift for a chief, also verb 'to dash'

DC
— District Commissioner, generally senior District Officer responsible for administration of district within province, known in earlier days as Native Commissioner, in the Sudan as Inspector (v. 'district')

debbie
— 4-gall. petrol can, serving variety of functions from roofing material to water container

dhobi
— laundryman (EA; Anglo-Indian)

district
— area of administration within a province, varying greatly in size and population; in Nigeria the area administered by the Native Authority official

doki-boy
— groom (N. Nigeria) from doki – horse (Hausa); known in EA as syce (Anglo-Indian)

dona
— bwana's wife (CA and EA; Portug. Swahili)

| | |
|---|---|
| double-*terai* | – double-layered felt hat (Anglo-Indian) |
| *dubas* | – tribal police (Kenya NFD; Somali), lit. red turban |
| *duka* | – shop or store (EA and CA; Swahili), usually run by Indian trader |

### E

| | |
|---|---|
| ED | – Elder Dempster, shipping line dominating W. African sea route, founded in 1868 |
| *effendi* | – lord, term of respect for official (Sudan, N. Nigeria; Turkish) |

### F

| | |
|---|---|
| first-timer | – newcomer on first African tour, also known as 'first-tour man' |
| *fitina* | – bearing of false witness and accusations (EA; Arabic) |
| *foo-foo* | – side-dish of pounded yams, served with palm-oil *chop* (WA; pidgin) |
| furlough | – home leave, nineteenth-century term most often used by missionaries |

### G

| | |
|---|---|
| *gadgets* | – canapés (WA; pidgin) (*v.* 'small *chop*', 'toasties') |
| *gari*-moto | – motor-car (Anglo-Indian) |
| governor | – in Sudan senior administrator in charge of province, more usually governor of colonial territory |
| GRA | – Government Reservation Area, section of town reserved for houses of officials and Europeans |

### H

| | |
|---|---|
| *harambee!* | – hauling cry, 'let's pull together' (CA and EA; Swahili) |
| *hodi!* | – term of greeting (EA; Swahili) the reply being '*karibu*' |

### J

| | |
|---|---|
| *janbo* | – greetings (EA; Swahili) |
| *jigger* | – (*chigga*) *pulex penetrans*, soil insect carried on (and in) naked feet (WA) |
| *jilumchi* | – (*chilumchi*) canvas-covered basin or bath, used on tour (Anglo-Indian); also known as 'safari basin' or '*bakuli ya safari*' (EA; Swahili) |

# K

K
— knighthood, usually of the Order of St Michael and St George (KCMG), sometimes known as 'Kindly Call Me God' (*v*. 'C')

*kapasu*
— chief's messenger or constable (N. Rhodesia)

KAR
— King's African Rifles, formed soon after turn of century with battalions in Kenya, Uganda, Tanganyika and Nyasaland, with a detachment in Somaliland

Kenya stiff
— derogatory term used outside Kenya to describe its prouder European inhabitants

*kiboko*
— rawhide whip (EA; KAR), known also as *balala* (WA; WAFF), traditionally made from rhinoceros hide

kitchen-kaffir
— CA equivalent of 'kitchen-Swahili' (*v*. 'Swahili')

*kuku*
— cook (WA; pidgin) thus '*kuku matey*' – cook's mate or apprentice, traditionally said to carry at all times a jar of yeast, also chicken (EA; Swahili)

*kururu*
— ululation (CA)

# L

*liwali*
— local Moslem headman appointed by Government to deal with affairs of local Mohammedan community (Kenya, Tanganyika; Swahili)

load
— luggage, divided into loads of no more than 56 lb. for portering, earlier 60 lb.

# M

Ma
— traditional term of address used by servants (WA; pidgin) from 'Madam', also 'Missus', 'mama' or *memsahib* (EA)

*mallam*
— scribe or teacher of language (N. Nigeria; Arabic)

*mammy*
— African woman (pidgin), thus '*mammy*-wagon' – simple bus much used by market women (WA), and '*mammy*-clothes' – Western garments foisted on East Africans by missionaries

*mammy*-chair
— enlarged bosun's chair used for the disembarkation of passengers off Accra and (until First World War) Lagos

mess
— bachelor quarters shàred by several Europeans in larger stations

messenger
— government or district messenger, often regarded as

DO's right-hand man (*v. askari kanga*, dubas, kapasu, tarashi)

MMRA — Miles and Miles of Ruddy Africa (more commonly MMBA)

mosquito boot — usually black leather (for men) or white canvas (for women) boot worn in the evenings

*m'pishi* — cook (EA; Swahili)

*mzungu* — white man (EA; Swahili)

## N

NA — Native Administration, Native Authority, operating side by side with the colonial administration as part of the dual mandate

*ndaba* — official gathering or meeting (N. Rhodesia; Zulu *ngoni*) (*v. 'baraza'*)

NFD — Kenya's Northern Frontier District, extra provincial district, under the charge of a senior administrative officer known as the Officer-in-Charge, colonized in 1946 with Turkana to form a province

*ngoma* — tribal dance (EA; Swahili), lit. drum

## O

oil rivers — rivers of the Niger Delta used in the transportation of palm oil; in the 1890s briefly an administrative region of what was later S. Nigeria

old coaster — experienced West Africa hand, usually trader, known in earlier days as 'palm-oil ruffian'

## P

pagan — animistic tribe as opposed to Moslem (Nigeria) thus a DO in a pagan area was known as a 'pagan' or 'pagan man'

*palaver* — talk, dispute (WA; Portug. pidgin *palabra*), thus '*mammy-palaver*' — women's talk

*panga* — bush knife (CEA; Swahili)

PC — Provincial Commissioner, the equivalent in the Sudan being known as Provincial Governor and in Nigeria and Buganda as Resident

pidgin — WA lingua franca developed for trading purposes ('pidgin' being supposedly a corruption of 'business') using basic English and simplified grammar,

|  |  |
|---|---|
|  | sometimes known on the Gold Coast as 'Coast pig-gin' or 'Kru-English' |
| PK | – portable lavatory (CA) or thunderbox, said to be derived from *piccanin-kaya* – small house (CA; kitchen-kaffir) |
| *punkah* | – fan, properly one suspended from ceiling and pulled by a *punkah-wallah* (Anglo-Indian) |
| PWD | – Public Works Department |

## R

|  |  |
|---|---|
| remittance man | – a form of Kenya settler said to depend on remittance from UK sent to stop him returning |
| Resident | – see 'PC' |
| rest-house | – simple staging house built by the PWD or local authority for official travellers on tour, more wide-spread in WA than in EA and CA |

## S

|  |  |
|---|---|
| safari | – journey (EA; Swahili) (*v.* 'touring') |
| *sarki* | – chief (N. Nigeria; Hausa) |
| SCC | – Sudan (or Somaliland) Camel Corps |
| Scotch club | – informal club or outdoor gathering from the first phase of administration when Europeans on station supplied their own drinks, chairs and lamps |
| scratch box | – unofficial term for secretariat (WA), in N. Rhodesia 'biscuit box' |
| *shamardan* | – classical Arab lantern, with large glass bowl (Sudan) |
| sleeping dictionary | – African mistress, also known as 'native comfort', '*bibi*' (Anglo-Indian) or '*bint*' – young woman (Arabic) |
| spine-pad | – felt pad worn to protect spine from sun |
| station | – government post where district officials live, thus 'out-station' (*v.* '*boma*') |
| *stoep* | – uncovered verandah (WA, CA and EA; Afrikaans) |
| stud book | – Staff or Civil Service List (WA) |
| sundowner | – drink taken at 6 p.m. and thereafter |
| Swahili | – EA lingua franca developed for trading purposes (supposedly from the Arabic *swahele* – man of the coast), more properly Ki-Swahili, thus 'kitchen-Swahili' as spoken with servants and 'Ki-settler' – ungrammatical Swahili as spoken by settlers |

# T

| | |
|---|---|
| *tamasha* | – display, parade (EA; Anglo-Indian) |
| Tanganyika boiler | – hot water system (EA) consisting of piped water from a heated 40-gallon drum |
| *tarbosh* | – Turkish fez |
| *tarishi* | – native messenger (Tanganyika) |
| *toasties* | – canapés (EA; Anglo-Indian) (*v.* 'small *chop*', '*gadgets*'), thus 'first *toasties*' before supper, 'second *toasties*' (savouries) after |
| *toto* | – kitchen assistant or 'small boy' (EA; kitchen-Swahili), thus 'cook's *toto*' (more properly *mtoto*); also child |
| tour | – usually the term of service between leaves, varying from 1–2 years (W. Africa, Uganda) to 3–4 years (Kenya, N. Rhodesia), thus feeling 'end of tourish' – run-down and in need of recuperation (*v.* 'touring') |
| touring | – the practice of trekking (Afrikaans) or journeying on official business through the district, known variously as 'going on safari' (EA), 'going to bush' (WA) or 'going on *ulendo*' (CA) |
| *tumbo* | – species of fly (WA), known in CA as *puttse* |
| *turawa* | – white man (N. Nigeria: Hausa) (*v.* '*bature*') |

# U

| | |
|---|---|
| *umpeschie* | – cook (EA; Swahili) |
| *ulendo* | – *v.* 'touring' |

# V

| | |
|---|---|
| valise | – bedding roll |

# W

| | |
|---|---|
| WAFF | – (Royal) West Africa Frontier Force, with regiments or battalions in Sierra Leone, Gambia, Gold Coast, Nigeria and British Cameroons |
| WAR | – West Africa Regiment |
| WAWA | – 'West Africa Wins Again' (also Hausa for 'fool'), term used to express irritation at local ways and means, also 'YCHA' – 'You Can't Hurry Africa' |
| *wishi-wishi* | – white-faced teal found in Nigeria (pidgin), also known as '*wishy-washy*' |

## Y

Yellow Jack — yellow fever; the last serious outbreak occurred in W. Africa in 1927

## Z

*zaki* — lion, honorific form of address (N. Nigeria; Hausa)